DO IT AGAIN, LORD!

DO IT AGAIN, LORD!

By Dr. Shelton Smith

SWORD of the LORD
PUBLISHERS

Post Office Box 1099 • Murfreesboro, Tennessee 37133

For a complete list of books available from the
Sword of the Lord, write to Sword of the Lord
Publishers, P. O. Box 1099, Murfreesboro,
Tennessee 37133.

(800) 251-4100
(615) 893-6700
FAX (615) 848-6943
www.swordofthelord.com

Printed and Bound in the United States of America

Contents

Do It Again, Lord!
Do It Again!

"LORD, *thou hast been favourable unto thy land: thou hast brought back the captivity of Jacob.*

"*Thou hast forgiven the iniquity of thy people, thou hast covered all their sin. Selah.* ["Selah" was probably injected to remind the singers to repeat part of it.]

"*Thou hast taken away all thy wrath: thou hast turned thyself from the fierceness of thine anger.*

"*Turn us, O God of our salvation, and cause thine anger toward us to cease.*

"*Wilt thou be angry with us for ever? wilt thou draw out thine anger to all generations?*

"*Wilt thou not revive us again: that thy people may rejoice in thee?*

"*Shew us thy mercy, O* LORD, *and grant us thy salvation.*

"*I will hear what God the* LORD *will speak: for he will speak peace unto his people, and to his saints: but let them not turn again to folly.*

"*Surely his salvation is nigh them that fear him; that glory may dwell in our land.*

"*Mercy and truth are met together; righteousness and peace have kissed each other.*

"*Truth shall spring out of the earth; and righteousness shall look down from heaven.*

"*Yea, the* LORD *shall give that which is good; and our land shall yield her increase.*

"*Righteousness shall go before him; and shall set us in the way of his steps.*"—Ps. 85:1–13.

The question is asked in verse 6: "Wilt thou not revive us again: that thy people may rejoice in thee?"

What is it that he is asking? Once there was a time when things were running full throttle. Once there was a time when the Israelites were up and going, excited and thrilled about being the people of God. Yet something has happened. There has been a waning, a slacking off, a turning to the left or to the right, a looking away from the focus of things as they ought to be. The psalmist is saying, "Lord, there was a time when You had filled us with the life of Heaven, when the great things of God were injected into us with full vigor and vitality. What we had then we got from You. Dear Lord, we have lost some of what we had, and we need what we used to have. Please, Lord, do it again!"

Let verse 6 speak to all of us. Let this be our prayer: "O God, revive us again. Do for us again what we had in yesteryear. Give us that great anointing of revival so that Your people may in fact rejoice in Thee as they ought to rejoice."

I was preaching in north Florida a few months ago. I flew in on a Saturday night, got into the hotel and turned on the news at ten o'clock. There was a story on about a single-engine aircraft that had landed that day on one of the freeways. A man was flying from Point A to Point B. Right over the city of Jacksonville he ran out of gas. When in a single-engine aircraft, you either hope you're close to an airport or someplace where you can glide that thing to safety. In his case, spotting a freeway below him, he put that little single-engine aircraft down there. Thankfully, it only damaged a portion of one wing where it nicked a car, and nobody was hurt. They showed on the news its being dragged off down the freeway after some investigation.

When flying an airplane, you are heavily dependent upon what is in the fuel tank. It may be a nice-looking airplane and well constructed; there may have been great plans by engineers and others in putting it together; but if you don't have enough gas in it to keep you going the full distance, you are going to crash somewhere.

I was on a commercial aircraft right after that. As we were sitting on the tarmac waiting to take off, the pilot came on and said, "Our fuel gauge is not working. We can fly without the fuel gauge, but we have to check it manually." I sat there and watched out the window. A man who looked like the Pillsbury doughboy put a ladder up against a wing, climbed it, unscrewed the cap on the wing, took what looked like a yardstick and put it down in the wing, looked at it, looked around at the pilot and gave the "okay" signal. (Man, the technology in this age is impressive to me!) The pilot came back on the speaker and announced, "We've checked it. There is fuel in the tank. We can go."

You have to get it fueled up if you're going to run the aircraft.

I borrowed my wife's car the other day to drive to Nashville. I have a rule which I never violate. I know that anytime I get in her car I have to look at the gas gauge. I don't know what keeps her from being on the side of the road all the time. However, that day I forgot my rule, and I didn't check it. I had just pulled out on Interstate 24, and after two or three miles the car sputtered. I looked. It was set on empty. I kicked it in neutral, turned it off and let it coast as far as it would, because I couldn't see anything that even looked like a place to get off. I got down to about twenty miles an hour, turned the engine back on, dropped it in drive and gunned it forward three or four times. I finally got to an off ramp and into a filling station. It was dead when I got there.

There are times when we come to Sunday morning and have nothing more than routine, nothing more than our Baptist ritual—and there's nothing more right or holy about a Baptist form and ritual than there is about an Episcopalian liturgy. One is as dead as the other. We go through the form. We're set in our motion, and it is dead, dead, dead from start to stop.

We get back on Sunday night, and what was dead on Sunday morning has already begun to stink. Sunday night we get a few people together and discuss in slow motion how to bury what died.

Wednesday night we only have a few survivors who come and huddle around a little podium down front. We sit around that little podium and weep and moan and complain about who's not there and what's not happening. The whole place is coming apart simply because we don't have anything in the tank to get us going and get it flying and get it moving.

What do we need? We need the holy unction of God, the breath of God breathing in the preacher, the teachers, the bus workers and the soul winners. We need a mighty anointing of God that gets us up when snow is on the ground, when the air-conditioner doesn't work and when everything is coming unglued.

On some holiday weekend when half the crowd is gone, instead of going through the motions and saying, "Well, it will be better next week," get up and do something for God.

We need the kind of revival that it talks about here, where God does it again. Don't misunderstand me. I don't want some phony phenomenon. The charismatic crowd, according to their magazines that come to my desk, have meetings now where, right in the middle of the service, gold flakes fall off the ceiling and descend upon the crowd. Every one of those accounts which I have read has said, "Now they have not certified that it was real gold, but they just pronounced it to be so." If it were real gold, they'd be scooping it up and paying off those big buildings they built.

In others of their meetings, people have been testifying that their amalgam fillings have turned to gold right in the middle of the service, and they're calling that revival. One Toronto charismatic got in front of the cameras one night and declared that his filling had turned to gold. His dentist, who was watching, called him and said, "Man, I filled that tooth twelve years ago with gold." So the man came on and apologized the next night.

I mention those things because I have absolutely no use for this charismatic gobbledygook that's going on. When the Devil fools and fouls people up and gets them to buy into things that relate to the flesh instead of looking for the power and anointing of God, he has sold them a package of goods. God's people must not buy into those phony phenomena.

An anointing of God will give us an unction when church time comes that will make church like church ought to be—that will get Christians to be Christians like Christians are supposed to be and get us to raise families like families are meant to be.

The psalmist asked, "Wilt thou not revive us again: that thy people may rejoice in thee?" God is expecting something out of you and me. God's people, regenerated, born again, washed in the blood, ought to be responsible, righteous, godly people. This tomfoolery where we try to see how close to the world we can get and how much like them we can become and if we can go to all the places they go and do all the things they do—cut it out and get back to being a responsible, righteous, godly and holy people!

The writer asked, "Wilt thou not revive us again: that thy people may rejoice in thee?" If God did it again, what would we have? This chapter says that when revival comes, our holy God, the great God of creation, will be at work in our midst. What do you reckon that would mean? In a lot of cases it would mean purging. People would come to the altar, fall on their faces and tell God they had things in their lives that needed to be cleaned up and thrown out.

When God begins to work in our midst, there may even be some pruning. If you have a pastor's heart, no matter who may leave the church, you're going to bleed, and you ought to. When revival comes, when the breath of God is blowing hot on Sunday morning, Sunday night and Wednesday night, at soul-winning time and at other times, there will be some pruning. Some goats who haven't become sheep will not like what happens in God's vineyard, and they will walk out. This pruning process will come when God is at work in our midst.

When God begins to work in our midst, our puny sermons suddenly begin to produce. I was amazed to see some of the people who got saved at our church in Westminster go on to do something for God. I could hardly believe it when some told me that God had called them to preach or God had called them to be missionaries or God had called them to do other work in His vineyard. It scared me. It frightened me. Down deep inside I was thinking, *I can't imagine that!* but God had been at work. We might think, *There is no way that can happen to him or to her!* Nevertheless, because of the mighty working of God, He has taken the outcasts, the rejects, the broken—people we couldn't imagine could ever be used—and done some mighty things through them.

When revival comes, God does again in our midst what we want to have happen. This verse indicates God's people will get in form: "...that thy people may rejoice in thee." We have far too many grumps and grouches in our crowd. We have far too many people sitting on the pew just looking for something wrong, just hoping that they will have something to grunt and grouch about. If anything breaks out of the norm, they come unglued.

The preacher may do something a little different. Let's suppose he walks up to the mike some Sunday morning and says "hello" before they sing a song, or suppose he says, "I'm going to read my text, take the offering, then preach." When he does something different, you say, "Why would a preacher change things? Why would he do something out of the norm?" To challenge you!

At times God may put a test in front of us just to see whether we have bitterness down inside. Some people spew it out easily and fast. God help us to see that when He does in our midst what needs to be done, He is at work.

I know some good preachers, some good churches, who have worked hard, yet haven't had the success they expected. To those pastors I would suggest that they get on their faces and tell God that they need

His help, that they can't do it with just programs, with just personnel; that they can't do it just by promotion. Surely you know you must have more than that.

Second, this passage indicates that when God does it again, His mercy will be demonstrated. "Shew us thy mercy, O LORD, and grant us thy salvation" (vs. 7). When this begins to happen in any church—whether you have 50 or 500 or 5,000—people will come in out of the woodwork. They won't all come in driving a Mercedes or a Cadillac or a Lincoln Town Car. I promise you that the blessing of God will bring you all types of people when God begins to work and stir the hearts of people. Drunks will come and get saved, clean up and begin to walk with God. Dope addicts will come and get straightened up and become profitable servants of God. Those who have lived wicked, ungodly, immoral, absolutely abhorrent, abominable, despicable lives suddenly will become as straitlaced as they can be. How is that possible? By the mercy of God.

I can organize a class and teach drunks how to be sober but get little results. It takes the Gospel of Jesus Christ to clean out the cracks and crevices of wicked hearts and give people an appetite for the things that they didn't have before and shut off the old appetite. Only the mercy of God can do that.

When God does it again, we begin to listen to what He says: "I will hear what God the LORD will speak" (vs. 8). All across this nation some schools couldn't open this fall if they started listening again to what God had to say. They would have to modify their curriculum and buy new textbooks. Government offices in every state in the Union would have to shut down, clean their places out and start all over. The courts and other places would be in an absolute upheaval simply because somebody with authority walked in and said, "Starting now, we are going to listen to what God says."

"Well, that's not likely to happen," you say. It's not unless we get a breath from God that brings revival to this nation. We will never be able to vote that in. We will never be able to decree that. We will never be able to put enough social pressure on our culture to make it happen.

If the breath of God is breathed into the lives of God's people often enough and long enough and we begin to say, "God says, and that's what we'll do"—then things will begin to happen.

There are standards in the Bible to help one determine what his own standards should be. Don't sit around and grouse about that. Simply live by them. There are commands in the Bible—commands, not just suggestions. When God commands something, it's not for us to sit in some committee and argue, "Well, now, this is what I think about that"; "Well, I don't know whether that really means what it says or says what it means." If God has given a clear command, we decide to be obedient or disobedient. Why not be obedient and just do it? There are rules in the Bible for us, very pointed, specific instructions.

The liberals and new evangelicals seem just to love the Sermon on the Mount. They act as though it's plain vanilla and there is nothing in it of any pointed instruction. The other day I went through the chapters of the Sermon on the Mount looking for what kind of pointed commands I could find. In chapter 5 alone I found twenty-one specific, pointed commands—things we are to listen to in what God is saying.

When revival comes, we follow the standards, the commands and the doctrines in the Bible.

The Promise Keepers and a lot of these crowds have said over and over, "No doctrine." Up in New England a church marquee said, "Love unifies. Doctrine divides." You know, they are kind of right about that. When the Bible talks about "sound doctrine," there has to be some unsound doctrine somewhere. There's good doctrine, bad doctrine, sound doctrine, unsound doctrine. Doctrine does divide. It divides the apples from the oranges, right from wrong, good from bad.

When we have the breath of God, like this passage is advocating, we again listen to what God says.

Verse 8 also has an admonition in it that indicates that we will be kept from foolishness when that breath of God blows again.

We've talked this week about the contemporary church, which we think is foolishness. When we listen to what God says and when the breath of God is breathed on us, purging, cleansing, directing and giving us instruction and we pay attention, that kind of foolishness shouldn't appeal to us. When we feel the will of God effected in our lives, we don't want the soup diluted; we want it strong and powerful.

When men say, "Let's tinker with the Word of God, and let's rearrange it; let's amend it; let's correct it; let's change it; let's get it more palatable for the modern mind," it is foolishness. When men say, "If we talk about all the things that are in the Bible, it will turn a lot of our people off, so let's not do that except to a tiny group on Wednesday night with the most seasoned and mature people," no wonder our families are letting their kids go to Hell; no wonder our families are coming apart at the seams; no wonder people are jumping out of windows. This all happens when we don't give them the whole counsel of God.

This passage goes on to indicate that when God revives us again and does again in our midst what ought to be done, we'll again have a proper view of Him. Verse 9 says, "Surely his salvation is nigh them that fear him...." Not much is wrong in America that a proper fear of God would not solve. Acts 20:21 says, "...repentance toward God." That means getting a right attitude, a right spirit, a change of mind about God.

Psalm 85:9 indicates that when revival comes and God does again in our midst what we desire for Him to do, we will have glory in the land again. Truth and right will prevail, verses 10 and 11 indicate. The abundance of God's goodness will fall upon the land. There will be glory in the land.

No matter what the revisionists say, there was a time in America when this nation followed Christian principles. We no longer have that, but we can get it back. It will take a Holy Ghost revival to get it.

Verse 13 shows that when this revival comes, we will follow His leadership again: "Righteousness shall go before him; and shall set us in the way of his steps." Matthew 4:19 reads, "Follow me, and I will make you fishers of men." If you say, "Well, I'll think about following Jesus," you are disobedient already.

When our children were small and I told them to do something, it was not a matter of our sitting down and talking it over. I put the pressure on, and they did it. Jesus said, "Follow me, and I will make you fishers of men." If we are not fishing, we are not following.

You say, "Oh, but I'm a good Christian." You are not following Jesus if you are not fishing for souls.

You say, "But I'm shy; I'm bashful." The breath of God will give you boldness.

When I surrendered to preach in 1957 as a fourteen-year-old lad, I was one of the most introverted young people you ever saw. God enabled me to overcome this. When we have the Holy Ghost of God, the breath of God, the revival that God wants to give, we will say, "Wherever He leads, I'll go."

In 1978 when Betty and I moved to Westminster, Maryland, I was thirty-six years of age. We began to win souls and saw the church grow to become the largest fundamental church in the whole Northeast. I look at that work and pray, "O Lord, do it again. May some young man up in New England or somewhere else in that section do it again."

Let me mention a few of the men who speak regularly in our yearly conference at Walkertown.

In 1956 Bobby Roberson, hometown boy, became pastor of Gospel Light Baptist Church in Walkertown, North Carolina. Not too long after that he suffered a heart attack and went through many struggles and difficulties. Many left the church, but he stayed put; and he has gone on to be used of God to build the largest church in the Carolinas. I look at North Carolina and South Carolina and pray, "Lord, there's a hometown boy somewhere in one of these towns in North Carolina or South Carolina. O God, do it again in the Carolinas."

Twenty-five years ago Larry Brown, a boy from North Carolina, went to Washington, Iowa and bought an old Presbyterian church building a half block off the square. The Lord used him to build the largest church in that state. I say, "O God, do it again, please, out there in the corn country in the Midwest."

Twenty-five years ago R. B. Ouellette became pastor of a fifty-member First Baptist Church in Bridgeport in a Saginaw that has been "sagging" every one of those twenty-five years. He tells me nobody moves into Saginaw, but people move out every day. In a city where the economy has been so bad so long, the Lord has used him to build the largest Baptist church in Michigan. I simply pray, "O God, isn't there some young man somewhere, just graduated from college, who will go to the frozen northland of Wisconsin and the Upper Peninsula of Michigan and into Canada? O God, do it again."

Twelve years ago a young Mexican pastor named Alejandro Cordova went to a La Espada conference in Guadalajara. God set his heart afire. He preached to a hundred people then; right now they run 1,600, 1,700 and 1,800. He has built the largest Baptist church of any kind in the nation of Mexico. I pray, "O God, for some of those young Mexican preachers and pastors, do it again! Oh, do it many times over down there!"

Thirty years ago Don Sisk turned over the church he had started in Osaka to the first man he led to Christ. Today the largest independent Baptist church in Japan is pastored by Dr. Ogawa. I preached in his church. I'll go back there to preach again. I marvel in that great,

15

thronging megalopolis there and pray, "O God, there's another Dr. Ogawa somewhere; help us to find him. Please, dear God, many hundreds of times over, do it again!"

Fourteen years ago Paul Chappell took twelve people and founded the Lancaster Baptist Church in California. Two Sundays ago they had over 3,300, and that's a fairly normal Sunday. He has the largest independent Baptist church and, I think, the largest Baptist church of any kind in California. You heard him preach here last night. He's only thirty-eight years old. I pray, "O God, please give us some more men like him. Dear God, please do it again!"

Thirteen years ago Clarence Sexton left a thriving work in Paterson, New Jersey to come to, of all places, Knoxville, Tennessee. If he had asked me, I would have said, "Stay in Paterson." You know the story of what has happened in north Knoxville. I look at Clarence Sexton and pray, "O God, on those hills of East Tennessee, give us a hundred men who'll do it again!"

Twelve years ago his brother, Tom Sexton, started Gulf Coast Baptist Church in a very affluent city in Florida—Cape Coral. In just twelve years' time they have carved out a niche in that city. When I go there to speak, I pray, "O God, give us some more Tom Sextons. O God, do it again!"

Ron Baity started a church in Winston-Salem sixteen years ago. The radio station that is carrying this broadcast literally around the globe is owned and operated by that church. They have a thriving church here in this city. Oh, that there were somebody who would go to every city in the Carolinas and start a work like Ron Baity did sixteen years ago!

Max Barton took a church in the eastern part of this state that was in deep trouble. A resurrection occurred. Now they have a great, thriving work. I pray, "O God, do it again!"

Sam Davison went to Oklahoma City, took a church that was strong and, in a matter of ten years, has seen it double and more than double and become a great church. I pray, "O God, do it again."

Tom Malone went to Pontiac, Michigan in 1943, and you know that story. I pray, "O God, do it again! Give us another Dr. Malone who will go to Pontiac or to Detroit or to Chicago or to Cleveland."

Dr. Lee Roberson went to Chattanooga in 1942. He told his wife not to unpack—he didn't think he would be there more than six months. He only missed his estimate by forty years! You know his story as well. He built one of the largest churches in the world. I pray, "Do it again! O God, please give us another one like him."

Lonnie Mattingly has been in Louisville twenty-five years in an inner city and in a bad neighborhood. He has literally created an oasis and built the largest church in that part of the world. I say, "O God, give us another Lonnie Mattingly, another Lee Roberson, another Max Barton, another Sam Davison. Dear God, please, in every town and in every village may the breath of God be upon us and may we have the kind of revival that will burn in our midst and produce men like these."

Curtis Hutson went to a conference like this in Atlanta in 1961. The only difference was, there weren't very many people present. Dr. Rice and the other men thought the conference was a failure because so few people came. During that conference Dr. Hutson got his heart set on fire. You know how God used him so mightily for the rest of the days of his life. I pray, "O God, please tonight in this service give us another one like him. O God, do it again!"

When Dr. John R. Rice began thundering across the pages of history in the 1920s and '30s, nobody knew what fundamentalism was; nobody cared whether evolution was being taught in the colleges and seminaries. He began to cry aloud and spare not. When he began the SWORD OF THE LORD in 1934, he could not have dreamed how God would use him so mightily. I pray, "O God, tonight give us somebody with courage and backbone like Dr. Rice, someone with the determinate power of God in his life who will not give in nor give up but will stay in the battle and fight fiercely for what is right."

May our prayer be that of this blessed Book, "Dear Lord, do it again! and again! and again!"

Don't Close the Casket!

If I were not a Christian and didn't believe the Bible but were advised of the composition of Psalm 119, I would be forced to contemplate very seriously the matters of becoming a Christian and the validity of the truthfulness of the Bible.

Psalm 119 contains 176 verses, making it the longest chapter in the Bible. It is divided into stanzas, not just in English but also in the Hebrew text. Each stanza has eight verses. In the English text those eight verses are very carefully delineated as the *Aleph* section, the *Beth* section, the *Gimel* section, the *Daleth* section, the *He* section, the *Vau* section, etc.

The *Aleph* section, equivalent to the English *A*, is so designated because all eight verses in this section begin with a word, the first letter of which is an *Aleph*.

The *Beth* section, equivalent to the English *B*, is so designated because all eight verses in this section begin with a word, the first letter of which is a *Beth*.

The *Gimel* section, tantamount to the English *G*, is so designated because all eight verses begin with a word, the first letter of which is a *Gimel*.

That same scenario is consistent in each of those eight-verse sections of the entire chapter.

By tinkering with both language and vocabulary, you could perhaps put some words together that would be composed so as to have eight words that start with the English *A*, eight words that start with the English *B*, and so forth; but to do it poetically and in the way that it absolutely makes good sense so that the rhyme and rhythm and flow are in place, I pronounce it impossible for a group of writers or poets to do.

Psalm 119 was written a long time before there were any computers, but even if you had a massive computer and worked diligently to put something like that together, I think you would be hard pressed to do it.

God's Word is something greater than one man's little mind, something greater than I can possibly imagine. Whenever I read a passage like this and see what underlies it, it is absolutely staggering to the imagination. I remind myself that holy men of God spoke as they were moved by the Holy Spirit of God and that "all Scripture is given by inspiration of God, and is profitable" (II Tim. 3:16).

I thank God that we have a holy Book, God's Book, and I stand here before you holding the Word of God. This Book—every word, every letter, line upon line—is the divine, inspired, inerrant, infallible, totally reliable Word of God. Amen!

I read just the *Daleth* section of Psalm 119:

"My soul cleaveth unto the dust: quicken thou me according to thy word.

"I have declared my ways, and thou heardest me: teach me thy statutes.

"Make me to understand the way of thy precepts: so shall I talk of thy wondrous works.

"My soul melteth for heaviness: strengthen thou me according unto thy word.

"Remove from me the way of lying: and grant me thy law graciously.

"I have chosen the way of truth: thy judgments have I laid before me.

"I have stuck unto thy testimonies: O LORD, put me not to shame.

"I will run the way of thy commandments, when thou shalt enlarge my heart."—Vss. 25–32.

My text is taken from verse 25: "My soul cleaveth unto the dust: quicken thou me according to thy word."

There is a conflict between death and life, and there is a relationship between the body and the soul: the soul occupies the body, and the body lives for a time, but the soul lives on forever.

The body is a very carefully created and orchestrated accumulation of chemicals and molecules. God composed the human body in a very special way. He lifted out a little spade of dirt, took a sample of all the chemicals and components and made the human body with that same exact composition of elements. The dirt of the ground and your body are exactly the same chemically. The difference is the breath of God through which you have life.

As times goes along and our lives are spent, we will come to the natural point of death. Our bodies will be placed in the ground, and we will once again revert to dust. Inch by inch, piece by piece, the human body will deteriorate; and nothing will be left but the dust of death.

The psalmist says, "My soul cleaveth unto the dust." There is a relationship between body and soul. The soul and the spirit of a man cannot rise above the circumstances of his situations. The soul is locked into a human body—a fleshly, frail, faulty and fainting human body.

Life at its best is fragile, but for those who have not what God can give them, life has to be perplexing beyond imagination. If they have not our hope in the Lord, if they have not the anticipation of eternity that saved people have, they have to be frustrated people—facing an enigma they don't know how to solve. No wonder there are literally millions standing in line and paying big money to get on the psychiatrist's couch. Living and hurting and seeing themselves aging and dying, they know not what to do about it.

Whenever you and I face aging and our old bodies are beginning to groan, we know that death will come sometime. Surely we too say as the psalmist, "My soul is hanging onto the dust. O Lord God Almighty, breathe into me life, and breathe into me that everlasting life. O God, quicken me according to the truths and promises and mandates of Thy Word."

My old flesh is nothing but dust, but I will live eternally because of the promise of the great Almighty God who gave His word that He would let me live, dust or no dust. I love it! I park here, and I camp right around this little place, and I say, "O God, the dust, dirt, death—all of it—let it come and let it run its course; but, O God, I am cleaving to You because I have the hope and the promise that I am alive forevermore in the Lord Jesus Christ!"

Hundreds of times over the years I've walked into mortuaries and seen a casket with a human body inside. At times I've stood and looked into the face of someone I knew—a church member, a friend or family member whom I've loved very deeply—and thought, *Oh, wouldn't it be wonderful if he really were not dead! Even though he is in that casket, wouldn't it be marvelous if he would just sit up and live again!*

Sometimes I've looked very closely to see if there were just a little, shallow breath across the midsection. Of course I have never seen that, but I've imagined somehow that somebody might say, "Wait a minute! He's breathing! He's not dead! Don't close the casket!"

I'm saying to you, your body is mere dust. Your life is here, and like a fog in the morning, it burns off and is gone. It is something supernatural, the very work of God that breathes the simple things of life into these old, lifeless bodies—a hope, a dream and a vision that give us perspective beyond our frailties. It is God who breathes life into us and gives us hope for a grand tomorrow.

I. The Contrast Between God's Ways and Our Ways

Psalm 119:26 says that there is a contrast between our ways and God's ways. The psalmist, understanding himself and recognizing he had deficiencies, said, "I have declared my ways...." After confession to God, he said, "...thou heardest me: teach me thy statutes [thy ways]."

We all need to do that—understand that we are mere flesh. We're here, then gone. We don't need to run to the university; we need to run to God! We don't need to run to a psychiatrist; we need to run to God!

Folks, there is a contrast between our ways and God's ways. Those who sit in front of us on Sunday have a tendency, a propensity, for doing things their own way. Every time there is trouble in the church, somebody got off God's way and said, "I'm going *my* way!"

There is a contrast here, and you and I need to ask God constantly to teach us to learn His ways so we won't foul up things through our own ways.

II. The Correlation Between Wisdom and Wonders

Verse 27 shows there is a correlation between wisdom and wonders. He is talking about miracles. "Make me to understand the way of thy precepts [God's wisdom]: so shall I talk of thy wondrous works [the might of God, the miracles of God]." He is saying, "If You will help me to understand Your wisdom, then I will be able to talk about Your miracles."

Why don't we go soul winning? Because we don't understand the wisdom of God. Why do we have trouble dragging ourselves to the church house? We say, "Oh, Sunday again. I don't know if I want to go"; or we grumble, "Oh, won't that preacher ever stop! Oh no, that same guy is going to sing again!"

When we are grumpy and grouse our way around, we get out of fellowship with everybody. Then we don't have wisdom to know good from bad. We don't understand the wisdom of God. Not understanding His wisdom, we cannot understand His ways and His mighty workings.

One speaker said, "No wonder people are not getting saved at our altars. We head out the door to get to a Big Mac before the Presbyterians do!" What is wrong when we have a bigger concern in our stomachs for a burger and fries than we have in our hearts for people dying and going to Hell? when someone is rescued from the pit and we simply don't care?

We don't have a focus on the wisdom of God! We're wrapped up in our flesh—our big-screen TVs, our big cars, our boats and motor homes, our houses and clothes and all that other "stuff"! I'm glad for a nice suit of clothes. I'm glad to drive a nice car, but if clothes and car and house and all my "stuff" get in the way, I've got a problem. The wisdom of God—understanding the things of God—can help me catch hold of His ways.

When I was pastor in Maryland, I didn't want to have "regular services" on Sunday. For years we had a double service on Sunday morning. The first service was at 8:30. Some people think that is a good time to roll out the overhead projector or a chalkboard. After all, people are not really fired up at 8:30, are they? No, but their preacher ought to be! Forget the overhead projector and preach the Word with concern and vigor!

How can you get stirred up at 8:30 in the morning? By getting hold of the wisdom of God and the power of God. Those in that early morning service needed to hear something out of the Word of God.

When we get wisdom, then we will capture what God is trying to do.

III. The Comfort Between Our Tears and Our Troubles

Just as there is a contrast between God's ways and our ways, and just as there is a correlation between wisdom and wonders, verse 28 indicates there is a comfort amidst sorrow and our efforts to survive, between our tears and our troubles.

In our neighborhoods there may be tragedy and trauma and cause of tears, but what does verse 28 say? "My soul melteth for heaviness [that's all kinds of trouble]: strengthen thou me according unto thy word." The psalmist had disappointments and defeats. All kinds of things weakened and crippled him, but he found a way to survive the drought. In spite of the pressure, he found a way to make it.

I wonder how many preachers have said, "Where I am pastor it is a very hard town." May I say this? You don't just get up one Sunday and find a great crowd floating into a big complex of buildings. Your town is a hard town, you say. Let me tell you, all towns are hard towns.

"My heart is breaking. Like the psalmist, I'm weakened and crippled," you say. Where do you get strength? The psalmist says that strength is in the Word! That's one reason I don't like all these strange new twists on the Bible. People carry all of these Bibles (versions) that read like newspapers, but they don't memorize from them, and when they have some real problem, they often don't know where to turn for help, for comfort.

I went into a restaurant the other day and lifted the tops off some things on the buffet. Now I like soup that is soup, but sometimes I see nothing more than colored water. I don't like watered-down soup. When I dip the ladle into the soup pot, I want it to come up with some chunks.

Don't water down the Bible. Don't dilute it. Read the Word of God to get the strength you need. There you will find comfort and encouragement for your heavy burdens.

I know it will not be easy, but turn off that stinking Hell's Box Office (HBO) and read your Bible. Concentrate on it, focus on it, study it and memorize it.

All of us sit with mouths open when Dr. Barber stands in the pulpit and quotes long passages. We say, "Oh, I wish I had a mind like that." You and I may not have a mind like his; we may not be able to memorize chapters at a time, but we can memorize a verse or two here and there, if we are of a mind to.

Turn off the video games and memorize some Bible verses. Start with John 11:35: "Jesus wept." Start with those little towers of truth in I Thessalonians 5:16, 17: "Rejoice evermore. Pray without ceasing." Learn Scripture and memorize Scripture. Get yourself interested in the Bible, and you will be strengthened and encouraged.

IV. The Choice Between an Inspiring Testimony and an Expiring Testimony

"Remove from me the way of lying: and grant me thy law graciously."—Vs. 29.

I think the real meat of this little eight-verse stanza starts with this verse which talks about convictions.

Maintain Your Convictions

Verse 25 tells us not to close the casket because the corpse is still breathing. Why is it breathing? Verse 29 tells us that the convictions that we have are the basis for living. It is convictions that ground us.

I can tell you my preferences in food if you want to prepare me something to eat. I really don't have convictions about them; I have some preferences—but when it comes to the things that are really important, we need convictions. The psalmist says that convictions are what will ground us: "Remove from me the way of lying: and grant me thy law graciously." In other words, let's clean up our acts.

Colossians 3:9 exhorts, "Put off the old man with his deeds." Even if you are a young person, there is an old man inside, so put him off. Put off all fleshly carnalities. When that stuff comes crowding in, put it off!

Don't go to the closet every morning and say, "I'm going to put this on and go out of here and have a mad spell. I'm going to be an angry person, and I'm going to blow my top today!" The apostle tells you to put off the old man, put off that carnal anger, put off that fleshly anger. You say, "If I put off all those things, there will be nothing left."

Read the very next verse: "Put on the new man, which is renewed in knowledge after the image of him that created him."

Find out what it is to be a good Christian, then try to be one. Clean up your act; then cling very closely and tenderly to the commands of God.

"Grant me thy law graciously" (Ps. 119:29). In other words, "O God, in Your compassion, let Your law make its impact on me. Let it be so overlaid on me that that is what people see in me."

These kinds of convictions will affect our lifestyles, our behavior, our demeanor and our spirits.

Some people have no backbone. Your back should be made up of vertebrae, not spaghetti. Be strong and solid; but, bless God, don't get a fractious, ugly, cantankerous spirit. Maintain your heart, your fight, your drive, but don't let it put acid in your soul.

He says, "Grant me thy law graciously."

Choose the Way of Truth

"I have chosen the way of truth: thy judgments have I laid before me."—Vs. 30.

Not only are the convictions vital, but then there come choices. "I have *chosen* the way of truth."

You ask me, "How did you get to be a fundamentalist?" I decided to be one. As a young man, I was pastor in a little Southern Baptist church. I went to the mailbox one Friday and found a copy of the SWORD OF THE LORD. I'd never heard of Dr. John R. Rice or this paper, but my spirit immediately witnessed with the spirit that I found on the pages of that newspaper. I thought, *There is something amiss with this junk I've been associating with. I don't know who these Sword people are, but I like the looks of them, and I like the sound of what they say!*

Then when another one came, then another and another, my whole life began to change. Then my ministry began to change. I allowed some retutoring and reschooling to take place out of the pages of the SWORD.

If you had mentioned the word *fundamentalist* to the crowd I was running with, it would have taken a committee of dialogue about it to ascertain whether or not it was properly defined.

After a little while I said, "You know, I am a fundamentalist!"

Some folks today will say, "Well, let's be fundamentalists," or, "Let's be evangelicals." Some will sign onto anything and everything.

They ask me, "Aren't you an evangelical?" Not in the sense that that word is used today.

Some say, "But aren't the charismatics wonderful?" I don't know whether they are personally wonderful, but I know that what they teach is not wonderful.

They say, "But the news media makes such negative vibes about fundamentalism." I know they do, but I'm a fundamentalist. How did I become one? One makes some choices, one decides some things, and I made my choice.

Some folks say, "But a lot of things I like are happening today with those crowds." All right. That is your choice, but I won't even get in the neighborhood where they are. I'm not going that route because I made some choices.

My choice is not to have that honky-tonk music on my platform. I don't want those standing on the outside to wonder if the music they hear is coming from a bar or a church. I made some choices. I know not everybody is going to like them, but I made some choices.

We make some tough choices, and those choices impact who we are.

Get your convictions settled and make the choices you have to make; then shut the door on all the other considerations.

Our decisions can make or break us. Many have made weak decisions, and those decisions are killing their ministries. God help you to make the right choices.

Get Stuck on the Right Stuff

"I have stuck unto thy testimonies: O LORD, put me not to shame."—Vs. 31.

This verse talks about continuing: "I have stuck unto thy testimonies." Brother, be sure you get stuck on the right stuff and plan to stay.

I heard Dr. Tom Malone say, "I've lived in the same house for fifty-some years. I've had the same phone number for fifty-some years. When I get something good, I just stick with it!" I said, "Amen, brother!"

You've got a Bible; stick with it!

You're in a good, fundamental church; stick with it!

You're living a separated, godly life; stick with it!

"Eureka!"

"Princes have persecuted me without a cause: but my heart standeth in awe of thy word.

"I rejoice at thy word, as one that findeth great spoil.

"I hate and abhor lying: but thy law do I love.

"Seven times a day do I praise thee because of thy righteous judgments."—Ps. 119:161–164.

Verse 162 is the text for this message:

"I rejoice at thy word, as one that findeth great spoil."

Immediately upon reading this verse, there came to mind the word *eureka*.

Eureka is more than just a single word; it is an expression. It means "I have found it!" It's not the term you would use if you found an old, worn-out pair of shoes stuffed in the backside of the closet. You would not pick them up and say, *"Eureka! Eureka!"*

Ladies, if you were to lose the diamond on your finger and knew it was in the room somewhere, you would search high and low for it. If you didn't find it, you would sweep the floor. If you still didn't find it, you would in desperation call in the kids and maybe even the neighbors, and perhaps still you would not be able to find it.

Finally, after many days, you might happen to walk through the room, and as your eyes scan the carpet, you see it. You would be so excited you might exclaim, *"Eureka!"* ("I found it!") You would be delighted because that $2,000 ring had been found.

I lose things sometimes. Driving down the interstate one day, I got a call on my car phone. If you have to make a call of any duration, the meter ticks so fast on the car phone, especially during the prime hours, you look for a standard phone where the rate is less.

I saw an off ramp, and I got off. The service station was closed, but there was a phone booth. I got my phone card out to make the phone call. I thought I put the card back in my pants pocket. I looked in those trousers and in my shirt; I went through my duffel bag where I was carrying my clothes; I looked through the car. I looked everywhere, EVERYWHERE! No card. I haven't yet found that telephone credit card. Sure as the world, some joker is having an international gabfest at my expense!

I don't know what happened to the phone card, but just about the time I get it canceled, I'll get in the car and, lo and behold, *eureka!* There it will be!

This is a word of surprise, an expression of delight and amazement. Oh, how Christians need to learn to capture delight and amazement! So many folks profess to know the Saviour, yet they are as dead as the dark of midnight in their faith, testimony and Christian walk. They simply do not have any zip. Their get-up-and-go has already "got up and gone."

This passage in Psalm 119 tells us that it just ought not be that way, not with a born-again, Heaven-bound son or daughter of God.

Verse 162 says, "I rejoice at thy word, as one that findeth great spoil."

You say, "Listen! I found something spoiled, and I didn't take delight in it." What this is saying is not that the thing is rotten or worthless, but it is talking about a great prize, a treasure, like the booty, the spoils of war. When one nation invades another and literally takes over the nation, very often the conquering nation will take from the conquered nation whatever is there that they consider of value—the spoils of war.

The story of Daniel and the three Hebrew children is a case in point. The Babylonians had conquered Palestine and had taken the brightest and sharpest of the Jewish young people back to Babylon as prisoners of war. They were part of the prize for winning the war— booty, spoils of the war.

That's precisely the meaning of verse 162: 'I am as one who has found a great spoil, a great booty, a great prize, in that I have found the Word of God.'

When great effort has been made—such as in a war—to achieve a great victory, it is expected that there will be some prize for the victory.

The testimony of this verse declares a delight in unearthing the Word of God. Such a treasure causes the psalmist to break forth in great rejoicing. This spirit of rejoicing is the idea of *eureka*. It's the following idea: he has gone a long time without the Word of God; but suddenly, upon finding it, he says, "I've found it! What I have looked for, what my heart has longed for these years of my life, I have found!"

I've led an elderly person to Christ and seen him in a matter of hours or days literally turn from the way he had lived for so long to a bright, exuberant, happy and joyful person; and I've heard him say, "I spent all my life going in the wrong direction and doing the wrong things, but I've found it, and my life has turned around." It is that spirit of *eureka*. He has that spirit of rejoicing about him, the spirit of the rejoicing heart.

Notice what the whole passage in Psalm 119 says. The rejoicing heart sometimes has

I. The Opposition of Princes

The Hebrew word for "princes" in verse 161 is *sar,* meaning "a ruler." It can be any level of ruler, as the king or the president. He says, 'The princes (the rulers) have sometimes brought persecution against me, and without cause.'

Sometimes one's heart will rejoice at what he has found in the Word of God; nonetheless, he may have the opposition of those wicked rulers who rule adversely against him.

When wicked rulers rise up against us, it is no time to park our faith in some dark corner. When under duress and pressure, and when there are opposing forces waging war against us, it is then we need the rejoicing heart. We need the spirit of *eureka* ruling in us when the rulers rise against us.

So the psalmist says, 'These rulers have persecuted me.' Then quickly he adds, "But my heart standeth in awe of thy word"—in other words, "My heart is still gripped by the mighty Word; therefore, I rejoice at the Word as a great prize that is in my possession."

What a spirit! And what a heart for one to have!

II. The Obstacle of Persecution

The rejoicing heart sometimes has not just the opposition of the prince but the obstacle of persecution—pointedly and personally; not just some across-the-board thing where everybody is having a hard time, but where it comes directly and pointedly at the individual, where you have to stand back and ask, "Why have I been singled out? Why am I the one under the gun, under the pressure? Why don't they pick on one of those other guys? Why don't they get somebody down the street? Why is it being targeted directly at me?"

That's what the psalmist says: "The rulers have persecuted me. It's me they have come after."

It's not uncommon that such would be the case. As a companion passage and an illustration of this principle, note Paul's testimony in II Corinthians 11:23 and following: "Are they ministers of Christ? (I speak as a fool) I am more; in labours more abundant...."

You say, "Paul's just one of those 'Type A' personalities who get up early and stay up late to work. The guy's a workaholic."

Then he adds the second item: "...in stripes above measure...." They had whipped him more times than he could remember.

Paddling a child seems to have the ire and agitation of most everybody these days, even though God says that administering a paddling is not a bad thing; but here is an adult being not just paddled or whipped in some kind of a reasonable fashion but actually whipped with probably that old cat-o'-nine-tails whip. They most often gave the penalty of thirty-nine stripes with it. With the little bits of rock and bone they attached to those little leather strips, you can imagine what it was like when applied forcefully and roughly to the naked back.

Paul continues, "...in prisons more frequent...." He was spending a lot of time in the Hoosegow Hotel behind bars, locked in the dungeon.

"...in deaths oft." [A time or two he was beaten and bruised and left for dead.]

"Of the Jews five times received I forty stripes save one.

"Thrice was I beaten with rods [or clubs], once was I stoned, thrice I suffered shipwreck, a night and a day I have been in the deep [hanging onto a board or something else in the water for a night and a day];

"In journeyings often, in perils of waters, in perils of robbers, in perils by mine own countrymen, in perils by the heathen, in perils in the city, in perils in the wilderness, in perils in the sea, in perils among false brethren;

"In weariness and painfulness, in watchings often, in hunger and thirst, in fastings often, in cold and nakedness."—Vss. 23–27.

The next time you think things are tough, read this passage and compare your hard time to Paul's. When we have a bit of a negative day, we may think it's a hard time—but a hard time would be stonings, whippings or being thrown in jail because we're Christians.

The psalmist says that his heart is rejoicing and he is absolutely ecstatic; he has this spirit of *eureka* because he has found the precious Word of God.

You say, "Well, after all, he was the king!"

Yes, but there were rulers, people within his own administration, including one of his own sons, who rose up in opposition against him and persecuted him in a merciless fashion.

The rejoicing heart also has

III. The Occasion of Pain (Without a Cause)

Here is a man who was "blameless," according to Philippians 3:6; yet he is judged and penalized.

If you do something for which you deserve penalty, you may not like it and wish it hadn't happened, but you'll look at it ultimately and say, "I had it coming to me." You deal with it and take whatever penalty is coming.

When you have done nothing amiss, when there is no reason for which the opposition ought to be coming at you, no occasion for which these charges ought to be being brought, yet they *are* being brought— and brought unjustly—you are a sitting duck for becoming bitter unless down in your soul there is a rejoicing heart.

We want to be treated fairly. When treated unfairly, you may think you have reason to be bitter; but no matter how harsh the day nor how intense the persecution, we are under orders and mandate. We have example and precept. We have everything needed to maintain our hearts, to keep our spirits, to keep plodding onward and to do it with courageous hearts and souls and joyful spirits.

Don't give in to pressures. Don't give in when things don't go the way they should. "Well, it's unfair," you say. I know, but you show what kind of a Christian you are when something is unfair, when something comes at you that is so hard, so difficult, so unjust that there is no rhyme, reason or explanation.

IV. The Opinion of the Perpetrators

"I hate and abhor lying" (vs. 163). Remember, this is the man with the rejoicing heart, with this spirit of *eureka* about him; yet he says, "I hate and abhor lying." The rejoicing heart needs a softness, a tenderness about it; but the rejoicing heart has its opinion of the conspirators, its opinion of wrong things. It need not put its mind in neutral just because it's a rejoicing heart. The rejoicing heart will be able to look at the violations of God's law and say, "That's wrong."

We take strong stands. We have standards. Our opinions are anchored in the Word of God. We have to stand face-to-face and toe-to-toe with an angry world and cry out that what they're doing violates the laws of God; yet our heart continues to rejoice, and we maintain a rejoicing spirit.

I have to do things all the time that I wish I didn't have to do. I have to make a phone call tomorrow to someone in another part of the world and say, "You're about to make one more big mess! I'm urging you, don't do it!" Do you think he will take that news sitting down? I'm not even going to be able to see him when I give him the message. He's going to be coming up out of his chair, ready to swarm on me. It's already kind of been coming, and I see it coming again. The guy is going to say, "But I want to do it!"

I'm going to say, "But you shouldn't!"

He is going to reply, "But I'm agoin' to!"

I'm going to say, "But you can't!"

As soon as I get off the phone I'm going to get alone someplace and say, "Praise the Lord!" I'm going to go to lunch saying, "Amen! Amen!" I'm going home in the evening saying, "Hallelujah! Thine is the glory!"

I don't want to catch his spirit. I may go out and find a cat to chase just to give me something to do and keep me from catching the spirit of some guy who has an angry heart and spirit. I don't want his angry heart! We must keep a rejoicing heart.

You say, "But there's a standard to be maintained." I know. Maintain your standard, but don't lose your rejoicing heart.

You say, "Listen! We have to walk with God and do the things God says, and we have to go at it and attack some of the evils in our world." I know—but keep a rejoicing heart.

You say, "The world is engulfed in darkness, lost and going to Hell!" I know—but keep a rejoicing heart.

V. Optimal Attitude Toward God

The psalmist says, "Seven times a day do I praise thee because of thy righteous judgments" (vs. 164). The rejoicing heart keeps an optimal attitude toward God.

34

You may get disappointed on one hand; you may be agitated on the other. Don't measure God by those agitations and disappointments. Don't let your attitude with Him be a low-altitude attitude. Lift it up. Get it up. Keep an optimal attitude toward God, no matter what else is going on in your world.

How do you do that? You talk to God; you praise Him "seven times a day." Maybe that means the psalmist was praising every time he could think of it. With things being so tough for him, he probably had to set a time to praise God. You say, "If you have to set a time and force yourself to do it, that's not a good idea." It may be. It may be what keeps you going. If you go all day long with such a burden, being hit from all sides and not praising God, not lifting up your heart to Him and not reflecting on His greatness and goodness, you may get that old negative spirit and that carnal, angry and bitter heart.

When you get up, the first thing every morning, part the curtains and lift the blinds, look out and say, "Lord, good morning! It's me again calling." Have a little visit with the Lord.

When you start out the driveway tomorrow morning, say, "Lord, I'm driving out here, and about two-thirds of these people don't even know how to drive. Dear Lord, help me." (You who drive the rush hour each morning know what I'm talking about.)

In the afternoon your spouse meets you at the door, and if you haven't been praising the Lord along that crowded route, you are apt to be in a bad mood.

Praise the Lord as you go. If something doesn't go right at work, go into your office and pray, "Lord, I love You. You surely are good. A lot of things are not right, but, Lord, You surely are great!"

We have already seen that the writer had his hands full. There was unjust persecution. What are rulers for anyway? Certainly not to be a terror to you. They are to help the people, support the people, protect the people. These rulers ruled wickedly and brought pressure against him.

What is he doing? He is just talking to the Lord. He has a rejoicing heart. He is so excited because he has something he can hold onto, something that will anchor him when all other things go awry. What a privilege to know that there is a God in Heaven who loves us, helps us and supports us. We can have a rejoicing heart with an optimal attitude toward God. No matter what may go wrong, can you say, "Even though everything else is going sour, God is so good to me"?

Tuesday morning we left here near the crack of dawn and headed to Knoxville for a meeting where I was to preach. It is exactly five hundred miles from Westminster, Maryland to Knoxville, Tennessee. So we headed out across Harper's Ferry on our way to Charles Town, West Virginia, where there is a Hardee's.

Next to the freeway, a frontage road comes by Hardee's. Looking down that frontage road I saw a person in a motorized wheelchair right in the center of his lane, driving his wheelchair just like a car. I just knew somebody was going to run over him. He wheeled around and turned in at Hardee's. I expected him to go to the handicap ramp and roll that thing in, but he went to the drive-thru! After ordering, he wheeled back out on that frontage road and headed for home! Meals on wheels!

I looked that guy over carefully. He wheeled himself in, got his breakfast and wheeled himself out on the other side, smiling ear to ear. Here was a man confined to a wheelchair. I didn't know him from Adam, but I could tell by his countenance, by his spirit, by his behavior, by the way he wheeled that thing, that he had found it! For whatever reason he might have been handicapped, I can imagine there might have been a day when he discovered that thing with the motorization. I can imagine his saying, "*Eureka!* I've found it! I've found it!"

O God, help this preacher to have that spirit! I was able to walk in on two legs. I was able to drive in an automobile. Sometimes when the gravy is not the right flavor or the soda has lost its fizz, we whine and complain when we ought to be saying, "*Eureka!* God has blessed me, and I have found what I need!" We ought to be happy and thrilled, excited and joyful because God is so great!

I remember those three parables in Luke 15. A lady lost a coin; she swept the house until she found it. When she found it, she called her friends and said, "*Eureka! Eureka!*"

The shepherd had a lost sheep. "And when he hath found it, he layeth it on his shoulders, rejoicing. And when he cometh home, he calleth together his friends and neighbours, saying unto them, Rejoice with me; for I have found my sheep which was lost" (vss. 5, 6). In other words, "*Eureka! Eureka!* I have found it!"

That father whose boy went awry, that father whose boy betrayed him and went out into the world—when that boy came back home, the father said, 'My son was dead. He's alive again. He was lost; now he's found.' He was saying, "*Eureka! Eureka!* My boy is back!"

36

Here we are in possession of the great Word of God. A Saviour has saved us; consequently, we have every reason to rejoice. It's right here in this precious old Book that we find God, the Gospel, the truth, the secrets to success, the direction, the guidance that we need. We find the reason for peace, hope and joy. Oh, we ought to get up in the morning saying, "*Eureka! Eureka!* I have found it! I have found it!"

There is no prize of greater value, no treasure of greater delight, no spoil of greater necessity than what God has given us in the Scripture, in His Son and in salvation. One day He will give us a wonderful, beautiful place in which to live forever. We'll walk in the door of our eternal Home, and I suspect we'll cry in the spirit of "*Eureka! Eureka!* I have found it!"

"For Which Cause We Faint Not"

"For which cause we faint not; but though our outward man perish, yet the inward man is renewed day by day."—II Cor. 4:16.

"For which cause we faint not." There is a cause so dear, so precious, so worthwhile that we have given ourselves to it. We are committed to it with devoted and undying commitment. It is *our* cause, and it keeps us from fainting.

Fainting is a familiar phenomenon to some of you. Some, maybe all of you, will remember a time when you did faint. I remember fainting a couple of times. You're going along, doing really well. Then suddenly you get this rush of blood to your head and a strange feeling. Maybe the objects out in the distance aren't in focus quite as clearly. When you raise your arm or hand, it doesn't feel like it's attached. You see it, but it feels strange. The first thing you know, you pass into semiconsciousness or unconsciousness. If you're standing, you fall; and when you fall, you may actually hurt yourself.

A strange thing happens when fainting occurs. There's a faltering and fading, then come fainting and falling.

As I travel the highways, especially in the summertime, I see lots of cars on the road, sometimes at 3:00 or 4:00 in the morning. I ask myself, *Why are they not home asleep?* Of course, they're wondering the same about me!

Among all these cars on the road, every now and then will be a car stopped alongside the road. Sometimes a person will be pacing around the car with a frustrated look because his car has quit on him. Sometimes he will have the hood up, and steam will be seeping out of the engine. Other times one of the spherical objects that causes the car to be propelled along easily has lost its rotundity. (That's a flat tire!) The car sits to one side. For one reason or another, it has failed to work. It's a good automobile and cost a lot of money, but it fainted.

Sometimes when a plane is taxiing out from the tarmac to the runway, it will pass by one of the hangars where other planes are stored. When the big doors are open, you can see inside. A mechanic or two will be up in the body of a plane taking things out and putting things in. What are they doing? They are fixing the plane. I'm always saying to myself, *I hope if it decides not to work, it will decide while on the ground.*

The mechanics roll the planes out and say, "They are ready to fly." Then something on one plane doesn't work, so the mechanics park it in the hangar and continue working on it. I say to the man supervising the fleet of planes, "I'm sure you would like for that plane to fly today." He answers, "Yes. It doesn't make us money when it doesn't."

The plane ought to fly every day, but for some reason today it has fainted.

Christians Sometimes Faint

In the Christian life, a lot of things are like that. When preaching in a church where I have been several times, I may ask, "Where is So-and-so?" Then I will hear some sad story.

Things were going along great. Everything was operating normally. Then for some reason that person fainted in the process of his Christian life. He didn't die; he just fainted. He stopped soul winning, quit his bus route, stopped tithing and quit coming to church. He lost his sweet spirit. He fainted, and because he fainted, the dry rot of failure set in.

I believe this passage says to us that if we faint not, we fail not; but if we faint, we fail. It also makes clear that there is a cause so important that we must not faint—"for which cause we faint not."

I point out to you a particular verse—John 6:66—a verse with pathos dripping from it on every letter, on every word:

"From that time many of his disciples went back, and walked no more with him."

The disciples went along for a while. They liked what they saw. They enjoyed everything. Then they fainted. There came a day when one after another they said, "It doesn't suit me." Because that life didn't suit them, they faltered. Having faltered, they fainted; and having fainted, they fell by the wayside.

In II Timothy 4:10, Paul is reporting to his young protégé, Timothy, about Demas: "Demas hath forsaken me, having loved this present world." Along the way Demas had been doing a good work, but there came a time when he fainted in the process. His agenda and God's agenda did not match. Demas began to salivate for the things of the present world more than for the things of the eternal world.

In the same passage, look at verse 14: "Alexander the coppersmith did me much evil."

I thought all smiths were good Smiths! I read in the Bible about goldsmiths, blacksmiths and, in this case, a coppersmith; but I've discovered that this smith did a fellow Christian harm. He could have done good, but he didn't. Instead of bearing fruit, he fainted.

Was Alexander the coppersmith a Christian? Probably so, but there came a time when he did Paul much damage; and Paul warned Timothy, "Of whom be thou ware also" (vs. 15). In other words, "Timothy, be wary of him, because he may hurt you too."

What happened to Alexander? Everything operated normally for a while, but then a carnality grew up in his heart, and he fainted in the way.

In the same passage, Paul also says, "At my first answer no man stood with me, but all men forsook me" (vs. 16). No doubt his thoughts were: "Certain issues were raised; and when I gave my answer, not a single person would vote with me. Not a single person would stand by me. No one believed what I believed. Not one person would do what I wanted him to do. Instead, when it came time to do the will of God, all men forsook me. It was soul-winning time, but they forsook me. It was church time, but they forsook me. It was time to stand for truth and right, but they forsook me. I was there to lift the load, but not a single person was there to help me when I needed him. I was standing alone."

The Bible is illustrating for us the distressful stories of good Christians who fainted in their Christian lives. They didn't die; they just fainted; and in fainting, they failed.

Notice now what this key verse, my text, says to us: "For which cause we faint not"—meaning we have a cause to which we are committed. We have convictions about it and are so committed that we will not faint but go on, press on, stay at it.

The greater context of II Corinthians 4 gives us a number of reasons why we must not yield to fainting, why we must not give in, why we must not fail. Even if we faint, it must be only momentary. We must not

41

even contemplate the possibility of fainting. This passage gives us some reasons to go on.

I. The Source of Our Resources Is the Lord

"Therefore seeing we have this ministry, as we have received mercy, we faint not."—II Cor. 4:1.

(1) *We have mercy.* Our resource is from the Lord. We are getting a full measure of God's mercy. Getting mercy, we get blessings, and with blessings we get power. Having mercy, blessings and power, we have everything we need. God very mercifully bestows all of that upon us.

Having His resources fully delivered to us, we are then able to thrive in the ministry because we enjoy the blessing of God.

(2) *We have light.* Our hearts are strong because the light of God shines in our hearts in the midst of the darkness of this world (vs. 6).

True, we live in a world of darkness, and sometimes in the darkness we trip and fall. We stumble on things that bruise. Invariably we lose our way, thinking we are on the right path when we are not. However, the light of God shines in the dark, and this light never goes out. There is never a time when our batteries are low, never a time when we can say, "I can't get the light to work," because God's light is shining in our hearts. We never have an excuse for fumbling in the dark because the light of God is shining in us. With God's resources—so rich, so full, so powerful, so sufficient—we are kept from fainting.

(3) *We have power.* God gives His mercy, His light and His power (vs. 7). We are able to operate because "we have this treasure in earthen vessels"—the great treasure of the Gospel, the great treasure of all eternal things. In this body we can have a full supply of eternal helps.

One day this body will die. The earthen dam may get so much pressure upon it that it bursts and does not hold. Little earthenware vessels that sit on the shelves may get broken. Somebody may knock them to the solid floor, and they shatter into a thousand pieces. Then note that the treasure of God's great things has been entrusted to these earthen vessels. We are mere human vessels, but God's resources within make us able.

We ask, "But is it of us? Is the task so dependent upon us?"

The Bible says, 'The excellency of the power is of God and not of us.' We are the earthen vessels. These earthen vessels often fail, often break and cannot do the job; so we must look to God for power.

We faint not because we receive our resources from the Lord. We get mercy, light and power from the Lord (vss. 1, 6, 7). We get from the Lord every resource we need, so we will not, should not, must not fail.

II. The Stewardship of God's Word Is the Foundation of Our Strength

"But have renounced the hidden things of dishonesty, not walking in craftiness, nor handling the word of God deceitfully; but by manifestation of the truth commending ourselves to every man's conscience in the sight of God."—II Cor. 4:2.

We faint not because we are handling the Word of God. The Bible says we renounce dishonesty and craftiness and we refrain from handling the Word deceitfully. We are sustained by manifesting the truth and "commending ourselves to every man's conscience in the sight of God."

One major reason we do not fail is the Word we handle. The messages we have in the Bible guide and govern us. The promises upon which we build our lives are the wonderful, eternal words of the living God. In them we have something secure. It is not the word of mortals nor the word of some man or any man or all men—but the very Word of God.

We contemplate: *Why do we go on? Why do we press on? Why do we stay at it? Why do we live for God? Why do we serve God? Why do we go out to do the work of God every single day?* Because we have the Word of God upon which we build, the Word with truth unstained and without error.

Do we simply believe that man lives like a dog until he dies and then there is nothing more? or do we believe that man lives and dies and goes into a great eternity in Heaven and lives with God? Why do we believe that some golden daybreak Jesus will come? Because we have the Word of God.

We do not twist or distort the Word of God. We simply hear it, believe it and handle it carefully. Based upon the fact that this Book is God's inspired, inerrant, infallible and inexhaustible Word, we know we have something solid upon which we can build, so we don't faint.

You may say, "I've been slapped, kicked and bruised." Still, you have the Word of God, and you can bury your face in the Book; you can feed, be nourished and strengthened. Because we handle the Word of God conscientiously, carefully, correctly and compassionately, we faint not.

Always be a good steward of the blessed Bible.

III. The Situation Around Us Is Never Easy

The Devil is hard at work, but still we faint not. "The god [god with a little *g*] of this world hath blinded the minds of them which believe not" (vs. 4). The "god of this world" is the Devil. He is hard at work to blind the minds of those who will not trust the Saviour and believe the Word of God. He works to keep their minds blinded so they will not hear and receive. He is hard at work to deceive, to defile, to defame, to decimate, to dismember, to desecrate, to defeat and to destroy; but you and I must not be influenced. We must not faint or yield to the powers of darkness or to the god of this world.

The Devil has to work hard because we are building on the Word of God and on the resources of God, and we must not give in or yield one single inch. We will not be intimidated by the Devil. We will not faint. The great God of Heaven is far greater than the little god of this world.

"But it's such a hard world in which we work. So many things go awry. So many things don't go right," you say. I know, but we must not faint. With God's help we can overcome Satan's every effort.

IV. The Scope of Our Service Is Twofold

The text states, "For we preach not ourselves, but Christ Jesus the Lord; and ourselves your servants for Jesus' sake" (vs. 5). So we faint not in serving the Lord.

Let me ask you: Whose agenda is it—mine, yours or the Lord's? If we only serve ourselves, then when things do not go well, we can toss in the towel and say, "No more!" When we remember that it is the Lord whom we serve, however, we do not become cynical or bitter nor turn aside onto some other path or track; we stay on the agenda divinely set and faint not, nor do we fail.

It is Christ Jesus the Lord whom we preach, and it is He whom we serve. We are but His servants, and we present ourselves as such. We present ourselves not only in service to God, but "ourselves [as] *your* servants" (vs. 5). The toughest part of Christian service is not in dealing with the world and darkness but in dealing with other brothers who are standing in the light.

How do we do this? Why are we to present "ourselves [as] your servants"? The Scripture says it is "for Jesus' sake." Surely this is a concept barely afloat today! Serve God? Yes! Serve those who serve God? Yes indeed! We present ourselves as the servants of God and as servants to others because we are commissioned to do so. It is the Lord's agenda. We preach Christ Jesus the Lord and "ourselves your servants for Jesus' sake." We faint not because we are not serving our own plan. We are not working for self's sake. We faint not because we remember whom we are serving! We stand with the Lord and with other believers of like precious faith.

The scope of our service, then, is twofold. Because we understand what we are about, we faint not in serving the Lord. When Paul says, "For which cause we faint not," he is talking about the service of the Lord, which includes service to our brethren.

V. The Strikes Against Us Are Frequent

We faint not even in the time of adversity. Sometimes I think affluence is as great an adversity as is the normal context of adversity. In II Corinthians 4 Paul says:

"We are troubled on every side, yet not distressed; we are perplexed, but not in despair;

"Persecuted, but not forsaken; cast down, but not destroyed;

"Always bearing about in the body the dying of the Lord Jesus...."— Vss. 8–10.

So often the way we talk and live is like this: 'We are troubled on every side; we are perplexed, persecuted, cast down. We are always bearing about in our bodies the death of the Lord Jesus. We are about to die. We can hardly help ourselves.'

What does this Bible say? "We are troubled...yet not distressed." Paul says, "Listen! All kinds of crazy things are going on, but I'm not going to let them bother me. Sure, all kinds of things are coming down upon me, but I'm not distressed." Paul means, "I'm still sleeping well at night. I'll not lie here and worry, fret and stew; I'll press right on, go forward and faint not. Even though I have all these troubles and no exit from them yet in sight, I am not distressed."

Then he says, "We are perplexed, but not in despair." Perplexed? Well, Paul is saying to us, "I know not the answer nor where to go nor what to do next. I know not how to tell you the way out, but I am not in despair. I haven't lost hope, haven't thrown in the towel, haven't cashed in—not yet! There may not be a ready answer, but I'm going forward."

"Persecuted, but not forsaken." Friends like Alexander the copper-smith and Demas make life hard for you. All kinds of darts and arrows may be hurled at you. You look around and wonder, *Have I no friends? Yes, I do; but where are they? Well, I'll declare! I don't see any, so I guess I have none after all.*

You look around, and everybody has deserted you. Several have turned on you. You are having all kinds of persecution. Still you can say, "But I'm not forsaken. I'm never alone because the Lord is always with me."

Yes, "cast down"—walked on, stepped on, tromped on—"but not destroyed." You may come down, you may be hit so hard that you think you will die, but even in death you will win. So faint not, even in the time of adversity.

When I was growing up in Kentucky, some neighbors had a special breed of fainting goats. In many ways they were regular goats. Ordinarily a goat is a goat is a goat is a goat. If you've seen a goat, you've seen a goat! However, these fainting goats were very pretty animals, and they behaved like goats—except for one thing: Go up within twelve or fifteen feet of them and say, "Boo!" and their feet would fall from under them. They would fall over on their sides and lie there for five or ten seconds, then jump up and run off.

I have reason to believe a lot of Christians are just like that. Those little goats would faint when they were suddenly scared. They weren't *dead* goats but *fainting* goats.

We go along until some little something happens; then we fall over in a little faint or a swoon. We're not dead, just lying there in a faint. We'll wake up soon.

O God, help us that somewhere down the pike we won't wake up with five or ten years gone and wonder what happened during the time of our faint.

You say, "But I have been living in the lions' den. I have been living in the fiery furnace. All kinds of trouble have come my way."

Listen now: "Troubled…not distressed;…perplexed…not in despair; Persecuted, but not forsaken; cast down, but not destroyed."

We must not faint even in the time of adversity.

VI. The Season of Our Lives Is Short

We are born, we live, we die. As Christians we serve God knowing that one day we will die. "We…are…delivered unto death for Jesus' sake" (vs. 11). We die a bit every day. We "die daily," the Bible reminds us. The whole concept we have studied from this passage in II Corinthians 4 is: "We faint not," even though we know death is working in us; "we faint not," even as we approach the time when we too will die.

Dwight L. Moody served God. He did not faint, yet he died.

Jonathan Edwards served God faithfully and was greatly used. He fainted not, yet he died.

Charles Haddon Spurgeon, the great English preacher, won tens of thousands to Christ in the United Kingdom. He fainted not, but he died.

I could mention Lester Roloff, John Rice and many others who lived, who served God and fainted not; but they died.

We bear "in the body the dying of the Lord Jesus" (vs. 10). Paul says, "We...are...delivered unto death for Jesus' sake" (vs. 11). Verse 12 states, "So then death worketh in us, but life in you." Life comes in us because death has been worked in us. We work ourselves until death comes, in order that life may come in a few others. We faint not because of that.

Others will live because we die to self, die to hurt, die to personal ambition, die to criticism, die to whatever else may happen to us. We give up ourselves so that sinners will hear the Gospel and be saved.

VII. The Standards That Motivate Us Are Three

(1) We faint not, knowing that one day we will be presented by the Lord Jesus.

"Knowing that he which raised up the Lord Jesus shall raise up us also by Jesus, and shall present us with you."—Vs. 14.

It is that same presentation that Jude 24 gives:

"Now unto him that is able to keep you from falling, and to present you faultless before the presence of his glory with exceeding joy."

Oh, to know that one day we too will be presented by the Lord Jesus before the throne of God! Then He will say to us, "I have known you. I have blessed you. We have had fellowship through the years!"

Will you be able to say when your name is called, "I fainted not; I failed not but stayed at it"?

47

Oh, how wonderful to be presented before the throne of the glory of our Saviour and be able to say, "I fainted not!"

(2) We faint not for the glory of God. May we be able to say, "For God to be glorified, I will not faint!"

Let it redound to the glory of God that we faint not but stay in the saddle, that we work on, press on, never quit. For the glory of God we will faint not, even with pain, with sorrow, with suffering.

"For which cause we faint not" (vs. 16). We are committed to Christ, to the church, committed for souls; and because we have a cause to which we are committed, we serve, press on and faint not.

(3) We faint not for eternity's sake.

"For our light affliction, which is but for a moment, worketh for us a far more exceeding and eternal weight of glory;

"While we look not at the things which are seen, but at the things which are not seen: for the things which are seen are temporal; but the things which are not seen are eternal."—II Cor. 4:17,18.

Paul is reminding us that whatever pain we have is light compared to what it might be, and is but for a moment compared to eternity. The far more exceeding weight—the greater, heavier, weightier matter here—is not the little pain we have today but the great issue of eternity.

We look not at what we see but at what is not seen. We look not at what is temporal but at what is eternal, and for eternity's sake, we press on and stay at the task. We must keep on doing what we know to do, fainting not, failing not, but vowing that by God's grace we will be His servants, stand where we ought to stand, do what we ought to do and serve our wonderful Saviour day by day for eternity's sake.

For eternity's sake, for the sake of the cause we serve and for the glory of God, we have every reason to faint not!

Always Abounding

"Behold, I shew you a mystery; We shall not all sleep, but we shall all be changed.

"In a moment, in the twinkling of an eye, at the last trump: for the trumpet shall sound, and the dead shall be raised incorruptible, and we shall be changed.

"For this corruptible must put on incorruption, and this mortal must put on immortality.

"So when this corruptible shall have put on incorruption, and this mortal shall have put on immortality, then shall be brought to pass the saying that is written, Death is swallowed up in victory.

"O death, where is thy sting? O grave, where is thy victory?

"The sting of death is sin; and the strength of sin is the law.

"But thanks be to God, which giveth us the victory through our Lord Jesus Christ.

"Therefore, my beloved brethren, be ye stedfast, unmoveable, always abounding in the work of the Lord, forasmuch as ye know that your labour is not in vain in the Lord."—I Cor. 15:51–58.

"Always abounding in the work of the Lord"—engaged diligently, laboriously, zealously.

I. The Task

There is a task assigned to us. The Apostle Paul warned "that in the last days perilous times shall come." He goes into some detail about what those times will be like:

"For men shall be lovers of their own selves, covetous, boasters, proud, blasphemers, disobedient to parents, unthankful, unholy,

"Without natural affection, trucebreakers, false accusers, incontinent, fierce, despisers of those that are good,

"Traitors, heady, highminded, lovers of pleasures more than lovers of God."—II Tim. 3:2–4.

Today we can see all those things—not just in some little minuscule way but in great, wholesale fashion.

It is reported that in New York City alone, there are now over 200,000 drug addicts.

In Washington, D.C. there are more abortions than live births.

Our major cities now have multiple murders every single day. They say that in Miami thieves kill watchdogs with lead pipes and steal whole houses of furniture in broad daylight day after day. I'm told one cannot camp safely in any of our national parks. Ethnic gangs roam the city of Los Angeles like angry predators, with no morals, no conscience and no restraint.

The Bible says that "evil men...shall wax worse and worse, deceiving, and being deceived" (II Tim. 3:13). Hell has literally spilled its insides onto Main Street in America. The politicians, educators and social engineers are wringing their hands in desperation.

But I believe there is a greater tragedy than any of the things I've mentioned—the backslidden, carnal waywardness of professing Christians and the waywardness, backsliding and carnality of many of our churches that have good, strong statements of faith.

Both professing Christians and sound, fundamental churches have fallen into a lethargic state—apathetic, cold and indifferent—and they have left their first love.

"They will not endure sound doctrine; but after their own lusts shall they heap to themselves teachers, having itching ears;

"And they shall turn away their ears from the truth, and shall be turned unto fables."—II Tim. 4:3, 4.

Many churches are as lethargic as they can be. Others have been sapped by liberalism. In fact, almost anything liberal is a sap; and theological liberalism is a doctrinal poison.

So many churches that at one time were shooting straight are now using some kind of a diluted Bible, and it breaks down from there. The liberalism that we used to face and battle in the Convention, I fear, is getting some roots in our own movement.

There are not only problems of lethargy and liberalism, but there is a looseness among us that is of great concern. Our moral perspective is "anything goes," from the White House to the schoolhouse to the church house—no standards and being permissive in everything. There is a crisis brewing in America because of that.

We lambast the bureaucrats in Washington—and probably do as much of that as anybody else—but I believe the problem is mine and yours. The crisis that exists in America will exist as long as we will tolerate it and until we determine to get back on our horses and ride like we're supposed to ride.

The liturgical crowd have signs out that say they are churches, when literally that crowd is already "Ichabod." Other places I simply call liberal social clubs. Honestly, they are an odoriferous stench in the nostrils of a holy God.

Then there are the evangelicals. There is a difference between us and them. The evangelicals have diluted their theology. They are laid back, "me-centered," eroded by compromise and accommodation. I made a decision some years ago not to preach for those crowds. There are some places where we ought not go and lend our endorsement.

These new contemporary churches are taking over now. We had a couple of them in Westminster—the "have-it-your-own-way" church. One of the major news magazines did a spread declaring that the baby boomers have been away from church but they're back now.

Do you know what this new, contemporary philosophy is? The preacher has to take off his coat, tie and white shirt and put on a T-shirt or some open-neck deal. Let's get rid of the pulpit as well and just have a mike in front of us so our people can hear us. The preacher just slouches on a stool. In fact, they had such a picture in *Time* magazine with an article on it. This is the contemporary philosophy.

Some of our crowd (or those who used to be) are going around the country doing seminars, saying, "Hey, get with it! Let's do it! This is the way to do it. This is the way to build crowds." I was not too interested in my church's becoming a contemporary church.

A guy said to me, "I went to _____ [and he mentioned the name of the place]. I wore a short-sleeved, open-neck sports shirt Sunday morning; and, honestly, Pastor, I was overdressed. Cut-off shorts and tennis shoes were all I saw there."

The whole design of this new contemporary philosophy is to take the Bible out of the preacher's hand, take the preacher out of the pulpit and take the pulpit out of the church.

We have a great assignment, a great task, when we see these things happening.

I ask you, Is it time to get discouraged? I don't think so. Is it time for us to be defeated? I don't think so. Is it time for us to doubt? I don't think so.

These are times 'always to abound in the work.' We determine to go and do what we're supposed to do. Our command is, "Go ye therefore, and teach all nations" (Matt. 28:19). Jesus said, "Go ye into all the world, and preach the gospel to every creature" (Mark 16:15).

He said, "Go home to thy friends, and tell them how great things the Lord hath done for thee" (Mark 5:19).

These are times when we need co-workers who will abound with us, who are conscious of the commands of God and who are obedient to His orders and diligent in the duty assigned to them.

On occasion the Lord sent the disciples "two and two before his face into every city and place" and said to them:

"The harvest truly is great, but the labourers are few: pray ye therefore the Lord of the harvest, that he would send forth labourers into his harvest."— Luke 10:2.

Some in our town did not like what we did. Some in our town criticized what we did. However, I'm under contract. I'm not obligated to respond every time somebody voices a criticism. Every time somebody says, "Here's a new wave or trend," I'm not under obligation to follow that wave or trend. I am under contract from my Lord, and He said:

"Go out quickly into the streets and lanes of the city, and bring in hither the poor, and the maimed, and the halt, and the blind....

"Go out into the highways and hedges, and compel them to come in, that my house may be filled."—Luke 14:21–23.

All across this land we have the lazy, the backslidden and some in the ministry who say, "Well, it doesn't matter how large the crowds or whether or not folks come."

There is a ball team in Maryland called the Baltimore Orioles. They have a beautiful ball park seating 46,000. Once they went through a period of time when they had over 60 straight sellouts. Everybody said, "Man, that's great! Man, those Birds go out and play ball, and great crowds come!"

Are we so naive as to believe that 46,000 people buy those expensive tickets and show up every night just to watch baseball? Those crowds are orchestrated. Probably as many people are working behind the scenes to get the crowds as are on the ball field playing ball. They work at it. They have Home Run Clubs and other ways to get folks to come.

The Bible says, "The children of this world are in their generation wiser than the children of light" (Luke 16:8).

We put little signs out front that have the names of our churches on them and say, "You all come," and we wonder why the crowds are not coming. Some sit home, watch television or do whatever they like to do, then wonder why people don't come to church.

People asked me why we were able to do what we did in Westminster. I used to have some pat answers that I thought explained it, but I decided I was not sure I knew why. Aside from the fact that we tried to do what I've been telling you about over and over, I'm not sure, humanly speaking, that I can explain exactly why it happened; but I can tell you this: it helps if the preacher will get up out of his rocking chair Monday night, Tuesday night and Thursday night and make some house calls and phone several dozen people. He might decide that some of those buses the school system is throwing away are worth investing a few dollars in, and he might decide to run them up and down the streets picking up folks and bringing them in.

You have empty pews. Why don't you set folks on them? Are they not the quality to suit you? If you'll quit worrying about the quality and go for the quantity, God might give you some quality.

You are looking at a preacher who is not ashamed that he believes this Book. When you come to our church in Westminster, you won't have to check to see which Bible we are using. It is always the King James Version.

When you come to our place, you won't have to ask, "Are you having service Sunday night?"

I'm surprised at the number of places where the church door is no longer open on Sunday night. I'm surprised at how many churches have no service on Wednesday night.

I went way up in the Northeast—in Vermont, New Hampshire and Massachusetts. I went to Northampton. I visited the church where

Jonathan Edwards held forth and where his grandfather had preceded him for many years.

I thought about the sermon he preached in another place in 1741 that literally ignited a revival across the great Northeast, where now there are a dearth and a deadness that liberalism has brought in.

I thought about Jonathan Edwards who preached that mighty sermon on sin and judgment and salvation. Right down the street is another church that he later opened because the first church ultimately came to say, "We don't want to hear about sin and judgment and salvation anymore," and by a 10-to-1 margin voted Edwards out of the church.

As I stood and looked at the house where he had lived and where his grandfather had lived, those streets where he no doubt had walked so many times, I thought, *Was there not a great burden on that man's heart? Did it not cut him to the quick when people said, "We don't want to hear your message anymore"?*

In Heaven, no doubt, Jonathan Edwards has long since been reminded that his message was right, and it got through and took a whole generation of people to Heaven because he did not give in to pressure and criticism.

I remind you that we are under contract to go out and get people. In our commission Jesus said, "As my Father hath sent me, even so send I you" (John 20:21). His commission took Him to the cross. Our commission is to take the cross and the Christ of that cross and His message to men so they may hear it and be saved.

Jesus said, "I have chosen you…that ye should go and bring forth fruit, and that your fruit should remain" (John 15:16).

Those truths may be disavowed, denied and disobeyed; but if we stick to the Book, we cannot debate them nor disobey them without some twinge of conscience.

II. The Power

The task that we have is one requiring power. This text says "always abounding." All kinds of pressure are on not to do that today. All kinds of things beckon us this way and that way. So our task requires a power that only God can give.

How do we get that power?

The Bible says there is power in salvation:

"I am not ashamed of the gospel of Christ: for it is the power of God unto salvation to every one that believeth."—Rom. 1:16.

One Sunday a man and his wife walked down the aisle in our second service and gave their hearts to Christ. The next day, unbeknownst to me (I learned of it later), the gentleman, who had just completed a brand-new bar in his home and had it stocked full, within twenty-four hours of the time they walked the aisle and gave their hearts to Christ, emptied that bar. That's the power of salvation!

Less than a week from the time that man was saved, a relative was on the line telling me, "You've got to do something about this guy!"

I said, "Dear lady, we already did!" It's the power of salvation.

The Bible also talks about the power of the Spirit:

"Ye shall receive power, after that the Holy Ghost is come upon you."—Acts 1:8.

Parenthetically, that doesn't mean you will jabber like a baby and act like an idiot. The verse goes on to say that when you get the power, you will witness.

The Bible also talks about the power of supplication:

"Now unto him that is able to do exceeding abundantly above all that we ask or think, according to the power that worketh in us,

"Unto him be glory in the church."—Eph. 3:20,21.

The Bible talks also about the power of the Scripture:

"The word of God is quick, and powerful, and sharper than any twoedged sword."—Heb. 4:12.

There is also the power of sincerity:

"Our gospel came not unto you in word only, but also in power, and in the Holy Ghost, and in much assurance; as ye know what manner of men we were among you for your sake."—I Thess. 1:5.

There is power in holy, godly, sanctified living.

"That ye might walk worthy of the Lord unto all pleasing, being fruitful in every good work, and increasing in the knowledge of God;

"Strengthened with all might, according to his glorious power, unto all patience and longsuffering with joyfulness."—Col. 1:10,11.

III. The Determination

When we have revival in our churches, the Spirit of God is openly manifest, and we almost immediately have reaction. Everybody wants to critique it. Committees are formed, and the cooldown begins.

Following the reaction to revival, there is a reticence, a lukewarmness, an apathy, then the meltdown that soon leads to the complete breakdown and ruin.

We're like Israel of old, like a Yo-Yo—up and down, off and on. We wonder what happened to the folks who walked down the aisle. We wonder what happened to the folks who were baptized every Sunday.

Determine to beat the odds and don't let it happen where you are.

You say, "I can't get my deacons to go along with the program." If they will go for souls, they will go along with your program.

"Is it going to be the fate of my church that it falls into liberalism and disarray?" It might be, but not with your permission, not without a fight from you and not as long as you have breath.

Some things are worth fighting for; some things are worth standing our ground for. One of the biggest jobs preachers have is to say, "No!" but to please the Lord, you have to say it a lot.

A couple came to our church a few Sundays. I called and made an appointment, then went to see them.

I walked up and said, "Hello. How are you?"

He said, "Just fine. Come in. Sit down, please."

I sat down and started to say, "That's pretty. That looks nice," but I didn't get a chance.

He said, "Preacher, I'm glad you came. The Sundays we were there, you talked about what you call 'saved.' People sang, and people went forward each Sunday. What do they do when they go forward? Can you tell me about it?"

I said, "I think I can help you with that," and I did.

In Westminster I went to a hospital to talk and pray with one of our members. Just across the hall a fellow was standing in the doorway in his bathrobe. As I walked out of the hospital room of my member, he looked at me. I thought he started to say something, but I nodded to him and kept walking. As I turned my back to him, he said, "Excuse me."

I turned and said, "Yes sir?"

"Would you mind coming in and saying a prayer like that in my room?"

"I wouldn't mind at all. Let's go in."

He sat on the edge of his bed and said, "I heard you praying with the other fellow across the hall, and I need somebody to pray a prayer like that for me."

I said, "Well, sir, I'd be glad to pray a prayer like that for you; but let me ask you a couple of things first." I had the privilege of leading that man to Christ.

He told me, "I will come to church on Sunday."

His wife told me later that two or three days after he got out of the hospital he said, "Now, as soon as I can walk, I want to go to that church and get baptized."

Ten days later when she went in one morning to wake him, she found him on his knees, leaning over on the bed. He had died in the night.

I was preaching in one of the big cities in the Northeast. On Tuesday afternoon the ones who were preaching with me said, "Let's get in the car and go do something."

I said, "I know a place in the immediate area that everybody ought to see—a church that used to be a great ministry. I think you would enjoy seeing the campus and the facilities. Let's drive over there."

We drove about twenty minutes across town, found it and went in. The kindergarten teacher said, "The church is locked up, but the janitor is over here, and he'll let you in."

The janitor came over and said, "Hi. I'm Joe." We introduced ourselves, and the four of us started in. He took us in through the furnace room.

A buddy of mine who was walking in first asked, "Hey, Joe, do you enjoy coming to church here?"

"Oh, I don't come here to church." (I've never understood why churches will employ people who do not attend the churches that employ them.)

My preacher friend said to him, "Well, Joe, if you don't come to church here, where do you go?"

"St. Stephen's."

About that time he opened the door into a big 1,200-or-so-seat auditorium. Joe moved around and turned on a light. We came in. I walked up and stood behind the pulpit, looked around and began to quote Scripture, just voicing it out.

I turned to my friends, laughed and said, "See there! I've preached in So-and-so's church! Mark it down"—just joking around.

A couple of the men were walking around looking at some of the other things. I was leaning on the pulpit.

I asked, "Joe, what kind of a church is St. Stephen's?"

He told me, and it was about what you would guess.

I said, "Well, Joe, I don't know about St. Stephen's, but let me ask you something." About that time my three friends scattered and went off into the rest of the building to give me time with him. Sometime later they came back. I had said, "Now, Joe, when these fellows come back in, tell them what we just did here!"—and he did.

There are unsaved folks everywhere. You and I need 'always to abound in the work of the Lord.' The time is always right. Jesus said, "Say not ye, There are yet four months, and then cometh harvest?" (John 4:35). He said, "I must work the works of him that sent me, while it is day: the night cometh, when no man can work" (John 9:4).

When Moses crossed the Red Sea, had I lived in that time I wouldn't have wanted to have missed that.

When Elijah rebuked the prophets of Baal, had I lived in that time I would not have wanted to have missed that.

When three thousand were saved on the day of Pentecost, I would have hated to have been a Jew from Jerusalem and been off at Herod's palace in Masada on vacation.

Folks, when the buses ran at our place, I enjoyed seeing them roll off the lot every Sunday. When another preached at our place, I wanted to be there. When we went soul winning on Thursday night, I was not sitting home watching a ball game while our folks were out trying to win folks to Christ. Yet folks do that all the time.

They brought a little boy to Jesus. He had just a lunch that wasn't much, but God took it. It wasn't gourmet food, but God blessed it. It wasn't filet mignon, but God used it.

"It's not enough," you say; but God will multiply what is given to Him.

With all that is going on, remember, we are on the winning side. We need to play the role of a champion—get up, get going and determine to go for it.

"We shall all be changed, In a moment, in the twinkling of an eye, at the last trump: for...the dead shall be raised incorruptible."—I Cor. 15:51,52.

All of this leads us to one conclusion: this old world is as rotten as she can be. Regardless, you and I need to take heart and go back home from this conference and start doing what we know to do and keep on doing it, even if it harelips every imp in Hell.

"Therefore, my beloved brethren, be ye stedfast, unmoveable, always abounding in the work of the Lord."—Vs. 58.

From the Fullness Comes the Filling

"Let no man deceive you with vain words: for because of these things cometh the wrath of God upon the children of disobedience.

"Be not ye therefore partakers with them.

"For ye were sometimes darkness, but now are ye light in the Lord: walk as children of light:

"(For the fruit of the Spirit is in all goodness and righteousness and truth;)

"Proving what is acceptable unto the Lord.

"And have no fellowship with the unfruitful works of darkness, but rather reprove them.

"For it is a shame even to speak of those things which are done of them in secret.

"But all things that are reproved are made manifest by the light: for whatsoever doth make manifest is light.

"Wherefore he saith, Awake thou that sleepest, and arise from the dead, and Christ shall give thee light.

"See then that ye walk circumspectly, not as fools, but as wise,

"Redeeming the time, because the days are evil.

"Wherefore be ye not unwise, but understanding what the will of the Lord is.

"And be not drunk with wine, wherein is excess; but be filled with the Spirit."—Eph. 5:6–18.

Verse 6 mentions being deceived with vain words.

Verse 11 tells us not only to have no fellowship with the unfruitful works of darkness but to reprove them.

Verse 14 states, "Awake thou that sleepest, and arise from the dead," talking about the same person. He is saying, "Wake up!" This fellow is in such a deep slumber that he appears dead. "Wake up NOW! Don't act like you are dead! Let the light of Christ enable you to capture the day! Make full use of the time. Awake and know what the will of the Lord is."

He says in verse 18, "And be not drunk with wine...but be filled with the Spirit." Don't be intoxicated with distilled spirits, but get filled with the Spirit of God!

In Ephesians there are three emphases on fullness:

I. The Fullness of God

The first is in chapter 3, verse 19: "...all the fulness of God."

A lot of things are to be considered in that. When I think about God the Father, I think of Him as the Creator; I think of all the beautiful things He has made.

I went to east Tennessee last weekend and to east Kentucky the Sunday before. When I drove through the hills and valleys, I could not help but see and believe that there is a great God, the Creator who made everything, and "without him was not any thing made that was made" (John 1:3).

In creation, I see God in His fullness.

I think about the character of God, His multiplied attributes that are almost incomprehensible and beyond our ability to articulate fully with our limited vocabulary. I am absolutely astounded at the character of God, His flawless perfection, His immutability, His eternality, His sovereignty.

I think about the eternality of God. Once when a person quizzed me as to how it was possible that God had no beginning or end, I said, "It's like looking out into space."

"Well, space is infinity; it has no end to it," you say.

"Oh, there's got to be a stopping place out there somewhere," another says.

My position is this: if there *is* a stopping place, I'd like to know what's on the other side. Finiteness is much more difficult to describe than infinity. When you think about it, if there *was* a starting place, what happened the day before? If there was a time when time began, wasn't there something five minutes before that?

In the same kind of way, God is an eternal Being. He has no beginning and no end. The day I was conceived was the beginning for me, but God had no such day. The fact is, we see the great God in all His fullness: in His creation, in His character, in His eternality, in His omnipotence and omnipresence. We see the absolute vastness of God.

When I think of that, I say, "Surely if there is a God like that, I ought to give Him a place in my life!"

II. The Fullness of Christ

In Ephesians 4:13, we find "the fulness of Christ."

When I think about Christ in His fullness from His virgin birth to His triumphant resurrection and marvelous ascension, I rejoice at how great and wonderful He is.

The Bible also clearly depicts this virgin-born, resurrected Christ as taking part in creation. In Genesis 1:26 God the Father says, "Let us make man in our image." About whom was He talking? About Himself and God the Son and God the Holy Spirit. We see that fully delineated in John, chapter 1:

"In the beginning was the Word, and the Word was with God, and the Word was God.

"The same was in the beginning with God.

"All things were made by him; and without him was not any thing made that was made."—Vss. 1–3.

Here we see Him as the Creator, the great, eternal God— omnipresent, omnipotent and omniscient, just as the Father is.

Whenever I contemplate that my great Saviour is who He is and what He is, then see the statement that He is, in fact, the fullness of the Godhead bodily (Col. 2:9), I stand back and say, "If God in all His vastness and fullness is who the Bible says He is, and if Christ Jesus in His vastness and fullness is all that the Bible says He is, I ought to pay attention; I ought to listen very carefully."

III. The Fullness of the Holy Spirit

Ephesians 5 emphasizes the fullness of the Holy Spirit. Everything that God is, everything that Christ is, everything the Holy Spirit is, is expressed in the concept of *fullness*. We are admonished here to let the great Lord God Almighty in the Person of the Holy Spirit fill us to the full so that in our little container—our little human, fleshly body—we might be filled up to the full with this great Holy Spirit of God. In fact, it is a double command. He says certain things do not belong in your body. Do not allow yourself to be drunk with wine.

As a little boy, when we went places and saw someone drinking, my daddy would point to that person and say, "Son, see that? Don't you ever do that!" Folks, drill that into your kids! Show them that alcohol in all its forms—whiskey, beer, vodka, gin, rum, wine and however else they make it—is bad! Alcohol is a devil, and it ought to be poured in the sewer and run out of town!

This is not really the thrust of this sermon, but I never pass up an opportunity to beat up on alcohol. Beer—light or heavy, little cans or big cans, little bottles and big bottles—is bad stuff!

The sum and substance of this fullness is not just to be filled once but to be filled continuously with the Spirit. Every time there is a slight emptiness, let the Spirit of God fill you.

We have gotten a little spooked about being filled with the Holy Spirit. You may be dragging your feet in your Christian life. You sit here service after service and hear the preacher talk about soul winning but do nothing to win others. You are weak. You are not an "A" student. You barely passed at school. You know there is no way you can speak to others about being saved. You sit here and say to yourself, *That couldn't possibly be for me.* You are scared to death even to think about doing some of the things that are voiced from this platform over and over again.

The fullness of the Holy Spirit can help you.

IV. Religion's Distorted Doctrine of the Holy Spirit

The teaching, the doctrine, of the Holy Spirit is often distorted. Remember when I read the text and pointed out some things about being careful lest somebody deceive you? Pay attention, because I'm going to wave some flags at you.

Remember in that passage where it says there are certain unfruitful works of darkness that ought to be reproved? Okay, I'm about to shellac a few things.

When I say the teaching, the doctrine, of the Holy Spirit is often distorted across the land, what do I mean? Specifically, I'm talking about the so-called "speaking in tongues" that is so prominently flaunted on the American religious scene. The so-called "speaking in tongues" is actually gibbering nothingness!

How can I speak so knowingly about that? I simply know that what some call "tongues" today is as phony as a nine-dollar bill! It is counterfeit! What a lot of those folks have, they got from the *other source*, not from God. How do I know that? Because in the second chapter of Acts when the "tongues" were spoken, **they were real languages!** Foreigners present could understand the message. They heard the Gospel in their own languages, and three thousand people were saved!

In fact, when the Bible talks about this in the second chapter of Acts, it uses two terms: the first term is *glossa*, which always means "a language," not gibberish, ecstatic stuff. The second term is *dialektos*, which means "dialect." That's the reason those foreign Jews in Jerusalem on the day of Pentecost said, 'We heard the wonderful works of God spoken in our own *dialektos*, our own tongue' (Acts 2:6).

You say, "Well, look what happened at Corinth." Remember, Corinth was not exactly a spiritual church. They were steeped in carnality. In I Corinthians, chapters 12, 13 and 14, there is an attempt by Paul kindly and tenderly to correct the carnality in which the Corinthians were engaged. They knew what happened in Jerusalem on the day of Pentecost. Such a gift of language had not happened at their place, so they were trying to create the same thing there. Since they couldn't, they *faked* it! Now Paul was trying to straighten them out.

You ask, "How do you know what people do today is phony?" Let me say this: I was recently in Japan. What do the Pentecostal missionaries have to do when they go to Japan? Go to language school! Their tongues do not work!

When you watch television (and I hope and pray that you don't watch much of it), you see Benny Hinn or Swaggart or Parsley or Angley or any of the tongues-talking Pentecostals in Africa or some non-English-speaking country. They have an interpreter just like I had in Japan, because their "tongues" do not work!

The teaching of the Holy Spirit about tongues that is so highly touted in charismatic circles is phony. Not only the "tongues" but the "laughing revivals," the barking and baying, the rolling in the aisles, the slaying in the Spirit—all of that which they promote as spiritual is fleshly. It is like a carnival.

Right along with the tongues in that crowd is the "extrabiblical revelation." Some of you have seen Peter Popoff on television. He walks around in the audience, finds a guy he had supposedly never seen before, and says, "I know you. Your name is Mr. So-and-so, and you work for…" He can give the man's address and social security number. Supposedly he has an extrabiblical revelation from God to be able to do that. No. It was all done with a radio.

What the audience doesn't realize is that Popoff's wife and some workers are meeting the people as they come in the building and are taking really good notes. When the service begins and he is circulating around through the crowd, his wife is back in another room on a little FM transmitter (he's wearing a tiny hearing-aid-type receiver in his ear), saying to him, "Peter, this guy's name is Mr. So-and-so, and he lives at…," and she gives him all the information in bits and pieces. Then he calls it out as though he had a special word from God. In reality, he is a con man and a fake.

All of this was tape-recorded. I have a piece of the video tape showing this "back room" procedure. It blew him out of the water, and he went off television for a while, but he is back now. In fact, I saw him on TV the other day.

These guys walking around pulling off those charades in front of audiences are playing on people's emotions. It is *not* for real—and certainly *not* biblical! When you hear someone saying, "I've got a word of knowledge that someone in Atlanta is getting his gall bladder healed; somebody in Charleston has his corns falling off his big toe," it is phony, phony, phony!

A fellow from Tulsa said he saw a nine-hundred-foot Jesus. He got on TV and said that this nine-hundred-foot Jesus told him that if he didn't raise several million dollars, he was going to die. Let me assure you that he didn't see a nine-hundred-foot Jesus!

What happened to him? What made him say this? Probably he ate too much sauerkraut that night!

These guys are notorious for what the Bible describes as "private interpretation" of Scripture, which leads to false doctrine. By the way, I'll also mention the "healings." There are healing charades going on at a convention center in almost every city! Wonder why these guys don't go to the hospitals to have their healing meetings! Don't misunderstand me. I know God can heal. We pray for people to be healed all the time, and we should, but I am dead set against these characters who are making merchandise of these performances, declaring people healed when there is absolutely no evidence that they have been healed!

Let me tell you what they do when they have a problem. Some of you will remember Katherine Kuhlman, kind of the female patron saint of Pentecostalism. I saw her on television many times. When she got along in years, she had a heart problem. She went to the hospital and had cardiac surgery!

R. W. Shambach is on television to this day. About six or seven years ago he had a problem. He went in for heart surgery.

Just recently the pastor of the Brownsville Assembly down in Pensacola, where all that big hoopla is going on and where they have had somewhere around two million visitors in two and a half years, fell off a construction project and broke his collarbone, his pelvis and ribs. They took him to the emergency room. People came from all over the world to be in his healing lines every night, yet when he had a problem, he was taken to the emergency room.

I called down there and got one of the associate pastors on the line. I told him who I was, then said, "I hope you will not think I'm unkind, but I have a very serious question: Why did you take him to the emergency room?" There was silence on the other end of the phone.

I asked, "Are you still having services every night?"

He said, "Yes."

"Don't you still have healing lines?"

"Yes."

"Do you have people rolling in there in wheelchairs every night?"

"Yes."

"Why didn't you roll the pastor in there?"

"Well, it is just strange how God works."

I'm serious. I'm telling you exactly what happened and what was said.

I asked, "Well, how long has he been out of the pulpit?"

"About six weeks, but he'll be back this Sunday."

"Is he going to be able to preach?"

"No; he will be in a wheelchair."

"Well, are you going to put him in the healing line?"

He just kind of garbled something and never answered me on that!

Now, folks, please don't misunderstand me. Your Bible has John 3:16 in it, but it also has I John 4:1–3 and 6:

"Beloved, believe not every spirit, but try the spirits whether they are of God: because many false prophets are gone out into the world.

"Hereby know ye the Spirit of God: Every spirit that confesseth that Jesus Christ is come in the flesh is of God:

"And every spirit that confesseth not that Jesus Christ is come in the flesh is not of God: and this is that spirit of antichrist."

"Hereby know we the spirit of truth, and the spirit of error."

There is a difference! Not everyone who comes to town talking like a Christian is a Christian. The teaching of the Holy Spirit today is often distorted, but the fact is, there is powerful teaching in the Bible about the ministry of the Holy Spirit. What it says is that the Holy Spirit does the following things:

The Holy Spirit Is Our Teacher

"And when he is come, he will reprove the world of sin, and of righteousness, and of judgment:

"Of sin, because they believe not on me;

"Of righteousness, because I go to my Father, and ye see me no more;

"Of judgment, because the prince of this world is judged."—John 16:8–11.

"But the Comforter, which is the Holy Ghost, whom the Father will send in my name, he shall teach you all things."—John 14:26.

When you hear truth, pray that the Holy Spirit will communicate it to you. Even if it's not communicated in the finest, most articulate way, if you will listen and let the Spirit work, you will be taught something, and you will learn the great truths of God!

The Holy Spirit Is Our Reprover

The Holy Spirit is our Teacher; He is also our Reprover. The Bible says that He resides in us. "And I will pray the Father, and he shall give you another Comforter [the *Parakletos*, meaning "He who will come alongside you"], that he may abide with you for ever" (John 14:16). That is the promise God gives about the Holy Spirit.

The Holy Spirit Resides

He comes reproving, teaching and abiding. Then I Corinthians, chapter 12, states that He places us in the body of Christ.

That's another thing charismatics talk about—getting the baptism of the Holy Ghost. Listen, when you got saved, you got baptized by the Holy Spirit into the body of Christ! You don't need to seek a second blessing or a third blessing in regard to that. The baptism is the placing of the believer into the body of Christ.

The Holy Spirit Magnifies Jesus

The Holy Spirit not only reproves, teaches and abides with us, but the Bible indicates that He is also the One who magnifies Jesus.

"When the Comforter [the *Parakletos*] *is come, whom I will send unto you from the Father, even the Spirit of truth, which proceedeth from the Father, he shall testify of me."*—John 15:26.

In chapter 16, verses 13 and 14, He said, "He shall not speak of himself," but "He shall glorify me."

This is a composite of what I'm saying. When you see a meeting advertised and the great talk is all about the Holy Spirit, it may be that the Holy Spirit has nothing to do with it. When the Holy Spirit is really in charge, He doesn't build up Himself nor promote Himself nor advertise Himself nor preach Himself nor proclaim Himself. The Holy Spirit is in the background, and He always pushes Jesus to the forefront, making Him the big item.

When the Holy Spirit fills us, He doesn't magnify Himself in us, nor does He get us to go around saying, "Oh, how wonderful is the Spirit!" He gets us to go around saying, "Oh, how wonderful is Jesus!"

When the Holy Spirit guides, governs and controls us, we don't go around bragging on the Holy Spirit; we brag on Jesus!

The Holy Spirit Fills Us

The Holy Spirit reproves, teaches and resides in us and magnifies Jesus. Then He fills us with power so that we can do the job Christians are supposed to do.

Here I am, weak and trembling; and the pastor preaches that we ought to do this, and we ought to do that, and I say, "That's good for all those strong folks; but I am weak! That's good for all those longtime Christians, but I haven't been a Christian very long, and I'm still struggling."

You need what this passage talks about—the filling of the Holy Spirit to give you power. Acts 1:8 says that when the Holy Spirit comes in you, He will fill you and give you power. *Power!*

Have you ever tried to pick up something that was bigger than you? What if I claim I have a lot of muscles and can pick up the piano with one hand and move it? You'd say, "Man, you're losing it!" Well, so I can't move the piano like that. Maybe I'll just grab the pulpit and give it a toss up into the balcony! "Man, you're way off. You can't do that!"

When I think about coming to a place like this, or I go out and sit down with someone who is lost and living in darkness, or I think about communicating with someone about what it means to go to Heaven and miss Hell, to have Christ and be forgiven and get saved, it scares me to death. I say, "Me? There's no way I can do something like that! No way can I possibly make that happen!"

Over the years, the Lord has allowed me to lead hundreds and hundreds to Christ.

Sometimes I go into churches where I've never been before, walk on the platforms and see them doing things with which I'm not comfortable—singing some oddball music and the like. I sit there and think, *O my soul! What's going to happen here?*

In a service a lady got up to sing, but first she started talking. She went on for about seven or eight minutes. I said to myself, *What's she doing? I won't have time to say anything, and they've brought me a long way.* Finally, I bowed my head and prayed quietly, *Lord, if that lady is going to sing, it's time for her to do it. Please shut her up and let her sing.* Almost immediately she began singing!

You can get into some difficult situations traveling around the country. How do I adjust to that? I ask God to help me, to fill me, to anoint me, to give me what I need so that those hearing me will get what they need—*dunamis,* the power of God. It is not in my flesh, not in my mind, not in my ability to quote Scripture or carefully craft a sermon; but in the power and energy of God I am able to minister.

How is it possible to live in a world of darkness and be the light we ought to be? By the Holy Spirit's power.

This passage says not to be like the old drunk; instead, be filled with the Spirit.

The old drunk gets intoxicated and loses control of himself. The same thing happens when you get filled with the Spirit. You quit trying to control yourself and let the Spirit control you.

That old drunk often gets a loose tongue. When the Holy Spirit controls you, your tongue will loosen, and you will be able to walk up to that fellow and witness to him! How did your tongue get loose? How were you able to speak freely? By letting the Spirit have control.

The old drunk lays aside all his ordinary cares and concerns. He will give you ten dollars if you ask him. He doesn't think about paying his bills tomorrow. When we get filled with the Spirit, the ordinary cares and concerns take a backseat, and we start thinking about eternal matters and what the Spirit impresses upon us.

Also, the drunk likes the camaraderie of his fellow drunks. They may not have bathed in a week, but those drunks wallow all over one another. They talk about what great guys they are. Christians have a whole different attitude about the people of God when filled with the Holy Spirit of God. You say, "Some of the Christians I know are not very lovable." You will find them lovable when you let the Spirit take control.

Every Christian needs that filling, that anointing, that empowering of the Spirit of God. Quit thinking pridefully about who you are. Quit thinking about whether you are going to succeed or fail. Just remember the commands and mandates of God and ask Him to give energy for what you must do.

We cannot do it ourselves. To get in the place of blessing, we must empty ourselves of self—and anything else that needs to come out—and ask the Lord to fill us.

Put away all those old, dead limbs. If there is trash hanging around in your life, get rid of it. Far too many of us have let rooms of our houses be occupied by other things. Walk around every room in your house—the house of your life—and open up the closets and let the fresh air of the Holy Spirit invade that place. Leave no room locked. Let nothing be privatized to the point that the Holy Spirit cannot have residence there. Do that, and you will sense the power and energy that come from God. You will see that He really meant it when He said He would give us power to do what He has asked us to do.

This verse and the context remind me of the fullness of God and the great magnitude of God the Father. They remind me of the fullness of Christ and all that we have in Him. I can stand in awe and see the great God Almighty, and I can declare, "Isn't God something!"

When I think about the fullness of Christ and how willing He is to save not just somebody important, but you and me, I'm absolutely astounded!

God Wants Something From You

God wants me to live like a Christian. He wants me to put my hands and my feet to the task of not only walking *with* Him but walking *for* Him. I think, *There is no way I can do all of that!* But He promised to give us the power we need. He said He would provide the fare, the vehicle, if we would let Him fully invade every room of our lives. That's the filling of the Holy Spirit.

The fullness of God? Yes! The fullness of the Lord Jesus? Yes! The fullness of the Holy Spirit? Yes! All are available to fill us up and make us into something special.

God has in mind to do something in your life. I wouldn't even begin to try to tell you what it is, for I don't know; but if you will listen closely, God will make it abundantly clear to you as you go about your business from day to day, talking to people, witnessing and trying to get people saved.

Getting Back the Years the Locust Ate Up

Joel 1:1–4:

"The word of the LORD that came to Joel the son of Pethuel.

"Hear this, ye old men, and give ear, all ye inhabitants of the land. Hath this been in your days, or even in the days of your fathers?

"Tell ye your children of it, and let your children tell their children, and their children another generation.

"That which the palmerworm hath left hath the locust eaten; and that which the locust hath left hath the cankerworm eaten; and that which the cankerworm hath left hath the caterpiller eaten."

Verses 13–15:

"Gird yourselves, and lament, ye priests: howl, ye ministers of the altar: come, lie all night in sackcloth, ye ministers of my God: for the meat-offering and the drink-offering is withholden from the house of your God.

"Sanctify ye a fast, call a solemn assembly, gather the elders and all the inhabitants of the land into the house of the LORD your God, and cry unto the LORD.

"Alas for the day! for the day of the LORD is at hand, and as a destruction from the Almighty shall it come."

Chapter 2, verse 1:

"Blow ye the trumpet in Zion, and sound an alarm in my holy mountain: let all the inhabitants of the land tremble: for the day of the LORD cometh, for it is nigh at hand."

Verses 12–16:

"Therefore also now, saith the LORD, turn ye even to me with all your

heart, and with fasting, and with weeping, and with mourning:

"And rend your heart, and not your garments, and turn unto the LORD your God: for he is gracious and merciful, slow to anger, and of great kindness, and repenteth him of the evil....

"Blow the trumpet in Zion, sanctify a fast, call a solemn assembly:

"Gather the people, sanctify the congregation, assemble the elders, gather the children, and those that suck the breasts: let the bridegroom go forth of his chamber, and the bride out of her closet."

Verse 18:

"Then will the LORD be jealous for his land, and pity his people."

Verse 21: "Fear not...."
Verse 22: "Be not afraid...."
Verse 23: "Be glad then...."
Verses 25–29:

"I will restore to you the years that the locust hath eaten, the cankerworm, and the caterpiller, and the palmerworm, my great army which I sent among you.

"And ye shall eat in plenty, and be satisfied, and praise the name of the LORD your God, that hath dealt wondrously with you: and my people shall never be ashamed.

"And ye shall know that I am in the midst of Israel, and that I am the LORD your God, and none else: and my people shall never be ashamed.

"And it shall come to pass afterward, that I will pour out my spirit upon all flesh; and your sons and your daughters shall prophesy, your old men shall dream dreams, your young men shall see visions:

"And also upon the servants and upon the handmaids in those days will I pour out my spirit."

Verse 32:

"And it shall come to pass, that whosoever shall call on the name of the LORD shall be delivered: for in mount Zion and in Jerusalem shall be deliverance, as the LORD hath said, and in the remnant whom the LORD shall call."

The last two verses of chapter 3, verses 20 and 21:

"But Judah shall dwell for ever, and Jerusalem from generation to generation.

"For I will cleanse their blood that I have not cleansed: for the LORD dwelleth in Zion."

My text is chapter 2, verse 25. My message is "Getting Back the Years the Locust Ate Up"—getting back what has been lost.

I am very aware that Joel is a highly prophetic book. I am aware of the apocalyptic emphasis that it has. You cannot read it without literally, in almost every verse, hearing the cry of the last-day prophecies; without seeing the introduction of the Antichrist; without hearing the sounds of Armageddon; without visualizing God's plan being fulfilled in the promises that He has made to the nation of Israel; without visualizing God's ultimate and final plan, including His working through that tiny but historic nation.

You cannot read the Book of Joel without seeing the wonderful things that God is setting in place all the way into the millennial kingdom and extending to the fullest of His glory.

In the early part of the book, God begins to look at His people. He sees them in their roller-coaster living—up one day and down the next; over and over, up and down, hot and cold; never the same; no dependability, no consistency; running one day and saying, "I mean business for God," and the next day out on the backside of somewhere doing something other than what they have said they would do for God.

I. The Predictions of God

Here are the predictions that God makes in regard to this inconsistency. I want you to see not just what He says prophetically about things like the Antichrist and Armageddon, but I also want you to see the picture God puts in this passage to help us know that He is working now. He has plans for now. Before Armageddon, before the Millennium, God has plans for today.

God makes some predictions for those who are not His own—the unsaved. He says in regard to them, "They have cast lots for my people" (Joel 3:3). They had been gambling with the destiny and well-being of these blood-bought, blood-washed sons and daughters of the living God. These on the outside—the heathen, Gentile people—had gambled with the well-being and future of the redeemed.

In some very specific illustrations He says that those wicked heathen had taken little boys from Israel and made harlots of them. They had sold Israel's daughters just for the price of a drink, and they themselves had lived in drunkenness.

75

He says, 'They have taken my silver and my gold—the possessions that I put in their hands—and used them for all the wrong reasons. They have had much but have not honored Me with it. They have taken things that have been consecrated to Me, removed them from the house of God and put them in the temples of idols!'

Looking upon all of this, God says, 'Not only have they done all that, but they have used My people virtually as though they were slaves.'

God looks upon the nations of the world that are geared, guided and governed by that kind of mentality and promises that the hammer of judgment will fall. These activities cannot go on indefinitely without God's putting His hand heavily upon those responsible.

We here in America, with the great and illustrious heritage that we have, expect that we can plunder through the pits of paganism and turn our backs on God. We cannot without God's taking notice!

Do we expect God will say, "Oh, I have spent all My energies on Sodom and Gomorrah"? Are you kidding? What He does says is, 'I was faithful to carry out My word upon Sodom and Gomorrah, and I will do it upon America.' We can count on that. Just as surely as you can count on *anything* God says, you can count on *everything* He says! God will not be embarrassed by America or anybody else who determines to go against Him.

In fact, the other half of God's predictions in this passage concern those who are *His* people. So if we simply look at it and wonder how God deals with His people, we can find what He expects to do with us today.

Here are His people—up and down, up and down, inconsistent, irregular, doing what they ought not to do, promising one thing one minute, doing another the next.

God says in this regard, 'The palmerworm will eat up your crops. The locust will eat what the palmerworm leaves. The cankerworm will eat what the locust leaves, and the caterpillars will eat what the cankerworms leave.'

He further says, 'You will find that your vineyards will not produce, that the nation that comes against you, though it is smaller than you are—indeed, not strong like you—has teeth like that of a lion and jaws like those of a mighty, mammoth animal. Whenever that devourer comes, he will lay waste your crops, lay barren your trees and strip them bare and cast them away. The branches will be made white. The things that you bring to My house will not satisfy Me because they are only superficial, only tokenism.'

Then God says, 'As a result of all of this, the fields will be laid waste. The land will mourn, and it will be heartbroken. The crops will be wasted, dried up and languishing. Things will go to waste and perish in the land that ought to be thriving. For no explainable reason, the land will fall into the pit of despair. Where you counted upon the pomegranate, the palm, the apple and the other trees of the field, they will wither, dry up and not produce.'

God is talking about what is going to happen with His own people!

Do you wonder how in the world God can deal with His people like that?

Let me back up and tell you the story about these worms. The palmerworm, the locust, the cankerworm and the caterpillar are four stages of the locust.

Stage One: The Gnawer

The palmerworm is the first stage. He is called a *gazam* in Hebrew. Here is a little *gazam*. This is the worm stage of the locust—just out of the egg and without wings. *Gazam* in Hebrew means "a gnawer," a word we are not familiar with in English. A gnawer is one that gnaws and gnaws. He gets hold of the corn or the grapes or whatever and gnaws on them. He doesn't eat them all up, but he mars them. This starts the process of ruination.

Stage Two: The Swarmer

Then He mentions the locust. The word here means "swarmer," just moving into that stage where they are able to create a little swarm. They are not flying through the sky in great droves, but they are beginning to try their wings and do what little they can do. They have no legs—only tiny wings—and they are hardly able to fly; but these also do their damage. What the palmerworm—the gnawer—leaves off or doesn't do, this second stage of the locust takes hold of. Millions of this tiny insect grasp at every leaf for nourishment.

Stage Three: The Adult Locust

Then He uses the term "cankerworm," which is the third stage, the adult stage, of the full-grown locust. This word *yeleq* in the Hebrew means "the devourer," one that comes in with a huge, gaping mouth. He has an appetite that cannot be satisfied. When he has eaten, he eats again and again and again, but he is still not satisfied; he still wants to eat. By this time, the crops have been gnawed on and swarmed over. Now in this stage of things, they are literally devoured.

Stage Four: The Consumer

Then there is a final stage of the locust called the caterpillar, *chaciyl* in Hebrew, meaning "the consumer." What the palmerworm started, the locust came on board and worked on; and what the locust left, the cankerworm worked on, even in greater quantity. What was left, the caterpillar absolutely stripped bare. So nothing is left except sheer desolation, waste and destitution.

When the locusts come, we look in every direction and wonder what has brought them here: the very things I described a moment ago. God said, 'This is the reason they have come. They didn't just come on the heathen and the Gentiles but upon My people as well.'

Notice the other place where they are mentioned—in chapter 2, verse 25. He says in the last part of that verse, talking about the locust, the cankerworm, the caterpillar and the palmerworm: "...my great army which I sent among you." These are the privates, the corporals, the lieutenants, the majors, the colonels; these are the foot soldiers; these are the infantry, the army, the air force, the navy, the marines. They are the army of God. He sent them.

They stripped the vines of every grape, stripped the cornstalk of every grain of corn. The cupboards are bare. The table is empty, and little children are crying for something to eat. You can't run to the neighborhood market and buy it. It isn't there either.

God says, "This is My army, and I sent them." God says, "You might as well be prepared, because they are coming."

Somehow we have it all figured out. When an outfit like Iraq raises its head, we say, "We can take our smart bombs over there, and we will show them." Don't misunderstand me. Thank God for America and its strong stand. We ought to stand strong. I believe in a strong military and taking it to the enemy when necessity requires it, but it doesn't look like we solved the problem with Iraq.

We get over that, and the first thing you know, we look around and say, "Great day! We can't even pay our bills!"

Have you ever heard people talk about "the almighty dollar"? Mark it down, the dollar is not almighty. In fact, it is smaller today than it was yesterday.

We can't pay our bills. The Potomac is a little river compared to the rivers of red ink they are running through Washington. We can't even figure out how to pay for what we are doing, much less for what we would like to do.

What is going on? What is happening when we fail at every turn? Could it be that God has just turned the cankerworms loose on us? Could it be that God has just set the locusts loose?

He says, "I was good to you, but that didn't seem to help. So I will send a few little pests to buzz around you. They are My army. They will keep on gnawing, swarming, devouring and consuming until nothing is left. See then if your bombs help! See then if the dollar is king!"

God has predicted some things are going to happen—not only on this old, pagan, outside world, but to His people when they rebel against Him and run from Him.

II. The Plea of God

You say, "He sends this army to work on us. What does God want?" Let me show you what He wants. His pleas are in this passage. He makes the predictions, and He makes the pleas.

1. They start in verse 13, when He speaks to the leadership. He mentions specifically the priests and those who minister at the altar— the ministers of God.

By the way, that not only includes the pulpiteers but all those who serve in any kind of a function in the leadership of the nation's people. The politician—who is he? He is the minister of God to us! The policeman—who is he? He is the minister of God to us!

We think about other people who have positions of responsibility to the public. Who are they? We refer to them as public servants, but they are also the servants of God to us. Every leader, no matter what kind of position he has or how we think he came by it, is there by God's appointment.

God says He is looking to those of us in places of public responsibility, and He wants something from us. He wants us to cry aloud to Him and to put on sackcloth and to honor Him with the right kinds of things and not hold back from Him.

He says, "There are certain kinds of offerings, and I am expecting certain kinds of sacrifices."

He says, "You have been holding out on Me, not giving Me what is

79

My due and not doing what you said you would do."

He says, "Sanctify ye a fast, call a solemn assembly, gather the elders and all the inhabitants of the land into the house of the LORD your God."

Listen, God has always wanted us to fill up the house of God and cry aloud unto the Lord, and He still does.

We are talking about the pleas of God, as He makes His appeal to us.

2. The second plea is in chapter 2, verse 1:

"Blow ye the trumpet in Zion, and sound an alarm in my holy mountain."

Listen, God wants us in this place to sound the alarm, to cry aloud, to raise our voices for Him. In fact, if it be not done in the holy mountain of God, where in the world do you suppose it will be done? God wants us to blow that trumpet to call people to action.

3. The third plea is in chapter 2, verses 12 and 13:

"Turn ye even to me with all your heart, and with fasting, and with weeping, and with mourning: And rend your heart, and not your garments."

Don't put on some outward show, but give Him your heart. Turn to the Lord your God because He is gracious and merciful and slow to anger and of great kindness, but remember what I already said: God is the Commander of the army of the bugs, the pests, the locusts; and He will send them wherever He thinks He needs to. If He needs to keep them in dry dock, out of action, or in some other place, He will.

When I was growing up, we had army bugs. They would come through the land in the midst of the time of our crops. I remember Mother would say, "Get out there and…[do whatever it was that we did to forestall the army bugs!]."

I remember going to the garden and shaking stuff on the tomatoes and taking a stick and hitting the bugs and stepping on them. There were jillions of those rascals crawling all over the tomato plants!

They would make a swoop through for about twenty-four hours, and when they were done, those tomato plants would be standing there in stark, abject nakedness because the pests had invaded our little garden.

Did you ever try to control those rascals? They are not easy to control, but I know who their Commander is, and He has charge of every last one of them. He doesn't have to go out there with sprays and powders and dusts and sticks to try to hem them up or fence them out.

Every one of them has ears, and they are listening to the Commander.

You say, "Wait a minute. God is the Commander of that awful army, but He also says He is gracious and merciful, slow to anger, and of great kindness. Psalm 23:6 says, 'Surely goodness and mercy shall follow me all the days of my life: and I will dwell in the house of the LORD for ever.'"

I am telling you, this is right where we ought to tune in and say, "Lord, You won't have to send the bugs or locusts our way. We are going to thrive on mercy, on the graciousness that You extend to us. Lord, we are going to be greater Christians because You have been sweet to us and are kind."

So He says again in verses 15 and 16,

"Blow the trumpet in Zion, sanctify a fast, call a solemn assembly:

"Gather the people, sanctify the congregation, assemble the elders, gather the children, and those that suck the breasts: let the bridegroom go forth of his chamber, and the bride out of her closet."

III. The Plans of God

Then, finally, see the plans that God has. See what He is going to do for us if we listen, if we really get ourselves gathered right, not superficially and outwardly, but get our hearts bent toward God.

1. Here is the first of His plans. Look at Joel 2:18:

"Then will the LORD be jealous for his land, and pity his people."

He will minister to His people. God will look at the land and say to the devourer, "Hands off." He will say to that old cankerworm, "Leave it alone." God will build a fence to protect His people. He wants to be our Protector. He wants to be merciful to us and be our refuge.

When we follow what God has ordered up, when we hear His pleas, then His plan will go into effect. He will be jealous for the land and will show compassion to His people.

2. In verses 21–23 He says:

"Fear not...be glad and rejoice: for the LORD will do great things.

"Be not afraid, ye beasts of the field: for the pastures of the wilderness do spring, for the tree beareth her fruit, the fig tree and the vine do yield their strength.

"Be glad then, ye children of Zion, and rejoice in the LORD your God."

When we get right with God and serve Him like we ought to, our animals will go out and find grass to eat. Crops will produce because the blessing of God is there.

3. Verse 25 is the text for this message:

"And I will restore to you the years that the locust hath eaten, the canker-worm, and the caterpiller, and the palmerworm, my great army which I sent among you."

God says, 'The pests came and with great devastation swept across My people.' Then this next word is vital! 'There is still hope. When things are as dry as powder; when there is destitution that you cannot begin to describe, hear My pleas, and I will restore to you the years the locust has eaten. I will give it all back to you.'

God seems never to tire of us. He seems never to give up in despair when we are so stubborn. God seems to love us with a love greater than we can comprehend. He will give back to us what He had to take away. He will give back to us what we lost in our obstinacy. You thought all was lost! You thought you could never recoup from the locust invasion in your life! Not so!

There is not a person here but what, if he looks back at the kaleido-scope of his life, would say, "Some years were so lean, and I know why. I wasn't walking with or living for God, so He let that army come in and strip me of everything that was good. God gave leanness to my soul."

We could look at those years and say, "O God, those are lost, lean, almost forgotten years!" but God says, "I know, but I can restore to you the years that were destroyed by the devourer."

We think if it is lost, it is lost. We think about everything we have done—all the stupid things, all the rotten things—and think it is just out of sight and beyond. God is saying here, 'You do what I want you to do, really get your heart in place with Me, and I will restore it as though those years haven't even gone by. What I will give you, you can have only because of My gracious, merciful and kind generosity.'

Though all was lost, all is not lost! God is greater than the locusts!

4. God says in Joel 2:28:

"And it shall come to pass afterward, that I will pour out my spirit upon all flesh."

Is the day of revival over? No! Is the day past when people can get saved? No! Is it to the point now where you just can't do any of these things; you just have to be content with marking off how bad it is this year and how much worse it is going to be next year? No!

I know that the Bible says, "Evil men and seducers shall wax worse and worse" (II Tim. 3:13). Things are going to get more and more wicked. There will be more trouble as we go along, but in the darkest hour God wants His sons and daughters to shine the brightest. The light of the world is needed more during the darker hours than at any other time.

He made this promise: "I will pour out my spirit upon all flesh."

There may be other places where the blessing of God cannot come, but I want His blessing on my life. I want His blessing upon the church I attend. I want my people to have His blessing. I don't want pests swarming around my Sword staff. I want us to be living in the years of the blessing of God, where God has restored to us what He can give us.

God says, "In the last days, I will pour out my Spirit upon all flesh" (Acts 2:17). I believe we are living in a day and time when God can pour it out, dish it up and give it in great abundance.

5. Then, finally, notice what He says:

"And it shall come to pass, that whosoever shall call on the name of the LORD *shall be delivered."*—Joel 2:32.

Listen, when we are running with the world's crowd and trying to live like the Devil and play a little religious game on Sunday, restoration is not going to happen. God will let the pests come and take away from us everything we generate. Our need is to get right with God and serve Him and live for Him and mean business unapologetically. In fact, this passage in Joel twice says, "…and my people shall never be ashamed" (vss. 26, 27).

When somebody looks at you and laughs because you are serving God, let him laugh. You are going to have the last laugh.

Someone may have made fun of you at school last week. Just remember, if they are picking on you because you are a Christian, they are probably giving somebody else some rest.

God says His people shall never be ashamed. So, if you have a problem, just say, "Listen, Lord, I would rather have the scorn, the laughing, the heckling of some little person who works in my division, and have Your blessing, than for it to be the other way around."

God restores the years that the locust has eaten. We all have had some years that we gave away and wish now we could take back, but those years are gone. Don't go around dragging your feet and saying, "There is nothing I can do."

The thing you can do is to ask God to give it back to you. Tell Him, "I used to serve You. I used to live for You, Lord. I kind of slipped but I don't want to slip again. I want back those years; I want them back!"

Ask God to give you back the years the locust has eaten.

Has America Gone Too Far?

There is recounted in Psalm 105 an abbreviated biography of the major aspects of the life of the nation Israel. Several points are made which merit review:

(1) The point is made that the Lord is God. There is a God in Heaven; He is the great, eternal God of the universe; He is the Almighty. Like or dislike it, believe it or not, it's a fact.

(2) The point is made that God has not forgotten the covenants that He made with this nation. He does not forget the promises He makes to individuals or to nations. Whatever God promises, whatever covenants and contracts He makes, He keeps.

(3) His Word is always good (vs. 8), even to the extent of a thousand generations. Just because a little time has passed does not mean that God has relinquished His commitments or retreated from what He has established as absolute truth. His covenant is of an everlasting nature (vs. 10).

(4) God established leadership in the nation (vs. 26). He gave them a Moses to lead them day by day. Was God happy about the tyranny of the pharaohs and the slavery, the bondage, the captivity of His people? No! True, it went on for an extensive period of time; but, ultimately, on God's timetable of His determination, He gave them leadership to usher them out of bondage and take them to the land of blessing.

Moses was that man. Although a reluctant leader, he was the one chosen of the Lord, and his brother, Aaron, was given to be his assistant. God did many things to break the back of the Egyptians in order to get His people loose from the tentacles and shackles of their bondage.

Right at the end of the chapter, God "remembered his holy promise" (vs. 42). He does remember the promises that He makes. He remembered Abraham, His servant—a particularly important thing for us to note. We may sometimes think we're a forgotten commodity, but God remembers every one of us who serve Him.

(5) Everything God gave them was for the purpose that they, in turn, might serve Him.

"He brought forth his people with joy, and his chosen with gladness:

"And gave them the lands of the heathen: and they inherited the labour of the people;

"That they might observe his statutes, and keep his laws."—Ps. 105:43–45.

God did not give you the car you drive today just so you could coast up and down the highway in the lap of luxury. He gave you that automobile so you might serve Him in a better, more efficient way.

That could be said for everything that He has "loaned" to you. Moreover, you couldn't do much with any of it without a breath or two to draw today! He gives you every precious possession which you hold in your hand.

So keep in perspective that God gave all of this to Israel "that they might observe his statutes, and keep his laws."

(6) Rejection of God paves the way to Hell. "The wicked shall be turned into hell, and all the nations that forget God" (Ps. 9:17).

In our society, "hell" is a curse word. The intellectual elitists are convinced—and they have tried to convince all of us—that there is no Hell. Nonetheless, there is a very real place called Hell where people who turn from the Saviour will spend all eternity. Hell is an awful place. The Bible says that whole nations who forget God, who go against God, who refuse to remember God in their life and commitments, will end up in Hell.

We need not think, then, that just because everybody else is doing a thing, it's okay for us to do it. Just because Congress passes a law and says it's all right to do a certain thing does not mean that it's all right to do it. Abortion is still just as wrong today as it was the first day of January 1973.

The Bible says whole nations can go to the Devil and to Hell.

(7) Psalm 33:11 says, "The counsel of the LORD standeth for ever." His counsels are absolute.

Again, the intellectual elitists believe everything is relative and nothing is absolute. Listen to me carefully on this! Certain things are absolutely true. Absolute right and absolute wrong are absolute truths. They were right or wrong in 1910 and 1810 and 1710; they will still be in the same absolute rightness or wrongness in the Year 2010. "The counsel of the LORD standeth for ever, the thoughts of his heart to all generations."

This generation of Americans feel as if they have a graduate degree in understanding. Since they think they know everything there is to know, they think they don't need God. Well, the Bible says the thoughts of His heart stand to ALL generations. With all the technology and the nuclear age, the space age, the computer age, our generation needs God perhaps more than we have ever needed Him. With tools in our hands that could destroy the planet, we need to know God.

(8) Psalm 33:12 states, "Blessed is the nation whose God is the LORD; and the people whom he hath chosen for his own inheritance." Happy people are those who have given themselves to the Lord.

The establishment media will try to convince you that you will ruin your life if you go with the Lord. Their philosophy strongly suggests that to follow Him is about the worst thing you could do. It says your kids will be miserable! It says you will miss out on all kinds of good things if you follow the Lord. The absolute truth is, "Blessed [happy] is the nation whose God is the LORD." That means you! That means your kids, your family!

Do you want a happy heart when you are old? Then get with the Lord and stay with Him. That is how it works.

(9) In II Chronicles 7:12 it says:

"And the LORD appeared to Solomon by night, and said unto him, I have heard thy prayer, and have chosen this place to myself for an house of sacrifice."

God still sets aside places and says to us, "This is My place. This is My time. Give Me My time at My place." God has a claim upon us that He will not relinquish.

(10) In 7:13 He says:

"If I shut up heaven that there be no rain [He can do that], *or if I command the locusts to devour the land* [He can do that], *or if I send pestilence among my people...."*

Pestilence? We have read about the bubonic plague of years gone by, about the Black Death, the fevers—these things that literally wiped out cities and towns and broke nations apart. Today we say, "Well, that could never happen now." Yet in some of the Third World countries, tens of thousands of people have died because of the ravages of poverty, war and other tragedies. Even now, a scourge of AIDS is ripping across the world, particularly Africa, and thousands and thousands are dying; and if the great cover-up continues, there will be more than ever before.

God is telling us that He can send pestilence among His people.

"If my people, which are called by my name, shall humble themselves, and pray, and seek my face, and turn from their wicked ways; then will I hear from heaven, and will forgive their sin, and will heal their land."—Vs. 14.

God is talking directly about the response of His people.

(11) We can have the blessings of God now!

Some going up and down the streets would not think of turning in the driveway and coming into a church. They have no time nor use for God. They go on their merry way and do whatever pleases them. Yet God says if *His* people do what He says, then the nation can be turned around.

The secularists, the humanists, the liberals—those who have no use for God—continue to do what they want to do, not realizing that their philosophy is flawed and will fail. One day it will be too late for many of them.

You and I can see. We can know the will of God. We can follow the way of God.

"Now mine eyes shall be open, and mine ears attent unto the prayer that is made in this place.

"For now have I chosen and sanctified this house, that my name may be there for ever: and mine eyes and mine heart shall be there perpetually."—Vss. 15, 16.

God reminds us again of His presence "perpetually"—it will always be so. Amen!

When we look at a passage like the 105th Psalm, we see a beautiful composite of how God honored Himself, kept His Word and blessed a nation.

Nations Can Die!

A nation can go wrong, far wrong, so badly wrong that it falls on its face, defeated, disgraced and totally decimated. We could look at the stories of nations, dozens of them, who were birthed and flourished, then floundered and died. There is a scrap heap somewhere on which are piled the nations of generations past—nations that no longer exist. How did they die?

Some died (1) *by might*. Some enemy rose up, came and stomped and destroyed them.

Others died (2) *by their morals*. They crumbled from within. They lived lives of such dissipation that they absolutely destroyed themselves by their immorality or their amorality. Nobody had to come and ravage, pillage and destroy; they simply killed themselves off.

Some nations simply die (3) *for lack of morale*. They have no heart. They have no spirit. There is nothing to drive them anymore. Take a nation, tell the people there is no God, tell them there is nothing beyond the grave, and they will lose heart, lose their morale. They will become such a shiftless, lazy, apathetic, lethargic people that you won't be able to get half of them to work. Many will not be motivated by anything.

Nations do die—some by might, some by their morals, some by their low morale—and there are significant indications that America is in jeopardy on all three counts.

I understand that we have great military might in our country, but even there it is not where it was at earlier times in our history. There are forces at work in our nation now that would dismantle all the might that we have. How many times have you heard, "The cold war is over now"? Have we forgotten that the larger of the communist giants still lives and breathes well in Red China? They have atomic abilities and nuclear weapons in their arsenal. Even the little tyrants, straining to be somebody, continue to baffle us. Somehow we can't sort out all the little things that make our might seem not quite so mighty.

It's obvious to me that morally and in terms of morale in America, we have a problem; but the "spilled-milk syndrome," which is very, very popular among Christians, is not the solution.

"Spilled milk? Where did you get that?" We go around moaning and groaning: "Somebody let the gate down. The barn door was left open; the calf is out of the barn. Where did it go? Who left the gate open?" We whine and cry about how bad things are! We lament and we fuss! Spilled milk!

Folks, the "spilled-milk syndrome" is not the solution to our needs and to our situation. Our generation doesn't look good at all. A court decision doesn't go like we want it to go; some of the people in our society will go out to riot and loot, to rob and kill because something didn't go the way they wanted it to go.

Thousands of children are selling drugs, robbing, raping, even murdering. You ask, "Why are kids doing that?" Because they know that our judicial system is so fouled up they can do just about anything and get away with it.

The welfare system in this country has literally crippled millions. It has gotten people bound and gagged so that they cannot get off it. It is such a fouled-up system.

Parental rights are so seriously eroded that families can no longer legally exercise the kinds of controls that they ought to be able to exercise, and our families are in serious trouble because of it.

Hollywood has a social agenda, and they are pushing it. You turn on the television almost anytime now, and you will find one of these programs—it may be a sitcom, but it has a social agenda. There is something they're pushing. They have some liberal cause they're trying to get across to the American people; and their agenda is basically atheism, socialism, amorality, secularism and other variations of heathenism.

The philosophy of liberalism, though very faulty and always a failure, is now the theory of public policy in America. They are in control, but it did not just happen recently. They have been in control for more than thirty years now and, realistically, probably since the 1930s. Especially since the '60s, government at all levels has gotten bigger and bigger.

I can remember when we did not have as much "stuff" as we have now, and we got along really well, but we are to the point where we think we can't get along unless we have all this government to help us! We hear talk now about "essential services." We could do really well without a lot of the "essential services"—and if it's not essential, remand it to the private sector!

Along with the government's growing bigger and bigger, it has also become more intrusive by the hour. What are they after? With the liberals in solid control, we have begun to hear about "political correctness." That simply means that the liberal mind-set has determined what social things are acceptable, even what speech is acceptable. If you say the right things, think the right things, do the right things, you are okay, according to them. If you don't, the "thought police" are out there to jerk you around. They will have your name on the front page in the media.

If you are not "politically correct" on all these various things and not "thinking right" and saying something out loud that isn't "politically correct"—shame on you! They will get your job. They will have you strung out somewhere. They will shame you till you wish you hadn't said this or done that. We've seen it happen over and over and over.

References to religion have been systematically erased from textbooks and from the public forum all across our nation. At the same time, the crowd that has done that is vigorously defending pornography, vulgarity and nudity. All of those things are "A-OK" with them, but any reference to God or religious things has to be eradicated.

There was a time when George Washington's Farewell Address was considered to be the greatest speech ever made by an American president. There was a time when that Farewell Address was included in every history book.

(If you will pardon me the indulgence, I'll say this so you will know that I'm not a novice when it comes to historical things: I have some grasp especially upon American history by virtue of my training, my interest and my pursuing of it over more than thirty years. So I know a little bit whereof I speak.)

In the Farewell Address that Washington made, he basically explained, after his eight years in office, what had caused America to succeed in the early days following the Revolution and what had not only caused her to succeed, but what would enable her to continue on to greatness. Of the fifteen or so things that he mentioned, four were direct references to God and to religion.

We went through a period of about twenty years or so where you could not find that Farewell Address in a history book. I have hundreds of history books in my personal collection. I'm talking about all kinds of junior high textbooks, senior high textbooks. I have old ones and new ones.

Now in the last decade they have begun to put it back in some of the college textbooks. However, it has been edited, and those four references to God and to religion are nowhere to be found. That is just one tiny little illustration of what is happening to erase God from the minds of our American population.

I am an American. I'm very proud to be a citizen of this country. I have a good bit of Cherokee in me. I'm very proud of my heritage. I talk about Kentucky where I grew up. I'm very proud to be a native of

Kentucky. You ought to have some sense of pride in your heritage. I'm a citizen of this country, and I'm also a Bible-believing Christian.

I think I'm entitled to some freedom. When Sunday comes, I ought to be able to come here as I please and say the things I want to say. Frankly, I defend the right of everybody else to do the same thing. We ought to have freedom, no matter who we are, what we are. We all have the rights of citizenship in this country.

By virtue of the fact that I'm a Christian, I have a voice, and I ought not be restricted or restrained. I ought not be prohibited from standing up and articulating the values that I believe to be true. I should have the freedom to talk about God, Christ, the Gospel and whatever else, without government license, censure or permission.

A Nation Within a Nation

You see, the role that you and I have in this nation is like a nation within a nation. God has said to us that we are to be salt and light. The secularists don't like our salt, and they are working to put out our lights. They don't want our voice to be heard, and they don't want us to be able to do much. So they go around crying all the time, "Church and state."

You ask, "Where did they get that?" First, let me tell you where they *didn't* get it. Number one, they didn't get it out of the Bible. It is not in the Bible. Number two, they didn't get it out of the Declaration of Independence. It is not in the document. Number three, they didn't get it out of the Constitution. It is not in there. Those words do not appear in either the Declaration or the Constitution, and the First Amendment was never intended to keep religious values from public life.

In fact, they're trying to convince us now that our Founding Fathers were atheists, agnostics and deists. Patrick Henry said once:

> It cannot be emphasized too strongly or too often that this great nation was founded, not by religionists, but by Christians; not on religions, but on the Gospel of Jesus Christ.

John Adams, our second president, whose signature appears on the Bill of Rights, including the First Amendment, knew that our Constitution would only work for those people who could control themselves by religious values and religious standards. Adams said:

> We have no government armed with power capable of contending with human passions unbridled by morality and religion. Our Constitution was made only for a moral and religious people. It is wholly inadequate to the government of any other.

George Washington said in his Farewell Address:

> Of all the habits and dispositions which lead to political prosperity, religion and morality are indispensable supports. In vain would that man claim the tribute of patriotism who should labor to subvert those great pillars.

Up until the time of the Revolution, the Founding Fathers had been under British control. The constitutions of the various colonies had been British. When they went back home, they began, after 1776 (the Declaration of Independence) and 1789 (the Constitution), to put the constitutions of the various states together themselves; and the Founding Fathers did some very interesting things.

For instance, in Delaware, our first state, the original constitution of that state said:

> Every person appointed to public office shall say, I do profess faith in God the Father and in Jesus Christ His only Son and in the Holy Ghost, one God blessed forevermore; and I do acknowledge that Scriptures of the Old and New Testaments to be given by divine inspiration.

That was in Delaware's constitution. Does that sound like these men wanted to separate religion and God from public life? It doesn't sound like it to me.

What was true in Delaware was true in most of those early states.

John Quincy Adams, president number six (1825–29), on the 4th of July in 1837, said:

> Why is it that, next to the birthday of the Saviour of the world, your most joyous and most venerated festival returns on this, the 4th of July?

In other words, he is asking, "Why are Christmas and the 4th of July the two most popular holidays in America?" He went on to answer:

> Is it not that, in the chain of human events, the birthday of the nation is indissolubly linked with the birthday of the Saviour, that it forms a leading event in the progress of the Gospel dispensation? Is it not that the Declaration of Independence first organized the social compact on the foundation of the Redeemer's mission upon earth, that it laid the cornerstone of human government upon the first precepts of Christianity?

How about that!

And John Jay, first chief justice of our Supreme Court, said:

> Providence has given to our people the choice of their rulers, and it is the duty as well as the privilege and interest of our Christian nation to select and prefer Christians for their rulers.

93

There is much more to be said. The Supreme Court ruled in 1892 (just over a hundred years ago):

> Our laws and our institutions must necessarily be based upon and embody the teachings of the Redeemer of mankind. They must. Our civilization and our institutions are emphatically Christian.

Has America Gone Too Far?

However, we live in a time when much of that has changed. With America declining morally, spiritually and financially, is there any real hope? Will the bad news ever stop? Does it really matter whether or not you and I get involved? After all, isn't God going to make everything come out the way He wants it? (A lot of Christians have the idea that God is going to make it all come out.) Can we really turn things around in America, or has the country gone too far?

I want to tell you two things about that:

First, *yes, America has gone too far*. She has gone much too far down the pike, and there will be a bitter wage to pay for a long time to come.

Second, *no, America has not gone too far*. We are not to the bottom yet, we are not dead yet, and this nation is not done for yet. There is a way back. You and I need to sit up, stand up, show up and speak up. This is *my* country, and I want it back!

"Are you promoting politics?" you ask. No, I'm promoting people. If a good person is running for office, I don't care with whom he is affiliated. If he is a good person, standing where he ought to stand, then I'm for him.

Can We Make a Difference?

Can we really make a difference if we get involved?

A few years ago, just a few hundred yards from our church, a full-scale pornography store operated in one of these shopping centers. It took five years to get it closed and run out of the county. Opposition to it started in this pulpit. We began to beat on it, to pound on it, to drive on it until other people in this community got on board. Finally, some people in public office said, "We'll help you." We got it out of here.

There was a time when there were three "head shops" (drug paraphernalia stores) operating in our town—I mean, while I was pastor of the church. Somebody came to me and asked, "Do you know that there is a store right over here in this shopping center that sells nothing but drug paraphernalia?"

I said, "You've got to be kidding! That couldn't possibly be!"

I got on my horse and rode over there. I marched in just like I was "somebody" and looked around. My mouth is still hanging open! I couldn't believe it! I found out there were three of them in town.

I'll tell you what—they are not there anymore! They are not only not in Westminster; they are not in this county. They operate no more in the state of Maryland. The whole state is now cleaned out of them.

Where did it start? In this pulpit. I didn't do it by myself, but I began to beat on it, hammer on it, go after it. I went to see some people in public office. I talked to some people until some out there began to say, "We'll help you get it done!"

Can we make a difference? We can! I don't have time to tell you how many other good things we got done. I'm convinced we can make a difference. We have to do what we can. We must not throw in the towel, must not acquiesce to the liberals, must not lose heart in the process.

Somebody is always saying, "Preacher, why don't you ease up and not drive so hard? Why don't you get over there in the 'begat section' and preach on something that doesn't touch us where we live?"

I'm sorry. I'll help you learn the "begat's" too, if you are intensely interested in that, but we will continue to talk about things going on in our area of the world. I'm convinced we can make a difference in our city—and in our country!

What Can We Do?

A preacher named Stillwell was in Boston during the time of the American Revolution. He was pastor of the First Baptist Church there for forty-two years. He stood in his pulpit and preached in support of the American Revolution. John Adams and others often sat in his congregation and listened. He tremendously influenced the minds and thinking of some of our Founding Fathers.

The preachers across New England, by and large, supported the American Revolution. This was while we were still under the dominion of the crown of Great Britain. Were they afraid of politics? Evidently not!

You ask, "If we really want to do something, what can we do?"

1. *We can get right with God!* We can make an unashamed, unreserved commitment to God. We will not get anything done until we walk with God, follow Christ!

2. *We can give ourselves to serve the Lord through His church.* God gave us the church, and the church is where the action is. It is where we will get things done that need to be done and where the difference can really be made—more than Band-Aids, the *real* solutions. We should hold up this precious old Book, the Bible, as the inerrant, infallible Word of God with full authority in our lives.

3. *We can become ambassadors for Christ,* let our voice be heard and not be afraid nor intimidated by those who try to get us to shut up and dry out. Real ambassadors publish the Good News and the good tidings and get as many people saved as they can. Going soul winning regularly will make the difference in our society. If we get enough folks saved in this county, it will make a difference on the street where you live. It will be safer in your neighborhood. All kinds of good things will come.

4. *We can wage the war against the forces of evil* in our time, in our town. I mean, wage the war! If drug dealers try to come in, we wage the war; we say, "We're not going to have you here."

If the pornographers come in, we chase them out. If other devils come in, we say, "Not here! Not here!" We wage the war. We are willing to be counted.

You say, "But some may not like me if I do that." Listen! The Devil already doesn't like me. If anybody wants to line up with him and not like me, that is okay. You have to know that when you stand up for Christ you will take some hits, but we must not play it safe! We must get up and get at it! We can begin to exercise our freedom to its fullest.

When Moses crossed the Red Sea, wouldn't you have hated to have missed that? Probably some Israelites were off chasing some pretty rainbow somewhere and weren't there to see what happened.

When Elijah called down the fire from Heaven, I would have hated to have missed that. I would have wanted to have been there, wouldn't you?

Here we are in a new century. God wants His people to be on board with Him! We must stand up and be counted. I hope you don't miss that.

5. *We can catch the Spirit of Christ* and zealously and enthusiastically go out each day determined to serve God and be what we ought to be! Stay on the firing line!

6. *We can go to the polls* and cast our vote in the ballot box. Every Christian ought to vote in every election on every issue! Don't leave it to the worldly crowd. Vote without fail!

7. *We can put literature in the hands of the people* that will influence them and mold their thinking. The SWORD OF THE LORD is our source for it. I'm talking about good, solid material that stands straight and true—not the weak, anemic stuff so available everywhere.

I'm encouraged in one sense that a wave of conservative ideology has swept across the country. With all that the liberals have done, I think we may still outnumber them. They may have severely impacted about half of the American population, but there are some strong indicators that a lot of the people in this country still have some very traditional basic values. It doesn't mean they are all Christians, but the liberals have not succeeded in everything either.

I'm encouraged about that, but we're still waiting for revival to come. We need a sweeping revival where people confess their sins and get right with God, where folks turn out in bigger crowds at the church house than they do at the ball game, and where the old-time religion still gets top priority! Amen!

Has America gone too far? Yes, way too far! Has America gone too far? No, there is a way back, and we can bring her back, and should.

Don't be afraid to be counted. Show up, stand up and speak up.

Is God In?

"I cried unto God with my voice, even unto God with my voice; *and he gave ear unto me.*

"*In the day of my trouble I sought the Lord: my sore ran in the night, and ceased not: my soul refused to be comforted.*

"*I remembered God, and was troubled: I complained, and my spirit was overwhelmed. Selah.*

"*Thou holdest mine eyes waking: I am so troubled that I cannot speak.*

"*I have considered the days of old, the years of ancient times.*

"*I call to remembrance my song in the night: I commune with mine own heart: and my spirit made diligent search.*

"*Will the Lord cast off for ever? and will he be favourable no more?*

"*Is his mercy clean gone for ever? doth his promise fail for evermore?*

"*Hath God forgotten to be gracious? hath he in anger shut up his tender mercies? Selah.*

"*And I said, This is my infirmity: but I will remember the years of the right hand of the most High.*

"*I will remember the works of the* LORD: *surely I will remember thy wonders of old.*

"*I will meditate also of all thy work, and talk of thy doings.*

"*Thy way, O God, is in the sanctuary: who is so great a God as our God?*

"*Thou art the God that doest wonders: thou hast declared thy strength among the people.*

"*Thou hast with thine arm redeemed thy people, the sons of Jacob and Joseph. Selah.*

"*The waters saw thee, O God, the waters saw thee; they were afraid: the depths also were troubled.*

"*The clouds poured out water: the skies sent out a sound: thine arrows also went abroad.*

"The voice of thy thunder was in the heaven: the lightnings lightened the world: the earth trembled and shook.

"Thy way is in the sea, and thy path in the great waters, and thy footsteps are not known.

"Thou leddest thy people like a flock by the hand of Moses and Aaron."— Ps. 77:1–20.

My text this morning is verse 10:

"And I said, This is my infirmity: but I will remember the years of the right hand of the most High."

A young doctor moved into town awhile back. They came to church a couple of times. I tried to visit them; then I tried to phone them a few times, but they were never at home. Knowing that he had office hours on a Tuesday night, I went by his office. I walked up to the receptionist's desk and did something I'd never done before. I told her who I was, told her that the doctor had been attending church some and I wanted to see him.

"Is the doctor in?" I asked.

"Yes, he's in."

"Is he available?"

"Yes, I think so."

"May I see him?"

"Well, let me see."

Three questions: (1) "Is he in?" He was. (2) "Is he available?" Between appointments, he had some time. (3) "May I see him?"

She told the doctor I was there. (Maybe he was there, and maybe he was available, but maybe he wouldn't see me.)

So I asked, "May I see him?"

"Oh, yes, come right in, Pastor. You may see him." (Doctors can't be everywhere, just as preachers can't. We have limits as to what we can do, whom we can see.)

So many things are pressing upon us. Many difficulties abound. Violence stalks our streets. Our nation's capital has a murder every night. We have racial divisions and other kinds of divisions greater than at any other time in our history.

When I see all this pressing upon us—little boys and girls standing on street corners selling drugs, peddling their bodies and other things happening—the question pressing on me is not, "Is the doctor in?" or, "Is the pastor in?" but, "Is God in?" If He is in, is He available? If He is available, will He see me? Will He hear me? Will He help me?

In January of 1990 the Fox Network News in Washington reported on the evening news about a man who lived on the fourth floor of an apartment building. He got up at four in the morning to go to the bathroom and did not turn on the light. Even though he was half asleep, he realized something wasn't right, so very quickly he flipped on the light.

Kind of wrapped around the stool was a six-foot boa constrictor. Panic-stricken, in his night wear, he ran out of the bathroom, through the living room, burst out the door, rushed down the stairs to the third floor, the second floor, the first floor, and out the front door, then ran two blocks down the street to the phone booth. He commandeered a quarter from somebody and punched 9-1-1. The fire truck came. Standing out there on the street at four o'clock in the morning, he explained about that snake in his apartment.

They took the elevator up, and he gently pushed the door open. The fireman said, "Where is it?"

"It's right in there in the bathroom. It's wrapped around the commode."

They went in. They couldn't find it.

"Oh," he said, "but it was here."

They said, "Yeah, sure."

Here's a guy standing out on the street in his underwear in the middle of the night. He calls the fire department. They already realize they have a "loony tune" on their hands.

He got the fireman by the hand and said, "Sir, believe me when I tell you I'm not crazy. I didn't have a nightmare. I didn't dream it. I got up, turned on the light, and saw the snake coiled around the stool. It was right there."

He pleaded with them not to leave. They began searching the room; and sure enough, as they opened the closet door, lying among his shoes was this six-foot boa constrictor.

It turned out the snake belonged to a man who lived on the eighth floor. It had gotten loose in the apartment on the eighth floor, had gotten in the stool up there and had come down through the plumbing. It had found its way around in there and finally decided to surface again. This time it couldn't find its way back home, and it wound up in the bathroom on the fourth floor in a strange apartment.

This man never expected to find such a thing in his apartment.

You're going to find things that you never expected to find in the place where you work and live.

I've never heard a pastor say, "Listen! I just got called to this place as pastor, and it is a terrible place! Man, it's bad!" We always hear, "Oh, listen! I know God's in this. Man, this is going to be great!" Then we get there, and what do we find? Snakes in the closet. We find things in the dark of the night that we never dreamed could be. Three weeks later we find ourselves asking, "Is God in? and if He's in, is He available, or is He just sitting up in Heaven having a good time? Is God available when snakes are crawling all over the place? or, if God is in and if He is available, does He know where I live? Does God still know this little runt of a guy named Smith? Does God know that I exist? Is He in?"

Look at this passage. In the first half is a whole list of complaints. David said, "I cried unto God....I sought the Lord: my sore ran in the night, and ceased not."

He is saying, "I was about to bleed to death, and I couldn't stop the bleeding. Something had been punctured, and this thing was going down the tube, and I couldn't do anything about it."

David is saying, "I was so grief stricken; my soul was full of remorse and grief, and I refused to be comforted."

He is saying, "Everything people offered, I refused. I didn't want to hear it." David refused to be comforted.

He said, 'I remembered God, and I was troubled. I complained, and my spirit was so overwhelmed I could not sleep. I was so troubled that I could not speak. I considered the days of old, the years of ancient times. I called to remembrance how we used to sing in the night. I thought about how it used to be. I thought about those good old days.'

David is thinking to himself, *I wonder if God's still in. That's the way it used to be, but how is it now?*

David said, 'I talked to myself. I made diligent search. I even questioned my relationship with God. I'm beginning to wonder if God even knows me, if He will ever be favorable again. I wonder whether God will ever be merciful. I wonder if His promises will ever again come to pass in my life.'

David said, 'I wonder if He will be gracious again. I wonder whether He has even shut up His mercies so that forever His anger will be poured out and never again will we have the blessings of God.'

In verse 10 is the turning point: "I said, This is my infirmity: but I will remember the years of the right hand of the most High." This is where it all turned around. He laid out all these complaints.

Every now and then you and I need to recognize how it is. We need to look at the reality. It will not be bright sunshine all the time. We're going to have rain on our parade sometimes. We will have infirmities, but what will we do when we have them? That is the question I raise with you: What will you do when you have them?

David said, 'This is my infirmity. This is reality. This is what it is. This is where I am.' Then he also said, 'I determined that I would remember the years of God's right hand.' What does he mean?

I can do some things left-handed. I still play softball. I'm naturally right-handed, but I love to bat left-handed and do so most of the time. Ordinarily I throw right-handed, but I've practiced, and I throw left-handed a little bit. Still, if I really need the strength physically that I can give, I have to bat right-handed because that's my strong arm.

God uses that very illustration. He knew that we would know what He was talking about. My left hand will do some things, but it will not do all the things my right hand will do. My right is the one of strength.

God said to us through David, 'Remember the years when the right hand of God, the powerful, mighty right hand, was obvious, visible, in full demonstration.' That got David through.

I raise the questions with you again now: Is God in? and if He's in, is He available? and if He's available, will He see you?

I'm glad to give you a "yes" to all three of those. Yes, He is in. Yes, He is available. Yes, He will see us. In fact, it's exciting to note that God has been expecting us all along. He is thrilled when we come to Him.

David goes on in this chapter to tell us several things that God is in. In the last part of verse 11, he tells us that

I. God Is in History

"I will remember thy wonders of old."—Vs. 11.

We wonder what is happening in this world. I don't mean to shoot down your theological system, but you have to think through this thing.

God is not in control of everything. This world is spiraling out of control. You and I are trying to get the message out so that things will come under control.

I was in a conversation with a state attorney in our town the other day.

"Tom, how are you doing?"

"I'm doing fine, staying awfully busy."

"If I did a better job, you wouldn't have so much to do, would you?"

He looked at me kind of funny, then laughed.

"Seriously, if I do a better job, you will have less to do in the courts," I said.

A lot of things are running out of control, but they're going to get in control one day—in the Millennium.

We ask ourselves. "If God is not controlling, is not causing this, is He really in the course of history?"

Yes. God has with premeditation and purpose set an ultimate course. Even "the king's heart is in the hand of the LORD" (Prov. 21:1).

When I look at the nation of Israel, I see God's hand working in His people with His purpose. I know that that's yet to be fulfilled to the degree that God intends to fulfill it.

When I look at the United States of America, I see a nation that God has blessed beyond calculation. When it seems that our nation is bent so wrong so many ways, going the wrong direction, I ask myself, *Is there anything to the historical setting that is going on here? Is God doing anything in that?*

I walked into a classroom as a young preacher boy. We sat down to study history. We read Marx, Lenin, Paine, Ingersoll and others (no mention of Spurgeon and Moody and Wesley). I began to listen to what the professors were saying. "Listen to Marx. God's not in. Listen to Lenin. God's not in. Listen to Paine. God's not in. Listen to Ingersoll. God's not in."

I thought, *It will get better. I'll go over into the literature department.* There they spoon-fed me on classic works with little hidden messages saying, "God's not really in."

I've always kind of had a propensity for linguistics. I wanted to study Latin, so I signed up for Latin. I thought, *I'll go in and learn something about the languages.*

The dear old professor said, "You'll learn the finer points of this classic language, all right; but before you do, I'll refine your primitive mind and teach you something about evolution, Darwinism, natural selection and the origin of species." For the next two weeks he spent time in the Latin course saying, "God's not in. God's not in this thing. It just happened. It just came to be."

I drifted down the hall to the psychology department and took a class in what they called abnormal psychology. In the psychology department the professor said, "There's a reason you do what you do. Actually, somebody else is to blame. It's not your fault." Do you know what they're saying? "The reason the kids are in the streets, the reason we have riots in Los Angeles, is what somebody else does in Simi Valley."

Come on! Where are we? We rob and rape and maraud up and down the streets because of who *we* are—sinners. We're bent the wrong way. The psychologist who says somebody else is to blame is saying, "God's not in. God's not in."

I went to the biology department and there heard, "God may have made the little protozoa, but not the big multicelled human." No way! I listened really closely again, and I heard again: "God's not in. God's not in."

I drifted on down to another floor to the Old Testament department. In Old Testament class the professors began to say the first eleven chapters of Genesis were myths; the Bible was a book of faith but not a book of science.

I listened very closely to all of that. What he was saying was the same as I had heard in the other places: "God's not in. God's not in."

I thought, *Let's go over to archeology and see what he'll say.*

A very pious and studious man bowed his head and prayed a pious prayer, then immediately set out for the next two months through the Tower of Babel and the wall of Jericho, Hezekiah's tunnel and Solomon's pool and all of those other places. Over and over again I heard, "No, no, no. God's not in. God's not in this Book."

I thought, *Surely as I study systematic theology, I'll find somebody there who knows.*

They ran us through Brunner, Bultmann, Bonhoeffer, Bugs Bunny and a bunch of others like that. Those systematic theologians said, "The Bible is an ordinary book." (They always say it in a very pious way.) "The Bible is an ordinary book, written by ordinary men, a very nice, religious book; but surely it is not altogether true, not accurate in detail, and it is not the very Word of God."

I listened to that. Just like the evolutionists and the others, they were saying, "God's not in. God's not in."

In the ethics department we were given Joseph Fletcher and situation ethics and Harry Emerson Fosdick and H. Sloane Coffin and others who were saying, "God's not in."

Time would fail me this morning if I prevailed upon you to hear what I heard in philosophy and government and economics and a dozen other fields of study during the pursuit of some academic credentials. Over and over and over, again and again and again the sign on the door said, "Science—" or "Literature—," "History—," whatever, "God is not in."

We look back and hear David say, "I remember thy works of old." God is not only in history, but the great God Almighty, the God Adonai, God the Lord, God Yahweh, Jehovah, God Almighty Creator, who is my Saviour—that God is in this very day.

He is in when I go to the office. He is in for the 8:30 service on Sunday. He is in for Sunday night when I preach. He is in on Wednesday night. He is in when we go soul winning Tuesday and Thursday nights. He is in when we work our bus routes on Saturday. He is in. God is in—and He is in today.

I recently preached verbatim Jonathan Edwards's great sermon, "Sinners in the Hands of an Angry God." I told our folks I was going to preach somebody else's sermon.

A Congregationalist or no, Jonathan Edwards preached that great sermon on July 8, 1741, and revival broke out across this country.

I could tell of Wesley, of Whitefield, of Finney. We might still have slavery in America had it not been for a preacher named Finney. There might still be slavery in Great Britain except for a man named Wilberforce. Those men became the voices that spoke out, that cried out.

In the latter part of the nineteenth century, there were Dwight L. Moody and Charles Haddon Spurgeon; and into the twentieth century there came along men like John R. Rice and others sounding out the alarm. People in their day were saying, "Revivals? Who wants this?"

Revivals were not relics of the past then, and they're not relics of the past now. "This is the day which the LORD hath made" (Ps. 118:24). This is the day to hear His voice. Today, today, today! We can do it now.

In 1985 we built a new 1,500-seat auditorium at Westminster, Maryland. The excavators had cleaned off the spot. We were borrowing some money, and I felt the load and the burden of responsibility that go with that. About ten o'clock one night I stopped out by the side of the excavation. Having helped with the plans, I knew the pulpit would be in a certain place. So in the dark of the night, maybe one hundred feet from the road and with traffic passing by, I stood where I thought the pulpit would stand. As I looked at that flat, barren dirt, I thought, *In a few weeks a floor will be there, and there will be pews and an aisle there and another section of pews over here and a balcony up there and stairs that come down the side of the balcony.*

As I stood there, I quoted aloud what Scriptures came to mind. I sounded them out loudly in that place where for many years afterwards I stood week after week and preached. In my mind's eye that night in the dark, I saw those pews full of people. When the invitation was given, I saw people coming down the aisles. I saw them walking down those balcony steps before they were ever built. I saw people sitting in those balconies before they were there.

When we were starting to build, sticking our necks out and borrowing money and doing all we had to do to get ready to make that giant step, I had to ask myself, *Is God going to help me do this? Is God in? Are we going to make it? Are we going to be able to be in place?*

I said, based on what I found in this Book: "God is in—just as for Dwight L. Moody, just as for Dr. John R. Rice, just as for Charles Spurgeon. We can do it."

We don't have to give up and assume that somebody else had it all. God is in for us today.

II. God Is in His Sanctuary

Verse 13 says God is in the sanctuary. In the Old Testament there was one place where God was uniquely in. He met there and had special things there with His people.

In the New Testament the sanctuary of God, the habitat of God, where God dwells on this planet, is inside those who believe the Word of God and who have trusted Christ as Saviour. God comes into us; and because He comes in and stays in, pastor, you're never alone. You're occupied, inhabited by God Himself. So don't be afraid, don't be intimidated.

You say, "Well, somebody may not like the things I say."

America is sick because of the anemia in our pulpits. Preachers are afraid—afraid of the deacons, afraid of the budget committee, afraid of this, that and the other. God help us! We can get by without that. We don't have to have all those committees and boards telling us what to do. Churches can be run without those things. In fact, preachers might be better off not to get them.

What am I saying? God is in the sanctuary where you live. He is in you, and you are never alone.

Somebody is going to try to get you to stop your buses, to stop your soul winning.

On "Friend Day" in our church I preached on salvation. We had many visitors, and a number of people were saved. After the service I was sitting out in the lobby when some fellow came by, shook my hand and said, "I hope you don't preach a simple message like that *every* service."

I said, "I do my best to preach so people can understand it." (I wanted to say, "People like you!" but I tried to be kind.)

There are folks—you have them too—who continually say to me, "I wish you would talk about something other than salvation." If we do, then we're backslidden. When you are right with God, you are going to talk about salvation over and over again.

I preach on tithing, but I also talk to people about getting saved, and I give an invitation.

On Sunday you need to preach on a lot of things, but don't forget to preach the message of the cross, the message of salvation, and give an appeal for people to get saved. God is in to help you do that.

Don't be intimidated by the critics. Don't be afraid of them.

III. God Is In Supernaturally

Verse 14 also says God is in supernaturally. The work of God requires the power of God; and as the work of God goes forward, you will find that things break, things beyond your ability to fix. Some broken things only God can fix.

We must have God in power working in our lives.

I ask for God's help whether I stand before little groups or large groups. When I stand before people, I realize I'm handling the things of God; and I need His blessing, His anointing, His power.

We need it supernaturally.

IV. God Is In and Mighty to Save

Verse 15 says, "Thou hast with thine arm redeemed thy people." God is mighty to save. Jesus came to save sinners. The reason He came is the same reason you and I are here—to get sinners saved. It is not enough just to preach. We must preach to get people saved. I love great music and great hallelujah times, but that is not good enough. We are commanded to get sinners saved. God's unchanging mandate for us is to keep going after sinners.

I stood out there on that dirt and, with great apprehension, saw the building go up. I was fearful that when we went into that building, we would be comfortable and "uptown," that we would forget about the work of the ministry.

It is our mandate from God to take this message again and again and proclaim, "God is mighty to save!" Little boys and girls who ride our buses need to get saved. Those poor handicapped people who came to the Good Shepherd Department needed salvation. Thank God for those saved! We even worked out ways to baptize in wheelchairs. We worked out special programs for those precious teenagers who came in on the buses. We taught them what they needed to know.

Some said, "They're just trouble. They create problems. They run all over the building. They steal things." I know, but God is mighty to save.

God was mighty to save a Boston shoe clerk named D. L. Moody and a Chicago baseball player named Billy Sunday.

I sometimes called my office "The Salvation Center." People by the hundreds walked into my offices over the years. I seated them and told them the sweet story of Jesus and got them saved.

Our soul winners got people saved in the home.

I am thinking about a lady we led to Christ. Another man and I went into her home. She had a crying baby. I said to my partner, "Why don't you play with the baby?" So he did. I sat on the couch, took my New Testament out and led her to Christ. When we got back in the car, I said to my buddy, "You did a wonderful job! I really appreciate your keeping the baby entertained and quiet." He showed me his messed up clothes and said, "Yeah, look what I got too!"

His reward in Heaven will be great! We have to sacrifice for the Saviour.

One of the staff men and I visited a man who had been to the church the previous Sunday. We sat down with him at his dining room table. We found they had moved from Baltimore. I said, "Tell me a little bit about your church background. Where did you go to church down there?"

He mentioned the name of a certain Baptist church.

I said, "I've heard of that. Have you been going there for a long time?"

"For ten years."

"Is that where you got saved?"

"Well, we've done a lot of things there. I've been very active in the program."

"That's wonderful. And that's where you got saved, huh?"

"Well, I just enjoy doing all the things we have to do there."

When I pumped him more intensely and asked him if he knew for sure that if he died that day he would go to Heaven, he said, "Well, now, I'm not sure about that"—and he had been going to a church with "Baptist" tacked on!

I said to myself, *What in the world! Do we not know that God is mighty to save? We spend our time on all of this stuff when we need to make an impact on society.*

I hate abortion, but the solution is in places like Gospel Light Baptist Church in Walkertown, North Carolina; Church of the Open Door, Westminster, Maryland; Franklin Road Baptist Church, Murfreesboro, Tennessee; and other fundamental, soul-winning churches.

The solution is not in just manning the precincts; we need to man the bus routes, the Sunday school. When we build our churches to overflowing and get people saved and teach them what we've been taught, as the Great Commission advises us to do, we will impact our society. If we get our job done, the politicians will think twice before doing stupid stuff, because they will know we have enough strength to vote them out.

One of our men ran for the state senate and won. One of my deacons was state senator when I was pastor in Maryland. In one of the news conferences, his liberal opponent held up a copy of the SWORD OF THE LORD and said, "Hey, folks, vote for that man [talking about our deacon], and this is what you'll have in Annapolis [our state capital]."

I wanted to stand up and shout, "Well, bless God! We need some of that!" I wish all that crowd would read the SWORD OF THE LORD.

A great God in Heaven has a great plan. The Lord Jesus Christ came to this earth. He was birthed in human flesh to seek us out, to save us, to seal us, to secure us, to sanctify us, to strengthen us, to supply for us and to send us out to do the job all over again.

V. God Is in the Flock of His People

One final thing in that last verse: "Thou leddest thy people like a flock."

Many of our churches have been "sky-jacked" by well-meaning committees and boards. The wrong people are sitting in the pilot seat or holding the pastor's salary to his head—"sky-jacked."

The seat of authority and the scene of action are still the church. We need to be building Christian schools, bus routes and utilizing the media in our area in training soul winners.

We had one group of soul winners—120—whom we trained. Those 120 people alone led over 1,800 to Christ in three years. They handed out hundreds of thousands of pieces of literature all across our area.

At a National Sword Conference I heard Dr. Hutson quote Acts 19:10, which tells how, in the space of two years, the Gospel was heard in the entire area. God pressed that upon my heart. I figured it up: something like 250,000 people lived in a fifty-mile radius of Westminster. Then I began figuring ways we could get the Gospel to every one of them.

We ordered thousands of Sword booklets for our people to hand out. We did other things. One man gave us fifty thousand tracts. I said to our members, "Let's take these fifty thousand salvation tracts and give them out." They gobbled them up, and soon they were all gone.

We began to develop a network of radio stations in our immediate area. Every morning, Monday through Friday, at 8:30, we were on the air talking about the things of God. We did other things because of Acts 19:10. We called it our "1910 Strategy"—getting the Gospel to every single person who lived in our area.

Do you think all these came to Church of the Open Door? No, but some did. Were we able to do everything we wanted to do? No. Were we able to pay for everything we wanted? No, but we did what we could do because God is in.

Where I preached every Sunday was not a cathedral but a tabernacle, a meeting house, a lighthouse. People in darkness needed the light.

We operated a crisis center for people in trouble. They needed what we had to give. It was not a social action center but a salvation center.

A fellow came into the office and said, "I need to be born again."

I said, "You've come to the right place. I can help you with it." I began to explain how he could be saved.

He looked me right in the eye and said, "You don't know how I have hated you with a passion."

He didn't know it, but I already knew. In fact, I had looked him over very carefully when he came in, to see what he might have on him!

Nevertheless, he said, "I need to be born again, and I knew that you could help me with that."

I didn't even flinch when he said, "I hate you." I never even acted like I had heard it. I just passed on over it on my way to getting him saved. That is how you treat your enemies. Psalm 23:5 says, "Thou preparest a table before me in the presence of mine enemies." What do you think God has on that table?

You say, "We have all this battle to fight, all these who are the enemy. They hate Gospel Light Baptist Church. They hate Church of the Open Door. They hate the SWORD OF THE LORD. When they are fighting us, what do we do?"

Surely, if we're going to fight a war, we must have tanks, air support and all these other things needed to fight a war. "God, what are we going to do in fighting this war?" He says, "The weapons of our warfare are not carnal, but mighty through God to the pulling down of strong holds" (II Cor. 10:4). So I look at the table and say, "What has God put on the table?" I discover that He has not put on it guns and knives and bullets, but the table that God has set in the presence of mine enemies has on it the Word of God and prayer.

So I can look to Him, as all the rest of His multitude of children can. With the greatest communication system on the whole planet, we all talk to God at the same time, and He listens to all at the same time. There's never any mixup in the channels.

In the presence of our enemies, God has the Word of God on that table. He has prayer on that table. He has our stewardship on that table. What is the stewardship? Our tithes and offerings; the appropriations for funding the battle. Many things I wanted to do I couldn't do because we still had those trying to decide if it was the will of God for them to tithe.

It *is* the will of God. He put our stewardship on that table. He said, "You put the right stewardship on the table along with prayer and the Word of God, and you'll be able to confront the enemy successfully."

God put soul winning on the table in the presence of the enemy. Here I am facing the enemy. I say, "God, give me a Sherman tank. God, give me one of those Stealth bombers." What does He answer? "No, you have soul winning to work with."

I say, "Man, with all those enemies out there?"

God answers, "Snake your way out through the grass and among the enemy; then tell them about Jesus." In the morning when the Devil looks around, he will say, "Where is my front line?" Some of his henchmen will report, "They deserted during the night and went over to the other side." That's what soul winning is.

You say, "Where do we get the troops to run the bus routes, to teach the Sunday school classes, to do all the other things we need to do?"

We snake over through the grass into the Devil's territory and snatch out from him those he has in the ranks. I mean, we go over there and get his drunks. We go over there and get his addicts. We go over there and get his little harlots. We go over there and get his people who are bent wrong philosophically. We keep on until his ranks are depleted and ours are filled.

"Thou preparest a table before me in the presence of mine enemies." You have always wondered what was on that table. Now you know!

"Thou leddest thy people like a flock." God is in the midst of His church today. The church is still the center of action. The God of this universe is still the Almighty, the great eternal God, our Creator, the everlasting Father—and He loves you and me. He answers our prayers. He meets our needs.

I have pledged myself to love, to trust, to obey, to serve my God, my Saviour, my Lord.

Thank God He is in today! He is not only in history, but He is in today, and He is in the sanctuary where I live. He is in supernaturally; His power is available to me and to you. God is not only in supernaturally, but He is mighty to save. He is in the church, in the flock of God's people.

"Is God in?" Yes! "Is He available?" Yes! "Is He going to see me and help me when I'm working up there in my town?" Yes! "Can it be done where I live?" Yes. "Do I need to be afraid?" No. "Do I need to be intimidated?" No. "Do I need to pack and move?" No. "Do I need to dig in?"

Yes. "Why?" Because God's in. He is still alive. He is still real; and bless God, His power still works!

That beautiful Psalm 23 says, "**Thou** anointest my head with oil; my cup runneth over." When God fills your cup, it will run over. If your cup doesn't splash over every now and then, probably it is because you have some strange dregs in it. When God fills it, it will splash over.

I'm glad to tell you today: God is in, He is available, and He will help you. Don't despair. Knowing you have His presence, obey His commands today!

Just Do Your Duty

"So likewise ye, when ye shall have done all those things which are commanded you, say, We are unprofitable servants: we have done that which was our duty to do."—Luke 17:10.

Focus on the last part of the verse: "We are unprofitable servants: we have done that which was our duty to do." We will point out some things in chapters 14 to 16 to pave the way for understanding this verse.

Parable of the Great Feast

In chapter 14, Jesus gave an illustration, a parable. He said a certain man made a great feast and invited many. I suspect, from what I read there, that he invited those who expected to receive invitations to such prominent events. I imagine that the first invitations that went out probably included the mayor, the councilmen of the city, politicians, doctors, lawyers and other dignitaries who held positions of prominence in their area.

A number of them said, "We are going to be busy, we don't have time, and we're not really interested in what you're going to be doing at the feast." Maybe they didn't like what was on the menu. They all had some kind of excuse as to why they couldn't come.

The story goes that the master of the house said to his servants, 'You go out and find other people. The elite are invited, but if they won't come, then get the rest who live in that area—the maimed, the poor, the halt, the blind.' These are the folks whom others pass by. Even some religious institutions would say, "We really don't have seats at our place for those people."

Make note of this fact: Sometimes we fuss at the churches that don't want the handicapped or those who ride buses—and, without question, we ought to fuss when a church thumbs its nose at the downtrodden and the hurting. The fact is, however, some of our crowd turn up their

115

noses at the attorneys and lawyers, the doctors and university professors and others.

If I understand this passage, we have every scriptural reason to go after every single person, including attorneys and doctors, the handicapped, those who are in wheelchairs and others who ride buses. We ought to sit side by side with all of them in the house of God. We are to keep on pressing and pushing and doing all we can until we fill up the house of God. Those kinds of people—every one of them—should be there!

Even after he had sent out the first and the second invitations, the servants came back to report: "After doing everything you told us to do, there is still room in your house."

The man says, 'Go out again. Go beyond the borders and perimeters of the city. Go out into the highways and hedges. Go where people have not been, into the obscure places where some have hidden themselves, and bring them in as well. Stay at it until my house is filled.'

It is for this reason that we should leave no stone unturned, no area of town unworked. We should make it our business to go seriously and genuinely to reach every soul in our Jerusalem.

Parable of the Savorless Salt

In this 14th chapter of Luke, Jesus reminds us that we are salt. He is talking about being salt in the highways and hedges—where people live and work. He is talking about being salt in the lanes and the streets of the villages and cities—in the human arena. *You* are salt. If salt refuses to do its job, then those who live by the highways and hedges, by the streets and lanes of the villages and cities, will perish.

Salt acts as a preservative and a seasoning. If you don't put salt in at the right time in the right place in the right amount, then there are unfortunate results. Things that would be useful become unuseful. They perish! They fall apart! They decay! Why? Because salt was not applied.

He said, 'If the salt has lost its saltiness, it is good for nothing.' We learned in the Sermon on the Mount that we are the salt of the earth. If we're not willing to be the salt that Jesus intended us to be, even if we're doing something good, something religious, we are good for nothing.

You say, "But we live in a world that has gone bonkers! Our society is so sinful and corrupt. It is hard to do what we should in the place where we live!" I understand that, but Jesus said we are to be salt in just that kind of a world.

116

After having reminded us that our assignment is to go out and get people from all walks of life, from every corner of society, and seat them on the front seat, the second seat, the third seat—everywhere, until the house of God is filled—He says to each, "You be the salt. Go out and season! Get out and preserve!" In other words, do all that salt does.

Parable of the Lost Sheep

In chapter 15, Jesus gives three stories. First, He tells of a man who had a hundred sheep. On a given night, it seems one of them didn't come in. I can visualize that shepherd's counting them: "Ninety-six, ninety-seven, ninety-eight, ninety-nine…." He may even have said to his son, "Son, check back in there and count again. I must have miscounted."

Perhaps his son went back and counted again. He came back and said, "Daddy, you're right. There are only ninety-nine!"

Maybe the shepherd then said to his son, "Well, which one is missing?"

"Daddy, I think it's that little, scrawny runt. Remember the one that's been sick ever since it's been in the world?"

The shepherd replies, "Yeah, dirty little old rascal. Just a runt. It's threatening weather, and there is no telling where he is. He's probably lying out there somewhere in a gully, in a ditch. I'm not going to fool with him. If he wanted to come in, he should have come with the flock! He knows this is the sheepfold, and he ought to get himself in here!"

You say, "What Bible are you reading out of?" Oh, I'm glad you're listening! What I've just described is not the heart of a shepherd—not at all! The shepherd looked at the situation. He counted and double counted. He knew the one missing was that little, scrawny, sickly runt. Instead of the conversation I related to you a moment ago, I think he said, "Son, go get my heavy coat and that extra lantern, and you get your heavy coat and come with me."

The reason I suspect it was like that is that I grew up on a sheep farm. About the time I got into high school, Daddy thought his boys ought to have things to do.

I will never forget the day when that cattle truck rolled up at our place, dropped the tailgate, and those woolly muttons started coming off the truck. There were nearly a hundred ewes (mama sheep). It wasn't long before we had four-footed woolly creatures all over the farm.

Dad worked at a public job and, in the wintertime, got home after dark. Almost every night when he walked in the door, he would ask, "You got the work done?"

I would answer, "Well, yeah, Dad, we got the feeding done." Then sometimes I had to say, "Dad, we got one missing tonight."

"Which one?" he would ask.

"It's old Dessie," or whichever one it happened to be. (After a while you give them names.)

"She hasn't had her lambs, has she?" he would ask.

"No."

"Let me get a bit of supper; then we'll go see about her."

We would both get a light. Even on nights when it was cold and maybe snowing, we would walk fifty, sixty or seventy feet apart through the fields, shining the lights in one direction, then another. One of us would spot her down in a little ravine. More often than not, she didn't come in because she had had a couple of little lambs down there. When you have a new mama, you approach her very carefully. We took those little lambs in our arms. It wasn't an easy job when those newborns were covered with snow, rain, sleet and sometimes mud.

Yes, I know what the shepherd does.

You say, "But ninety-nine are in the house already safe." I know, but one is lost; and as long as there is one—even one in my family or your family, in your city or in my city—we are to remember the heartbeat of the Shepherd.

Parable of the Lost Coin

A second story in this 15th chapter is that of a lady who had ten coins and lost one. Because these were her valuables, she swept the house, rolled up the rugs, moved the furniture—whatever was possible to do—looking for that lost coin. When she found it, she hooted and hollered and called her neighbors and said, "Rejoice with me; for I have found the piece which I had lost." She became so excited when she found that one coin.

Sometimes we lose our heartbeat, our zeal. We find the coin or little lamb missing. When the lamb comes back, we don't even get up to check on it. Every time we find even one that was lost, we ought to show excitement.

118

I like what the preacher did here yesterday. When folks were lined up across the front, people came out of the pews to welcome those who had come forward. We must have sung forty-eight verses of one song!

A precious and valuable coin is brought in; it has been found! We will celebrate and rejoice because a valuable one has been found!

Parable of the Lost Son

Another story is in this chapter—the best known of the three. A certain man had two boys. One day the younger boy said to his father, "Father, give me the portion...that falleth to me" (vs. 12). His father gave him his inheritance. The boy went out into the far country. There he spent his inheritance, and when his money was gone, his friends were gone too.

For a Jewish boy, nothing was more despicable than having to make his living in a hogpen; but there he was, grappling for a few husks to feed himself. One day when he came to himself in that hogpen, he said:

"I will arise and go to my father, and will say unto him, Father, I have sinned against heaven, and before thee,

"And am no more worthy to be called thy son: make me as one of thy hired servants."—Luke 15:18, 19.

I am grateful that the boy wanted to go home, but I am a little bit enamored with his dad.

Let me editorialize a bit. I think there were some times during the days his son was gone that this gray-haired dad sat on the front porch in the late of the day and watched strangers pass along the long lane. Probably there were days when he sat up on the edge of his seat, looking closely at them. Many times he was disappointed. He was looking for his son.

One day that boy comes down the road and turns down the lane. I can see that dad sitting on the porch. He sees his boy turn in the lane; he looks closer, squints his eyes, gets up out of the chair and looks again. He may even hobble over on a cane to the edge of the porch to look.

He turns and says to anyone around, "I'll declare, for the life of me, that looks like my boy! I've looked so many times and been disappointed, but it sure looks like him!"

In a minute he looks back down that lane, then says, "I recognize that form! That walk—it's familiar. That's got to be my boy! My boy is coming home!"

Remember now, this is the same son who took his inheritance and left. This is the same son who said, "Daddy, I don't want to hear it from you anymore. I don't want to follow your directions. I won't listen to you any longer."

That silver-haired dad loved his boy, and when that rascal came home, he fell on his face before his father and said, "Make me as one of thy hired servants."

The father answered, "Hired help, nothing! Get up off your knees! Somebody get those old, ragged clothes off him and put a nice robe about him. Get a ring and put it on his finger. I want everybody to know he is a member of this family."

Not only that, but the father said, "Go out there and kill one of those calves that we are fattening up for a celebration. Call the neighbors and friends and tell them my son who was lost is found!"

A few weeks ago down in the South, I preached on the Prodigal Son. When I finished, a lady came to me and said, "I have a boy like that. I've looked many an afternoon down that lane, but he still hasn't come home. Do you have any advice about what I might do?"

I thought for just a second, then I said, "The only thing I can suggest is that you be prepared with a robe and get a calf ready. You've waited, longed and prayed; now just be ready, because God will perhaps answer your prayer and bring him home one day."

We talk about soul winning, bus routes, building a Sunday school and having a great church; but when somebody comes along and sits where we've been sitting for the last four hundred years, we make an appointment with the pastor. "Some of those people coming from the east side of town are sitting in my pew!" We get upset about it instead of saying, "Bless God! I had to stand up this morning because people filled the pew where I had been sitting!"

Thank God that they found the little lost lamb and brought him in! Thank God they swept the house and found the coin! Thank God this boy—lost though he was, out in the world though he was, doing everything that he should not have done—came home!

Let's capture the spirit of that father who said, 'My boy was lost; now he's found!'

Now go to chapter 16 where Jesus reminds us that we ought to use every monetary resource, every physical resource we have, to make friends for Heaven for eternity's sake, for everlasting habitations.

Who Is Your Master?

He asks us, "Now who is going to master your life?"

Everybody takes orders from somebody. You and I eventually have to decide who is going to be the master of our lives, who is going to tell us how we operate, who is going to be the authority in our lives.

Jesus wants to be that authority. He told us about a lost sheep, a lost coin, a lost boy. He told us about the poor, the maimed, the halt, the blind. He told us about all these others who are going to be invited to the feast.

That sounds like work to me! It sounds like it is going to cost a lot. It sounds like our buildings are not going to be large enough. It sounds like we have to make great plans, have a great vision and plan on doing things that others in town are not doing.

Is Proverbs 11:30 still in your Bible? Are Daniel 12:3, Psalm 126:6, Matthew 4:19, Acts 5:42 still in your Bible?

"Yes, yes, yes," we are quick to answer.

Then who is the Master?

You say to me, "Sir, are you telling us we ought to have a soul-winning church? Are you telling us we ought to have soul winning every week and that we personally ought to go soul winning?

"Now, everybody knows that the deacons ought to go soul winning, that the choir ought to go soul winning, that the ushers ought to go soul winning—but not me! I'm the guy who sits over here in the back, hidden and out of the way," or, "I'm getting old; I've served my time. Besides, my arthritis is killing me. Surely you don't mean me!"

But Jesus asks each of us, "Who is your master?"

Just so we'll not forget it, He gave us another story in Luke 16—the story of two men who died. One went to Heaven, and the other went to Hell. It's not a parable but a real story.

Jesus said, "I want you to know that we're not just talking about sheep, coins and boys for the fun of it. We're talking about real people who die and go to an eternal Hell." It is at this point that He throws us into chapter 17 and verse 10: "We are unprofitable servants." What does that mean?

There are people sitting here saying, "Many in our church do a better job than I could ever do." We've made famous the saying, "Let George do it," but there are not enough Georges in the church.

121

Some fellow comes in and says, "I'm the greatest gift this church ever had. I can just do everything." That guy will not amount to anything. He is just a lot of huff and puff, and I dare say, he talks a whole lot more than he walks. Often it turns out that way.

Then the one who comes in and says, "I don't know whether you can use me, but if you ever need anything done, just remember that I'll be glad to do something," is probably that one who will be the greatest blessing. He says, "I am unprofitable, but I will do what I've been commanded to do. It is my duty to do it, and I will do it!"

The Responsibilities of Duty

This passage makes very clear four things about duty:

1. Duty is never obscured by obstacles. You may say, "But I've been criticized. Some didn't like the way I made the visits." The fact is, duty is never obscured by obstacles, so welcome to the club. Others have been criticized, but criticism should never get in the way of your doing your duty.

You may say, "We wanted to have soul winning at our church, but we had opposition." Don't worry about opposition. You are not going to be voting on soul winning anyway. Just go do it! We don't vote on things that have already been voted on in Heaven. If God said do it, then don't have a business meeting over it!

You may say, "But folks don't like what we're doing." Never be surprised about such obstacles.

Verse 1 of chapter 17 says that offenses will come. You can do the best you can do, be the nicest you can be, but there will still be offenses.

Others may be foolish, but not you; others may faint in the process, but not you because you are locked into your duty. Never be afraid; just do your duty and trust God. The Lord is counting on you, and so are others.

Obstacles are sure to come—count on it, but do your duty. Offenses are sure to come—count on them, but do your duty. Opposition is sure to come—count on it, but do your duty.

2. Duty always observes the souls of men. Jesus said, "These little ones—you had better not offend them." You who sit around and carp about the kids who come on the buses, put a clamp on your tongue! In fact, if I read correctly, He says that you would be better off to go out to a lake and drown yourself rather than offend those little ones!

You say, "The ones I was looking at weren't all that little." I don't care who they are, each is a precious soul. Don't offend even one of them. Go drown yourself if you must, but don't obstruct the winning of souls. It is your duty and mine to win them.

You say, "But they're just little fish." It matters not what size fish they are, large or small.

When we first moved to Murfreesboro, we lived in the Rockvale area. A little man-made lake was at the back of our house. I don't like to fish, but my son does. So because he likes to fish, I went out there with him occasionally with a rod and reel. I would ask, "Where should I throw it?"

Marlon would answer, "Right over there."

So I tossed it over there, reeled it in, and there was nothing on it. About the third time that happened, I said, "All right, you guys. If you're going to get on that hook, you'd better get on. This is your chance." (You see, I'm not much of a fisherman. It's the same slack way some of us treat our unsaved friends!) But every now and then, I would throw it out in the water, and a little bass would get on it. I would pull it in, hold it up and holler toward the house, "Hey, Betty, I got one! I got one!"

My son would say, "Dad, put it back in the lake. It's not big enough to even bother with."

"But I got one! I got one!"

"Dad, it's not big enough to eat or to mount. Just take it gently off the hook and put it back in the lake."

"But, Son, I caught it! I caught it! It's mine!"

Are you hearing me?

Any fisherman wants to catch big ones, but when you're fishing in God's work and doing what He wants you to do, you make a big to-do about the little ones just like you do about the big ones. The little fish, the big fish—no matter—you don't throw them back and say they don't matter!

This man in Luke 16 said, "I have five brothers. Please don't let them come to this place of torment!" Duty under God sees every single one of them; and when you see the lost like God sees them, it will keep you going after them whether there are snow and sleet, criticism and opposition.

Do what you have to do. Work and press on. Do your duty. People are trusting every one of us to do his job. God is counting on us. Keep on fishing for souls!

3. Duty always operates by faith. This passage also talks about faith as a grain of mustard seed.

Sometimes we say we don't have enough faith. Let me tell you something: even when you think you have big faith, you don't have much! It's not big faith that gets the job done; it's little faith in a great God! Take the little mustard-seed faith you have and put it toward the right thing. Faith in God gets any job done.

"I don't know if we can get these folks saved." Sure you can—with faith in God.

"I don't know if we will be able to pay all the church bills." Yes, you will—with a little faith and trust in God. He will see you through.

"But what happens if we go out on the streets, give out Gospels of John and Books of Romans and salvation tracts? Might we be embarrassed?"

Don't worry about such trivials. Be willing to be embarrassed. Be willing to have someone slam the door. Be willing to listen when the one you visit says, "I don't want to hear it." Just go. Trust God. Do it because it is right. Follow where He leads. Trust Him. By faith do what He wants you to do.

4. Duty openly serves. No man is worthy to serve the Saviour. Just thank God for that privilege and go on and serve Him. Glory to God!

O God, give us some who will swallow their pride, give themselves up with deep devotion and say, "Whatever it is, Lord, I *will* do whatever I can. I *will* do my duty. I *will* serve You out of love and devotion!"

God help us who have our minds, our health, our physical strength and can go at leisure and do whatever we want to do, yet sit around and whine, complain and make up excuses!

You look at one with half your talent and wonder why God is using him. Why? Because he is willing to go. He may not do much, but he will raise the flag for his Saviour and do what he can because it is his duty!

Put aside your pride. You may not be the best in the house, but by the grace of God, do what is your duty to do!

It seems to me that it is my duty to believe every word in this Book, so I'll do my duty.

I think it's my duty to keep a warm heart, so I'll do my duty.

I think it's my duty to rejoice every day, so I'll do my duty.

I think it's my duty to walk with God, so I'll do my duty.

I think it's my duty to stay clean, so I'll do my duty.

I think it's my duty to give out gospel tracts, so I'll do my duty.

I think it's my duty to love sinners and to go soul winning, so I'll do my duty.

I think my duty is to be in church on Sunday morning, Sunday night and Wednesday night, so I'll do my duty.

I think it's my duty to give tithes and gifts, so I'll do my duty.

I think it's my duty to run with the *right* crowd and to avoid the *wrong* crowd, so I'll do my duty.

I think my duty is to support my pastor and be loyal to my church, so I'll do my duty.

I think it's my duty to stand against the enemy, so I'll do my duty.

I think my duty is to pray and to be Spirit-filled, so I'll do my duty.

I think my duty is to love what's right and hate what's wrong, so I'll do my duty.

I think it's my duty to separate myself from the world and live right, dress right, act right and smell right, so I'll do my duty.

I think my duty is to represent my Lord well, so I'll do my duty.

The Lord is looking for some old, broken-down vehicles that are not so impressed with themselves but are willing to do whatever He says to do. He is looking for someone who will say, "I'm an unprofitable servant, but I will do what is my duty."

Hear my appeal to you: Today, tomorrow, next week, next year—just do your duty!

11

"My Heart's Desire"

"Brethren, my heart's desire and prayer to God for Israel is, that they might be saved.

"For I bear them record that they have a zeal of God, but not according to knowledge.

"For they being ignorant of God's righteousness, and going about to establish their own righteousness, have not submitted themselves unto the righteousness of God.

"For Christ is the end of the law for righteousness to every one that believeth."—Rom. 10:1–4.

I ask you three simple but straightforward and very important questions:

I. Why Did Jesus Come?

The answer is found in Luke 19:10: "The Son of man is come to seek and to save that which was lost."

All who are not saved are lost. The Lord Jesus came to seek and to save. The fact is, we would get a lot more saved if we did more seeking. One of our biggest problems is, we seek out so few. The Lord set the pattern, the example, when He went about seeking and saving those who were lost.

The Bible also tells us, "I am come that they might have life, and that they might have it more abundantly" (John 10:10). Life is not like it ought to be until one gets saved. What He is addressing here is not *eternal* life, but *abundant* life. When we get saved, we get saved eternally, but we also get a dimension added to life that we could never have had without salvation.

I got saved when I was a kid. As a result, I missed out on a bunch of stuff, and I am excited about the fact that I've missed it! I've often thought about preaching a whole sermon on "Stuff I've Missed That I Don't Really Mind Missing."

Never once have I had a headache from a hangover. Why? Because I got saved early. It has added a dimension to my life that I could never have had, had I not come to Christ early.

I was preaching in Texas. One night while my wife and I were working the book table, I looked up. The fellow standing in front of me smiled and stuck out his big hand. I recognized him immediately. This Texan had come to our church in Maryland because he knew we had a program working with drug addicts and alcoholics. He had been a drug addict, and his family flew him up there. He came to our place, got saved, got his life on track and began walking with God.

As he looked at me with a little tear in his eye, he said, "Thank you for having a backbone when I didn't have one." He had been in trouble and now was thanking me for providing an answer.

Listen! I have never been afraid to see a drunk nor a drug addict walk down the aisle on Sunday, because Jesus came to give life and life abundantly even to druggies and sots. Jesus "came not to call the righteous, but sinners to repentance" (Mark 2:17).

Some people try to make you think they are so good. I don't try to put a guilt trip on anyone, but all of us need to understand that we are not so hot! No one can become good until he determines that he is bad. No one can really be righteous until he sees himself as a sinner. Jesus didn't come to call the righteous but to help downtrodden, Hell-bound sinners. You and I have a responsibility to help people see that they are sinners. Once they see themselves as sinners in their own sight, they can then lift their eyes up to the Lord—but not until they understand who they are and what they are in God's sight!

Why did Jesus come? To seek and to save, to give abundant life, to call sinners to repentance. "For this purpose the Son of God was manifested, that he might destroy the works of the devil" (I John 3:8).

The fact is, Jesus came to give the Devil a headache, to mess up his nest, to put up resistance to what he is doing.

Now, my second question is this:

II. What on Earth Are We *Doing* on Earth?

Here are some scriptural answers:

"Thus it is written, and thus it behoved Christ to suffer, and to rise from the dead the third day:

"And that repentance and remission of sins should be preached in his name among all nations, beginning at Jerusalem.

"And ye are witnesses of these things."—Luke 24:46–48.

Why are we here? To be witnesses. This message of the death, burial and resurrection of Christ and the salvation that comes when men turn to the Saviour is to be preached in the name of Christ in every nation. Jesus said that we are to bear testimony, be witnesses and give our lives to that fact.

The word *witness* is translated from the word *martureo*. What is a martyr? Someone who gives his life for a cause. It is for the cause of winning souls that you and I give our witness and our testimony for the Saviour.

Jesus said in John 15:16, "Ye have not chosen me, but I have chosen you, and ordained you, that ye should go and bring forth fruit." He picked us out, set us apart, gave us a mission and a mandate, made us messengers and set us on a course on purpose so that we might bear fruit.

I've heard it again and again, even from well-meaning people: "All God expects is that we be faithful." That is only half the truth. Indeed, God does expect us to be faithful, and we won't bear much fruit if we are not, but our Christian lives are not exclusively that of just being faithful. We are not only to be *faithful* but also *fruitful*.

Why are we here? Jesus said, "Ye shall receive power, after that the Holy Ghost is come upon you: and ye shall be *witnesses*" (Acts 1:8).

What are you going to do when you get the power of God on your life? Speak in tongues? No! That is not what happens!

Then when you get the power of God in your life, surely you will be museum quality, a living exhibition of what a Christian ought to be. No! When you get the power of God, "ye shall be witnesses." If we are not doing that, it simply means the power is not there.

So why does God give us His power? So we can be the faithful, fruitful and fervent witnesses He mandates us to be.

You may say you feel so feeble. Then get the power! You may say you are just a little, old, trembling, fleshly creature. God knows that, so He made His power available.

Why are we here?

"There is no difference between the Jew and the Greek: for the same Lord over all is rich unto all that call upon him.

"For whosoever shall call upon the name of the Lord shall be saved.

"How then shall they call on him in whom they have not believed? and how shall they believe in him of whom they have not heard? and how shall they hear without a preacher?"—Rom. 10:12–14.

Thank God, even the "five-pointers" can get saved! They don't think *others* can, but according to these verses *they can.*

What are we doing on this planet?

"I speak to you Gentiles, inasmuch as I am the apostle of the Gentiles, I magnify mine office:

"If by any means I may provoke to emulation them which are my flesh, and might save some of them."—Rom. 11:13, 14.

Do you see that?

What am I doing here? That I might get some of the unsaved saved.

Now for my third question:

III. Is There a Plan?

If to seek and to save is why Jesus came, and if bearing fruit (getting people saved) is why He came, and if that is why we are here, is there a plan for carrying out the task? I'm glad to report to you, yes, there is a plan; and Romans 10:1 makes it very clear.

1. Set up a partnership. Paul starts out with "Brethren," meaning partners. When you get your heart's desire and your prayer to God going, you will need a buddy, a partner, somebody to get in sync with you.

I've known some Christians who didn't want to get involved with church, but to my knowledge, not one of them amounted to anything for God or got anyone saved. You can personally win souls by yourself, but without the "brethren," you won't continue at it. We must tie ourselves in fellowship with our brethren. The Lord would have us tie together in fellowship in a local body, in a local church. I'm talking about a fundamental, New Testament, independent Baptist church. I've said over and over that I believe we had a church long before Pentecost. It's hard to add to something you don't have one of. The Bible specifically says "there were added unto them" that day.

The plan is: get together, build together and start a partnership together.

2. Get a heartbeat and a passion for seeing people saved. "My heart's desire...." Where my passion, burden and energy are is where I'll get involved and where I'll invest myself.

It is wonderful to have a computer on which to type your sermons, an office to work in and all these *things* available to us today. I look around this facility here. It is obvious that someone did some things with design and purpose. Everything is laid out on purpose, even to the stripes on the parking lot—but that is not really what our work is. Those are only the chores that we do so we'll have something to work with to do our work.

I grew up on a farm. We put in a workday, then went home and did the chores—which didn't count as work! A lot of us get fouled up on that. We just do the *chores,* but we never get around to doing the *work!* We talk about soul winning as though it were a Thursday-night activity only. Soul winning—seeing people saved—has to become a passion of the heart.

You say, "Man, we've got a nice building, and everything is going really well. Our crowds are up ten percent this year, and we've never raised so much money in all of our church life!"

Friends, if that's all you are doing, it is not enough. If that's all you're doing, you're backslidden, and *Ichabod* will soon be on the doorposts at your place.

It is not enough to have a nice building, clean floors, an orderly service; it is not enough to have a good crowd on Sunday and good offerings coming in. We need to be in the harness doing with a passion what we know how to do.

Does your heart get stirred up for those who are drunk or those into drugs, putting needles in their arms and doing damage to their families? Those are the ones who need to be saved, and it is our responsibility to reach them. Oh, for a holy heartbeat, a principled passion for seeing people saved!

In my early ministry, when a sermon went over well and a few shook my hand and told me how "nice" it was, I felt good. I got over that a long time ago. I'll thank you if you tell me a sermon was good, but when I preach, I'm not just thinking about giving some little highly honed homily! Alliterated outlines, warm-puppy stories and cute poems ring empty! When our passion for souls has dried up, our pulpit is dry! When we are not fervent for souls, we mock the ministry and bring shame to the cause of Christ.

It is likely that somebody is in church even on Wednesday night who needs to get saved, so give the matter your attention. Getting people saved must be your passion.

3. Get your prayers moving in the right direction. "My heart's desire and prayer to God...." When it becomes your heart's desire, then soon you will start praying about it. When you start praying, things start happening. You get answers from God.

I've talked to people in their homes who let me know after a few minutes that they were ready for me to leave. I've walked out in front of those houses, paused at the sidewalk and prayed: "Dear God, those folks didn't want to hear what I had to say. Dear Lord, stir them up a little bit. Get them ready so that when I return, they will pay attention to the message I bring."

I would drive down that same street two or three days later and pray, "Lord, remember those folks I visited with last week? Stir them a little today, Lord; I'd like to see them get saved."

Many times I would receive a phone call from a guy saying, "I don't know how your schedule is, but is there any possibility I could come by your office?" or, "You know, there have been a few things happening with us, and I wonder if you could stop by and see us again." Never am I surprised when that happens. I have been praying, so I expect it!

4. Pray pointedly and specifically for people. We get our partners, we get our hearts' desires (the great passion of our lives), we get our prayer lives moving in the right direction, and we point our prayers toward specific people. "My heart's desire and prayer to God for Israel is...."

You preachers and others here say, "My heart's desire and prayer to God for ___ [whatever your town, area, village, section of the neighborhood or countryside in which you are working] is that these people get saved. God, I want to bear fruit in this place!" Pray pointedly and specifically for people.

What is the purpose of it all? That they might be saved.

5. Organize your church budget for soul winning. When we go through church budget time, so often we don't give thought to planning the budget so people will get saved. You say, "Oh, well, we just organize the money that comes in." Organize it for souls! Plan to put some of it into what will get souls saved!

So often you figure out how to spend the money in the church and spend it so you will feel good and have things that interest and entertain your congregation. Instead, look over that budget and invest some of that money first in getting people saved!

"My heart's desire and prayer to God for Israel is, that they might be saved."

You ask, "Do people really need that?" Yes, because verse 2 of Romans 10 says there is a problem. The people have a record, and it is that they have religion, but it is a false one; they have a righteousness, but it is a bad righteousness. They have rejected the truth.

All of us owe a debt that we could not pay in a thousand lifetimes. That debt exacts of us what we could never meet, and we have a destiny that we could never change because of that sin debt.

The answer is found in chapter 10, verse 4:

"For Christ is the end of the law for righteousness to every one that believeth."

Not to everyone who believes and observes all the so-called "sacraments"; not to everyone who believes and gets "baptized"; but "to every one that believeth" that Christ is the answer!

6. Focus on getting people saved. Salvation is available to everybody.

You say, "I would go out and witness, but..." Why not say, "People are dying and going to Hell who ought to get saved. The Gospel works, and God wants me to take the message. I'll go, and if one person doesn't want to hear it, then I'll go next door and take the message there and on down to the next guy. I'll just keep going!"

Are you afraid that you might get insulted? Then be an insulted Christian in the will of God. Let your heart's desire and prayer to God be focused on getting sinners saved!

7. Start running with soul winners. Make your intimate friends those who are running on the right track.

Some of you preachers are going to misunderstand this, but I ask you to take a close look at who has been in your pulpit the last twelve to twenty-four months. Are you inviting preachers who have a heartbeat for sinners? a track record for souls?

I remember when people would come in for visitation and ask, "What kind of visits do you have to give me?" I would answer, "Just get in your car and go someplace. You can't take the Gospel to the wrong address!"

One time a fellow in the South told me, "I like to feel led when I go soul winning." If you are waiting to feel led, then somebody ought to get you by the nose, squeeze it hard and pull. You have a command to go soul winning, so don't wait! Don't dillydally around! Go! You don't feel like it? I've gone soul winning many times when I didn't feel like it.

Get a burden for souls and start driving around your town! Ask God to give you a burden for the bedraggled section of town where nobody has a dime. Go on out where those $400,000 homes are and pray for those people as well. The doctors and the lawyers, the educators and the politicians will be just as hot in Hell as someone who never had a dime! Folks running city hall don't need to be in those dead, liturgical churches. They don't need to be in some soft-soaping, wishy-washy evangelical mausoleum. They need to be in some place under the spout where the glory is coming out!

Get a burden for souls.

8. Get serious about going after souls. Get a burden for souls. Get on your knees for souls. Ask God to help you stay hot for souls. Get specific about it; get in the habit of winning souls.

You say, "Well, we're having this program"—a Christmas program or an Easter program or a patriotic program or a youth program. I'm proud for you, but do you plan on getting people saved while doing it? Everything you do ought to be anchored and geared, set and focused so that people can get saved. Get serious about going after souls.

The difference between good and great, between failure and success, between just so-so average and absolutely fantastic is elbow grease, midnight oil and—most of all—the power of God!

We talk about the power of God, but we're not willing to put our elbow grease to the equation. We want the power of God, but we're not willing to go soul winning more than just once in awhile.

I spent thirty-four years as a pastor. The first six or seven years of that I didn't have my act together like it needed to be. With some tutoring from Dr. John R. Rice and some things I learned out of the SWORD OF THE LORD, I got myself regeared.

I scheduled three times a week for working prospects. I won people to Christ at other times, but these were scheduled times. If I didn't have any prospects, I worked suspects! Don't be discouraged because you don't have some really red-hot prospects. Go out there and dig for some yourself.

I started getting other folks to help me. Then I started teaching my people how to do it. That church where I was pastor for all those years did it and is still doing it.

Somewhere along in the process, I determined that with the Lord helping me, every day I would try to witness to someone unsaved. I didn't always win him, but I tried. When I travel, I witness. When I'm at home, I talk to sinners. In a store, in a waiting line, stay alert; keep your vision; keep your burden for souls. Talking to people every day is part of the seeking.

A few months ago I began to pull books off the shelf—books by Spurgeon, Billy Sunday, Moody and others—looking for stories that I could share with others in the SWORD OF THE LORD.

I wondered if Spurgeon himself actually led people to Christ. Then I found stories where he told about leading people to Christ. Moody told about leading people to Christ. Billy Sunday told about leading people to Christ. These men were not just preachers; they were soul winners!

It humbles me to think that the Lord has allowed me to lead scores of people to Christ. There have been many times when I didn't explain the plan of salvation very well, times when I was tired and my mind wasn't clear, times when after I had finished I thought, *I didn't do a good job of that.* Still, the Gospel is powerful, and God let me tell the old, old story to sinners and see them genuinely converted and set on a course toward Heaven.

I attended my first Sword of the Lord Conference while I was still a student at a Southern Baptist seminary in the 1960s. When I read in the SWORD OF THE LORD that Dr. John R. Rice was coming to Kansas City, I said to my wife, "We're going over there. I want to see him." We went and sat in the back.

God set my soul on fire. I got unhappy with my meager amount of fruit. I told God that I wanted my life to count. I wanted to win people to Christ. I wanted to put my people to work. I wanted to train people to win souls. I wanted a church that was built on soul winning and getting people down the aisle and getting them out of the Devil's vineyard and getting them over into God's service!

God began to let me do some things. About five years later I went to a Sword Conference at the Sword auditorium in Murfreesboro and heard Curtis Hutson for the first time. That auditorium was larger than it is now. I think there must have been eight hundred to a thousand people there. When Dr. Hutson preached that sermon, "Building and Battling," my heart was stirred! It set my soul on fire, and I prayed, "O God, help me!"

People are lost and dying and going to Hell from my town and from your town! America is in trouble. It doesn't matter one bit what the Republicans and the Democrats think or say. They don't know the questions, much less the answers.

You and I have to get a fire burning inside our hearts that makes us unhappy to let our own towns die and go to Hell! Determine not to coast through this thing! Don't be just a yawner! Set out to get people saved!

"My heart's desire and prayer to God for Israel is, that they might be saved." Let's do something about that and do it now!

"O Jerusalem!"

"O Jerusalem, Jerusalem, which killest the prophets, and stonest them that are sent unto thee; how often would I have gathered thy children together, as a hen doth gather her brood under her wings, and ye would not!

"Behold, your house is left unto you desolate: and verily I say unto you, Ye shall not see me, until the time come when ye shall say, Blessed is he that cometh in the name of the Lord."—Luke 13:34,35.

From some vantage point, looking out over the city of Jerusalem, our Lord stopped to ponder her dilemma. With deepest compassion He wept for the people and pled the case on their behalf:

"When he was come near, he beheld the city, and wept over it,

"Saying, If thou hadst known, even thou, at least in this thy day, the things which belong unto thy peace! but now they are hid from thine eyes.

"For the days shall come upon thee, that thine enemies shall cast a trench about thee, and compass thee round, and keep thee in on every side,

"And shall lay thee even with the ground, and thy children within thee; and they shall not leave in thee one stone upon another; because thou knewest not the time of thy visitation."—Luke 19:41–44.

The text for this message is found in verse 34 of chapter 13: "O Jerusalem, Jerusalem." Jerusalem, the city, the home of the people for whom the Saviour felt such pathos, is a very special city.

It Is a Regal City
After all, it is the place from which David reigned. It is the place where Solomon reigned, as did others of the great kings of Israel. Many of them are buried in the little valley that runs between the Mount of Olives and the wall of the old city—in the Kedron Valley. That impressive line of ancient tombs is called the Tombs of the Kings.

Indeed, it is a city accustomed to regality. It is this royal city upon which the Lord looks so lovingly—the city to which He will be coming back as King of Kings and Lord of Lords.

Within the city's walls is the famous Eastern Gate, now sealed and forever shut until the great King of Heaven arrives to break it open. Such anticipation is befitting this city where royalty shall have its finest hour.

It Is a Religious City

If you go to Jerusalem today, you will find religion prevalent everywhere. Christians celebrate the things of the Lord on Sunday. The Jews make a religious to-do in the city on Saturday. Then another brand of religion takes place on Friday—the Islamic or Mohammedan religion. There is religion everywhere across the city. It is not always the right kind, but it is religion. The Bible uses the term *religion* almost always in a negative context. Much of Jerusalem's religion today is not the right kind. It has been that way for hundreds and hundreds of years. The city is steeped in religion. It literally has religion showing on the doorposts. In some places you'll find the Shema of Deuteronomy 6 posted in plain view. Signs adorn the city announcing its expectation of Messiah's coming. Everywhere things indicate the people have a mind about religion.

The city is indeed a very special metropolis, a regal city, a religious city—but that's not all!

It Is a Very Rich City

It is a very rich city in many ways—rich in tradition, rich in heritage. The whole line of its history runs through the vales and hills, up and down the length and breadth of the city of Jerusalem. It is a city replete with reminders that should speak to the hearts and minds of the people about their heritage and ancestry. The monuments, the graves, the archaeological digs, the ancient buildings and the testimony of the ages etched in stone—all contain a part of the story of a city rich in history. You see it everywhere as you walk the streets.

I would be remiss, I think, if I did not also tell you that

It Is a Very Ravaged City

No people on the planet have been so maligned as have been the Jews. For hundreds and hundreds of years the city has, once and again, many times over, been pilfered, pillaged, plundered and profaned. To this day, when one little rock is thrown on a back street in Jerusalem it makes news on the networks around the world. You can have a small riot in Winston-Salem, and probably nobody in South Carolina would ever know about it; or if there was one in Georgia, they might not even report it here. But let one little incident occur in Jerusalem, and it is flashed on the networks, and people around the world are soon advised of it.

Over and over Jerusalem has been ravaged. Armies and tyrants have scaled the wall, burned people out, stolen their young and bright, absconded with whatever loot appealed to them and left the city broken and in ruins.

You ask, "With all of that to its credit and discredit, what is the problem? Why is Jesus so distressed about them?"

It Is a Very Rebellious City

Defying God, desecrating the way of godliness and delighting itself in the way of flesh and carnality, it has set its course on a wayward path. Despite its religious roots, the city has found a way to endorse the ways of the world. It has adopted all the worldly carnalities that you might imagine.

Rebellion has expressed itself in various kinds of wickedness up and down the length and breadth of the city. Rebellion has most often held sway on the streets, in the marketplace, at the synagogue, in the modest homes and at the palace.

When I hear my Lord saying, "O Jerusalem, Jerusalem," it seems there is a sympathetic passion, a note of pathos ringing in those simple words.

It Is a Much Visited City

Jerusalem is not only a very special city but also a much visited city. All through the centuries the prophets have walked its streets. In the twenty-first century, the hope that wells from within the breast of every Jew is expressed in "next year in Jerusalem." It is the place to which every one of them, no matter where he lives presently or where his ancestors have been for the last hundreds of years, longs to go. It is the heart and hope of every Jew "by next year" for sure to make a visit to Jerusalem.

I have had the privilege on a number of occasions to go to Jerusalem. I've walked its streets. I've been up and down, back and forth, over and over again. There is something intriguing about the city. Unlike any other city in the world, there is something mysterious even as you walk the streets. You are enamored with every detail, even though you have seen it again and again.

Now, in this setting, where I have read the Scripture, the Lord God Himself, robed in human flesh, has come calling. Consider the matter:

Jesus has come door-knocking. Imagine the Great I AM making a visit in the city. When our blessed Lord Jesus surveyed this city, He said:

"O Jerusalem, Jerusalem, which killest the prophets, and stonest them that are sent unto thee; how often would I have gathered thy children together, as a hen doth gather her brood under her wings...."

Then there is not a more solemn statement in all the Bible than when Jesus said, "...and ye would not!"

I. His Charges

My heart is touched to see a congregation of people—and in this instance, a city of them—who "would not." It is not that they "could not," but they "would not." Rebellious and defiant, they turned their hearts away from God. Willingly, knowingly and decisively, they just "would not."

I know if I can understand something of the magnitude of that burden, surely the great heart of the Lord God Almighty must have felt a pervasive depth of compassion when He viewed the city and said, "O Jerusalem, Jerusalem"!

You ask, "What really is the problem with them?" He delineates very carefully their deficiency and declares the dilemma they face because of it. The charges leveled are straight and severe. What indictments did Jesus bring?

They Had Mistreated the Preachers

He said, "[Thou] which killest the prophets, and stonest them that are sent unto thee."

You say, "Well, those were prophets." The prophets were preachers, men called of God, men sent of God. They came to town on purpose. They were God's men with a message. They were ambassadors of the King, and somebody mistreated them. Somebody didn't do them right. Somebody opposed them fiercely, oftentimes killing them, stoning them, throwing them out of town, doing whatever they could to disenfranchise them and send them away. They purely and simply mistreated the preachers.

God's preachers are special people, and you and I need to treat them right. I'm a preacher, and I ought to treat every preacher I know as though he is a man of God. I ought to treat him right. I have no right to mistreat the preacher—I don't care who he is or where he is pastor;

I don't care what his name is or how big a church he has or how little. We are to treat the preacher like a preacher ought to be treated.

When America goes to judgment, there is going to be a long line of things in reference to how they've handled the preachers. One day the people in this nation will give an account for having derided and mocked the preachers. Ungodly things done to the men of God do not go unnoticed. Judgment will fall upon a nation that mistreats the preachers God sends to them.

They Misconstrued the Message

Jesus said that they misconstrued the message that the preachers, the disciples, brought. "If thou hadst known, even thou, at least in this thy day, the things which belong unto thy peace! but now they are hid from thine eyes" (Luke 19:42).

Had they understood what the men of God were saying, it would have done something for them. They would have been born again. They would then have had the Spirit of God living in them. They would have been new creatures and have had something they had never had. They wouldn't have been the heathen that they then were, had they heard the message and heeded it.

Get the message out. Give it plain and clear. Preachers sometimes get in trouble, not because they don't make it clear, but because they do make it clear. When you say something, spell it out plain and clear so those in the second or third grade can understand it. People may get perturbed and upset, but better it is that we please God than some worldly character who doesn't like the message.

That is true with reading the Bible. Folks say, "Well, I've had trouble reading the Bible. So much of it I don't understand." I never worried about what I didn't understand. It was what I understood that bothered me!

These rascals not only mistreated the preachers, but they misconstrued the message.

Let us learn a lesson from them! Don't foul up the message of God! Preach salvation plain, clear and straight as a line, as well as the great themes found in the Bible—the doctrines, the truths—without apology, without fear and without hesitation. Let us be sure we have them right, then go and give them out!

If you think your congregation can't handle that, I would work to find some way to get it to them. I would start with the Wednesday night crowd and work on them. Then I would go to the Sunday night crowd and do the same. Then on a Sunday morning I would bow up my back and preach it straight to *that* crowd. Preach it clear! Preach it hot! You can get the message across! America is dying because the politicians, the educators and the social engineers are running the country and running it into Hell. The only hope, the only salvation for our nation is for some beady-eyed, pointed-fingered, fire-in-his-bones preacher called of God to get up on his soapbox and preach the message! Mount the pulpit and preach. Let it fall where it will. Though some may misconstrue the message, be sure to give it to them undefiled!

They Missed Their Opportunities

Jesus said, "How often would I have gathered thy children together, as a hen doth gather her brood under her wings, and ye would not!" (Luke 13:34).

When I was a boy growing up in western Kentucky, my mother always had a few chickens, including at least one rooster with big spurs. Since some of you have no idea what those rascals can do, I will tell you. They can drive a six- or eight-year-old anywhere they want him to go.

The hens would periodically get really fussy—"setting hens" we would call them. A setting hen would often steal her out a nest somewhere and put an egg in it every day. After sitting on those eggs for a while, she would hatch out a little brood of chicks. There is nothing more tender and delicate than a little chick that's only a day or two old.

That old hen would come out of the thicket bringing half a dozen or more little ones. Now, Mr. Wise Guy, go over there and try to check them out! See how she handles it. See if she approves. See what you can learn and how fast you can learn it.

Let a storm start brewing and the wind start blowing the dust, then see what she does. She starts making clucking noises that those newborn chicks understand. She raises up her wings and makes room under there, and those little ones wisely and quickly just disappear to this safe place. Under pressure from storms or predators, it is a matter of life and death. She raises her wings, affording them the opportunity of shelter; she urges them fervently to come, and they respond.

Jesus used that amazing analogy to say, "In the midst of the storms brewing about you—times when predators might be coming or others who might be a threat to you, to your little children, to your little brood—how often, in view of the great, eternal damage that can be done, would I have gathered you together like that old hen gathers her little chicks. I would have done it over and over again. I raised My wings and invited you to come under, but ye would not."

Opportunity is afforded when the preacher preaches. Opportunity is presented when the soul winner goes out on the trail. Opportunity is there when you run a bus route.

You and I need to say to people everywhere, "Don't pass it up. Hear the message! Heed the call! Come to Christ! Be saved today!"

When you get done preaching on a Sunday, leave enough time to plead, enough time to make the appeal and urge the unsaved to come to the Saviour.

The Jews of Jesus' day missed their opportunities. Today many are following their ill-advised example and making the same woeful mistake.

They Mismanaged Their Resources

They have houses; but Jesus of necessity must say to them, 'You would not; consequently, your house is left unto you desolate.'

Winter before last we had a twister come through Murfreesboro about two miles from our house. I don't remember the figures exactly, but sixty or seventy homes were totally destroyed and another hundred or so, seriously damaged. I drove over there two or three different times after they got everything to where you could get in the area again. I drove through the neighborhood. We had seen it in the papers and on television.

For weeks, months even, after that twister came through, there were places where nice homes had once stood with nothing left then but the foundations. You could look out across fields and still see teddy bears and broken vases, remains of flower arrangements, people's underwear—all kinds of personal, private things. Now none of it was worth picking up, even if you knew it was yours. People found things several miles away that had been blown away by that twister.

It is a story repeated far too many times across the nation. Every resource, every good thing, all we thought we had, suddenly, in a moment, is damaged, doomed, destroyed.

Jesus said, 'I sent the prophets to you. They came with a message. They came with tenderness and love and compassion and devotion, but ye would not. Now your window of opportunity has passed! Now the only thing left is desolation and doom.'

They Misappropriated Their Future

We preach Heaven real and Hell hot, sinners lost and salvation the remedy. People who do trust the Saviour come out in good shape. To those who don't, you and I cannot but say, "Your house is left unto you desolate."

They mismanaged their resources and misappropriated their future. Jesus said, "Ye shall not see me, until the time come when ye shall say, Blessed is he that cometh in the name of the Lord" (Luke 13:35).

For the living or for the dead, there is a future. Jesus made things very clear. The charges He brought against Jerusalem are not unlike those that could be brought against my town or yours. If your future is important to you, then it's important for you to grasp the God-given opportunity to trust Christ as Saviour and follow Him!

II. His Compassion

Right in the midst of all Jerusalem—like Mount Everest surrounded by a mesa of molehills, as a giant standing among dwarfs—here is our blessed Saviour watching, warning, wooing and waiting.

The Compassionate Christ

The Lord Jesus is standing, looking out over the city of Jerusalem, looking at little hovels, nice homes, even great mansions perhaps. He is watching people come and go. He sees them set out to some center of religion. He sees them head out to some place of work. He sees. He watches. He looks them over. He scans them from head to toe. Then He says to them, one and all, 'Pay attention. Listen. O Jerusalem, Jerusalem, hear the prophets, the preachers. Listen to the message.'

The Calling Christ

Then He begins to woo them: 'I would have gathered you under My wings. I would have spared you from all that is coming.' Then He waits to see what they would do, and they did nothing. He then says, "…and ye would not."

When I look at my Saviour standing head and shoulders above the people of His time, I see Him like a mother hen watching her brood! I hear the compassionate Saviour, the comforting Christ, saying, 'Oh, I want you. I am wooing you. I am after you.'

The Conquering Christ

I also see Him belting out the words that He needs to give out, words the moderns dread to hear. They are the words of condemnation.

When you spurn the compassion and comfort of Christ, there will be a day when you'll have to hear the condemnation of Christ.

The liberals and modernists decry any thought of condemnation or judgment! These soft-soaping hirelings who stand in so many pulpits around the world today are not patterns of Christ's ministry. They are not willing to say a discouraging word to a generation on the skids to Hell!

Hear me! The God who loves you will one day be the God whose judgment will come. The same God who is the God of light, the God of hope, the God of salvation, will have to say, "You can't have the light; you can't have hope; you can't be saved now. Your opportunity is past."

Understand that the Lord is patient for but a while.

"He, that being often reproved hardeneth his neck, shall suddenly be destroyed, and that without remedy."—Prov. 29:1.

The Coming Christ
In this passage in Luke's Gospel, He is the conquering Christ and the coming Christ. He said, 'You won't hear this again until you say, "Blessed is He that comes in the name of the Lord."'

He is coming! I don't know when. That guy you saw on TV doesn't know when either. People who think they have it figured out, don't. We don't know when He is coming, but we do know He is coming sometime, and it could be anytime!

III. His Comparisons
We look at Jerusalem and see our Saviour there. Having heard His message to Jerusalem, can we fail to note its appropriateness for and its application to us? The comparison cannot be neglected.

I say that we, as Jerusalem, have been privileged, we've been prepared, we've been prompted, and we've been positioned. We, as they, have been entrusted with the great message of God. We, as they, have been given great responsibility—and we have lost our vision! We have grown fat and lazy.

We, as they, have squandered ourselves on ourselves. We have closed our eyes to the crisis about us. We have taken issue with the messengers of God. We, as they, have restricted our focus and not stayed on the message like we ought to have stayed on the message. We have resisted the will of God for our lives.

We, as they, have made a minor issue out of a major cause. We have given lip service to the eternal verities. Consequently, we have lost our moorings! We are adrift in a sea of unbelief and darkness. When we slide, we cannot hide! The comparison is staggering!

I remember years ago when I was a student, trying to be the pastor of a little church and doing everything I knew to do (which wasn't nearly enough), I had begun to get something of a vision. I knew God wanted to work through us and with us. I remember driving around that little town in the Southland where I was the pastor. I remember folks saying to me, "Now, we can't do that here, and we can't do that here, and we can't do that here."

I learned right away that if I asked anybody I would be told no; so I stopped asking and started trying to do some of this and a little of that and a little more of something else.

Honestly, a few little things I tried actually worked, much to the surprise of some folks who were standing around saying, "You can't. It just won't happen here."

I would drive all over the city and think about the people who lived there. I would wonder who lived in those houses. I began to knock on doors and to go here and there. The first thing we knew, things began to happen. I began to feel the burden and the heartbeat for my city. Souls were being saved! The church grew!

Years later the Lord moved me up into the Northeast, the mid-Atlantic. I went up there. I still remember so well that Betty and I sat across the street in a motel the Sunday that I candidated there. We stayed in what was then Room 48 and cried half the afternoon.

I never did ask why she was crying, and she never did ask why I was crying. We both knew why. We knew that God was putting it in our hearts to be there. He gave us a vision! It was soon to be our Jerusalem!

I remember later that I would drive around town, up and down the streets, and pray, "O God, give us people off these streets."

There were some little towns and burgs around us from which we had nobody coming. I went out there on more than one occasion and drove up and down the streets and prayed, "O God, can we reach these people? I don't know who they are, but maybe we can do something to reach them."

We began to set plans in motion—a little of this and a little of that. We went back there again and again. We put our people on the streets, knocking on doors, after souls, rescuing the perishing! This one came on board to help, and another pitched in.

Soon a flood of people were coming from north, south, east and west—from all over the county and beyond the borders of the county. People were coming simply because we began to pray over those places. We knew these people didn't need to be in some dead church, going to some place where they were being fed liberal propaganda. They didn't need to be getting spoon-fed on the Devil's poison. They needed to go where the preacher stood up with the Bible and preached the Word of God every Sunday. They needed to be in a church where the preacher said, "This is the Bible; this is the Word of God; this is what we are; this is what we believe"—where people went out every week to bring in the lost, give them the Gospel and get them saved.

Oh, if we are not careful, we, like Jerusalem, will disappoint our Saviour.

I wonder about my town, your town. O Winston-Salem! O Dallas! O Atlanta! O Baltimore! O Washington, D.C.! O Birmingham! O Omaha! O Winnipeg! O Toronto! O Honolulu! O Tokyo! O Bombay! O Paris!

Somebody somewhere needs to say with the loving tenderness of our blessed Lord Jesus, "I will go to my city and declare it my Jerusalem; I'll buy land here, build buildings, train soul winners, run bus routes, flood neighborhoods with the Gospel. I'll put on campaigns here, have big days, reach families. I'll get on radio, on television—I'll do whatever I can in order that my Jerusalem doesn't go down the tube into desolation."

O God, help us to get a burden and a vision for our towns and our cities and our neighborhoods, our little rural places out there where those churches are that You have placed in our care!

Acts 1:8 says we'll receive power after the Holy Ghost is come upon us: "And ye shall be witnesses unto me...in Jerusalem." I'm for the uttermost part, but it always has to begin at Jerusalem. When you have the anointing of the Holy Ghost, you'll not be apathetic about your Jerusalem. You'll be the Lord's witness there!

My Saviour said, "O Jerusalem, Jerusalem, which killest the prophets, and stonest them that are sent unto thee...!"

Dear friends, tonight there is a town where you live. There is a town where your church is located. There is a town where you are a pastor. It may not be New York City. It may not be New Orleans. It may not be

Los Angeles. It may be some town that hardly anybody has ever heard of; but if God has put you there, why don't you start praying, "O Jerusalem, Jerusalem"?

I hear folks say, "The people in my town are mean. There are crimes and all kinds of devilment." I hear them say, "People are steeped in religion here. All kinds of crazy things are going on here."

Whatever the problem, it doesn't excuse us from our responsibility. What needs to happen in every city and town, in every village and in the rural places is for somebody to get a vantage point, survey the area and weep over it like Jesus did, saying, "O Jerusalem, *my* Jerusalem!"

13

The Power and the Light

Some of you have come here with empty tanks. It may be some of you have come here terribly discouraged. Some of you may be facing terrible battles back home. It may be that some of the things that are supposed to be happening with you and in your ministry are not really taking place.

I'll read one verse for the text of the message today, and I hope I can be a blessing to you in these next few moments.

"No man, when he hath lighted a candle, putteth it in a secret place, neither under a bushel, but on a candlestick, that they which come in may see the light."—Luke 11:33.

Our world today lives in a great deal of darkness. The darkness is pervasive and widespread. Some of it is philosophical darkness. Some of it is moral darkness. Some of it is political darkness. Some of it is educational darkness—and, unfortunately, there is a great deal of religious darkness.

The darkness engulfing our society and the world has many dangers connected with it. Many dreads accompany those dangers. The traps that are laid therein can be devastating. Every one of us watches with a fixed stare and bated breath as our world grows darker and darker.

We saw the Soviet Union blunder along blindly in darkness for almost seventy years. From the time of the Bolshevik Revolution in 1917, literally millions were slaughtered by that giant governmental tyrant—but finally it crumbled.

Today the Arabs and Jews squabble. Darkness thickens between them. Mr. Arafat says some of those sites in Jerusalem belong to them and they're going to claim them. Darkness is hovering over the holy city.

There are all kinds of stories—stories of darkness—about Rwanda, Cuba, Haiti and other places.

A clipping in the paper the other day stated, "University of Kentucky Football Player Shot at Random and Killed." One of the notorious drug kingpins in Washington, D.C. was sent to the penitentiary for life. They rearrested him the other day in prison for running an international drug ring from behind bars. Interesting that you would arrest a man already locked up.

It is dark and getting darker.

Our world gets darker and darker philosophically. We cannot just state our position anymore and have everyone agree. Morally, everything is up for grabs. Politically it is dark. The educational arena has so little light. Religiously you and I are becoming more and more of a phenomenon in our society. People are looking up at us askance because they're not sure who and what we really are. A television reporter in Westminster interviewed me for a story that had been running amuck. She asked, with a kind of sneer, "Are you one of those fundamentalists?" I knew I had to be very careful about how I answered. It is dark and getting darker.

I went down to Carlisle County, Kentucky to see the old farm where we lived when I was a boy. Down the formerly dirt road, now graveled, I found where the little three-room house stood. A tobacco patch grows there today. The house is gone; the barn is gone; the big maple tree is gone. I walked out to about where I thought the house had been. I found the spot about where I thought the bedroom had been. I got down on my knees in the tobacco patch and remembered with sweet remembrance the Saturday morning in September when, as a mere lad, I knelt to put my faith and trust in Christ.

At that point I had not had a lot of exposure to the claims of Christ upon my life; but the first time I heard the Gospel, I knew my need, got on my knees and trusted Jesus. Something happened that I did not understand at that point. I was different.

As I knelt in the little tobacco field and looked up at the electric power lines running along that little, narrow, gravel road, my mind raced back again.

I spent my ninth birthday in the hospital with a bout of pneumonia. When I got back home from days in the hospital, they had put in the power lines. We hadn't had electric power up to that time. We carried one little kerosene lamp from the kitchen to the living room to the bedroom.

Boy, what an imaginative time I had when I found that they had installed in every room of the house—right in the ceiling in the middle of every room—one electric light bulb with a string on it!

I went into the bedroom, pulled the string, looked at the light, pulled the string, looked at the light go off, went into the kitchen, pulled the string, on and off, on and off—absolutely fascinated.

Daddy told me how they had put in the poles and then put the lines on them and ran the lines into the house, then how the electricity coursed through the lines down into the house so all we needed to do was pull a little twine string and the lights would come on. The power was the source of the light. No power, no light. When the light was burning, the power was there.

The mandate of our mission as individuals and as churches, the definition of our task, is stated and restated in the Bible. In Matthew 28:19, 20, Jesus said:

"Go ye therefore, and teach all nations, baptizing them in the name of the Father, and of the Son, and of the Holy Ghost:

"Teaching them to observe all things whatsoever I have commanded you."

We're to get folks saved, get them baptized, identify them publicly in profession of faith, get them into the church and teach them everything that He taught us. With this mandate, we are to do it and keep on doing it.

This mandate is repeated in Mark 16:15: "Go ye into all the world, and preach the gospel to every creature." "Every creature" means that the folks who drive in are to hear the Gospel. "Every creature" means that the folks we can get in on buses are to hear the Gospel. We are to preach the Gospel to "every creature"—young and old, rich and poor, black and white, fat or skinny.

We hear the command again in Luke 24:46–49:

"Thus it is written, and thus it behoved Christ to suffer, and to rise from the dead the third day:

"And that repentance and remission of sins should be preached in his name among all nations, beginning at Jerusalem.

"And ye are witnesses of these things.

"And, behold, I send the promise of my Father upon you: but tarry ye in the city of Jerusalem, until ye be endued with power from on high."

This is the Gospel: Jesus died, was buried and rose again. Salvation is available to sinners. Any sinner can be saved.

This wonderful story must be told. We are to preach it "among all nations." We are the witnesses for God to the hungry, hurting multitudes.

Human vessels are always weak, but Jesus supplies the power to energize the messenger. There's no excuse for any delay. Time is wasting. The harvest is failing. Souls are dying. The lighted torch that shows us a way in the darkness is in our hands.

In John's Gospel the Saviour's commission is given for us again:

"Then said Jesus to them again, Peace be unto you: as my Father hath sent me, even so send I you....

"Whose soever sins ye remit, they are remitted unto them; and whose soever sins ye retain, they are retained."—John 20:21–23.

We take the Gospel and give the message. All people to whom we take the message can be forgiven. Their sins can be erased from their record. If we do not get the message to them, their sins are still on their record, and they are held accountable for them.

The mission, the task, the commission is found again in Acts 1:8:

"But ye shall receive power, after that the Holy Ghost is come upon you: and ye shall be witnesses unto me both in Jerusalem, and in all Judæa, and in Samaria, and unto the uttermost part of the earth."

When the Holy Spirit "is come upon you," there is a bestowment of power. When the power is received, "ye shall be witnesses." So again we see the connection of the power and the light. You cannot shine without the power, but with the power you cannot help but shine.

Now with the eloquent testimony so ably stated and the abundant evidence so richly presented in Matthew, Mark, Luke, John and Acts, there seems no question about what our assignment is.

Understandably we are fickle, feeble, faulty, fainting and flighty. Undeniably the task is a formidable one and sometimes even frightening. We need to understand that to give light we need power.

Jesus illustrates in Luke 11:33 both the power and the light: "No man, when he hath lighted a candle...."

Why do we light a candle? To get light. It will not do its job and give forth light until the power is put to it.

"No man, when he hath lighted a candle [empowered the candle and made it burn], *putteth it in a secret place, neither under a bushel, but on a candlestick, that they which come in may see the light."*

This candle illustration is fascinating to me. Jesus refers to a candle, suggesting that it has been secured at some expense, at some effort. Then, deliberately and purposefully, the owner lights that candle. It is the nature of a candle to burn when lighted. We put fire to it to make it burn. We put fire to it because we know it will burn. As it burns, it is consumed. In consuming itself in its own natural task, it gives the light and does the job it is supposed to do.

I hear folks talk about "rust-out," "walk-out" and "run-out." More often they've just "turned out" and "rotted out." Folks fearfully lament about "burnout," but isn't that what we're supposed to do?

We're sitting up on the shelf resting, rusting, rotting and doing nothing! Folks all over this nation are going from church to church, sniffing to see if they like the fragrance, never one time plugging themselves into the power. Their candle is never fired. Since they are not burning, they can never be the light they are supposed to be.

I would hate to know I had lived my life to the end and had not burned every ounce, every bit of the tallow or whatever it is that I'm made of. I want all of it to be fully used up the day I die. Let it burn! Let the light shine. Once the light has been touched to the candle, don't put it in a secret place.

Folks, be willing to be vulnerable. Be willing to let your light be seen. Don't hide it someplace; display it in the open. Be transparent. You may get kicked around and bruised a bit in order to have your light seen by a world smothered in darkness, but whatever the personal price, don't hide the candle in a secret place. Remove the bushel and let the light shine.

We cannot content ourselves just because our light is burning in the church house. The message—the light of Jesus crucified and risen— once empowered, now burning, must be taken out beyond the four walls of the church. We must take it to McDonald's, to the playground, to the factory, to the new car showroom. We must take it to the streets, into the homes, up and down the streets. We must take it door to door, house to house. Why? Because the verse says don't hide it nor smother it but display it. Set the candle afire. Put it on a candlestick; get something to hold it with; then carry it.

Revelation 1:20 identifies the candlestick as the church. Jesus said in John 8:12, "I am the light of the world." We know that He is the Light. In John 12:46 Jesus said, "I am come a light into the world, that whosoever believeth on me should not abide in darkness." He said, 'I am come into the world to be a light that whosoever believes on Me should not stay in this awful, abysmal darkness.'

Now watch carefully. In another verse (John 9:5) Jesus said, "As long as I am in the world, I am the light of the world." Then what happened when Jesus left this world and ascended into Heaven? Did the light go out? He said, "As long as I am in the world, I am the light of the world."

Look in chapter 12 again:

"Then Jesus said unto them, Yet a little while is the light with you. [He is saying it again.] *Walk while ye have the light, lest darkness come upon you: for he that walketh in darkness knoweth not whither he goeth.*

"While ye have light, believe in the light, that ye may be the children of light."—Vss. 35,36.

Jesus said that you do not hide nor smother the lighted candle but display it on a candlestick. Then He reminds us that even though He is the Light of the World, things are going to happen because He is not going to stay.

In Matthew 5 Jesus taught carefully and clearly:

"Ye are the light of the world. A city that is set on an hill cannot be hid.

"Neither do men light a candle, and put it under a bushel, but on a candlestick; and it giveth light unto all that are in the house.

"Let your light so shine before men, that they may see your good works, and glorify your Father which is in heaven."—Vss. 14–16.

Jesus said, 'No man puts the candle in a secret place but on a candlestick, so others may see the light.'

People are living in darkness; we have the candle; we ignite it; it is empowered so we can give the light to those who are in darkness. As we give the light, they see Him who is the Light, even though He has already gone to Heaven. You and I are to keep the light burning, keep the torch lit and keep sending out the light. We must keep putting the power to the candle so the light may be seen by those in darkness.

I preached for years without a PA system. People talk about the "good old days." No, thanks! I preached for years when in the hot summertime I peeled off my coat, rolled up my shirt-sleeves and took off my tie. There were no screens on the windows, so bugs were flying in. I've ingested bugs—and other things—while preaching! I remember that, and so do some of you. We don't want to go back..

Still, the ministry is not about these beautiful buildings, not about this equipment. The ministry is about taking the light, getting it on the candlestick, whatever facilities or lack of facilities we have. The church, its facilities, its program, its ministry—everything is about giving the light.

Get the right kind of power, give the light, go out into the neighborhoods and stir up the people! We need to go in, kick the Devil's hornets' nest, create a furor and get things stirred up.

I don't want the liquor dealers in my town liking me too much. Respect me, yes—but I want them to know I'm not in harmony with them.

Some politicians in Westminster didn't seem to like me, and there were write-ups in the paper. I just sat back and enjoyed it. I had taken a stand! I'm not neutral. I'm for right, and I'm for him or her who is right. I promote and endorse what's right. That puts light on the subjects.

When you get the candle on the candlestick, some of those who are the proponents of darkness may try to snuff out your light. They may try to kick the candle over, break the candlestick and keep you from getting your appointed job done.

You and I have a great job. Let's get a candlestick, the best candlestick, the finest one we can find, so that we can show the light. Our candlestick should be crafted carefully, polished regularly and made beautiful. Your presentation, your candlestick, ought to be as nice as possible. Don't let your buses look like trash heaps. Some may run a little sideways down the road, but make them as neat as you can. If you can't buy new ones, buy the best used ones. If you have to run junk, buy the best junk.

There is no excuse for running dirty, slipshod, broken-down, unpainted buses and having unmopped, unwaxed, unpainted, trashy buildings. An ugly, diminished, less-than-our-best presentation to a lost world is unacceptable. You may not be able to have what some others have, but take what you have and "spiffy" it up. Present the candlestick as highly polished and as carefully crafted as you can present it.

Listen! You are not carrying out wastewater; you are carrying the light and the torch of the Gospel. You are representing the great King.

It is exciting to know that Jesus made us to be the light. Oh, I know that He is the Sun, the greater Light. The Son is in the spiritual world what the sun is in the physical world. He is the greater Light. I know that we are lesser lights, lights that have no source of light within themselves. We, like the moon, are unable to produce light, but we reflect the light from the Son. What an impact when every little reflected light is in its place and does its job!

When I try to negotiate without the lights on, I don't do too well. Sometimes in the night, while trying to find my way to a certain part of the house, I've gotten my shins skinned and my toes bruised.

We have one of those big, four-poster beds. Sometimes I have run smack into that thing face-on. Betty finally put a night-light in the bathroom. I can't sleep well with a light on, but at least I'm not running over the bedpost. Even with the light, I may stumble a bit because, being human, I'm a little inept. I don't have the perfect ability that my Saviour has, but with the light, I do better.

This passage in John 12:35 teaches that in the darkness the whole body is vulnerable and corrupt. Everything is in jeopardy. Character fails; politics corrupt; education, business—everything falls apart. Even religion breaks down rapidly when the light is not in place on the candlestick.

Our whole world needs to know, needs to hear, needs to see. People may throw reproach at us and be critical of us. They may not appreciate us, but they need to see us and hear from us.

A Pharisee in this crowd in Luke 11 was upset with Jesus because He didn't go through the ceremony of hand washing. It was not that he thought Jesus' hands were dirty; he just wanted Him to go through the ceremonial ritual.

Some in our society are like that. Some sitting in your church on Sunday are analytical, critical. They won't like anything you do, but when you stand up on Sunday, don't preach to the hardheads. The temptation is to fix up a sermon, something just right for them. Don't preach to that hardheaded, hardhearted crowd. Don't worry with some of those old stumps who have been plowed around for years. Find somebody who has a warm heart and preach to him. The same message you preach to the warm heart will penetrate that cold one, and you'll be in a lot better shape too. The light has a way of exposing, encouraging and getting inside the heart.

Jesus said, 'You clean the outside but pay no attention to the inside.' When the light of the Gospel goes in, it cleans up the inside, that part that needs cleaning up!

I look at someone's exterior and think, *Man, he's pretty rough!* How many times have we thought, *If we can just fix him up, put him in a new suit, clean him up, give him a haircut and a shave, it will get him started!* That won't do it. We have spent billions in this country trying through social agencies to fix people from the outside—but you have to take the light on the inside. When you clean up the inside, ultimately it will work its way to the outside.

I remember down there in Carlisle County, Kentucky that little house where I grew up with just three rooms: kitchen, living room and bedroom. Mama had two dishwashers—my brother and me. I hated two things about that: one, washing; the other, drying. I dreaded Mama's scrutiny. I could wash and wash them, and she could still find something on them. Even when I dried them over and over, she could still find little spots that needed further drying.

We can look and look, we can find plenty of dirty spots on things, but it is the light of the Gospel of Christ that puts the right kind of perspective on them. Even after you have been a Christian thirty or forty years, you can still find little specks when you dry. The light of Christ reveals that.

We take a stand. I preach on the issues. I preach on the abortion racket. I call the perverts the sinners that they are. I take a stand, and I ought to, but it is my conviction that those are not the sins that are killing America. The pet sins of the saints are killing America. We know we are supposed to have the candlestick. We know we are supposed to have the light. We know we are supposed to put the power to it and make it burn, but precious few do it. Most of those who come inside still have not gotten adjusted to exactly what it is we are supposed to do.

I'm convinced that one of the things God will hold America accountable for is our lackadaisical, ungodly attitude about keeping Sunday as the Lord's Day. We do anything and everything we want to do on His day.

People make car payments with their tithes. I'll sell my house or move into something smaller or do whatever is necessary before I will use God's money for myself.

Knowing what I know, for me not to be a soul winner would be a crime against God for which He will hold me in judgment.

We simply need to get the lights on in the church house. If we get the power on, the lights will come on, and we will be able to do the job we are called to do.

Jesus said,

"Ye do err, not knowing the scriptures, nor the power of God."—Matt. 22:29.

He said,

"Some of them that stand here…shall not taste of death, till they have seen the kingdom of God come with power."—Mark 9:1.

He said of John the Baptist,

"Many of the children of Israel shall he turn to the Lord their God.

"And he shall go before him in the spirit and power of Elias, to turn the hearts of the fathers to the children, and the disobedient to the wisdom of the just; to make ready a people prepared for the Lord."—Luke 1:16,17.

In the New Testament, "power" comes from two Greek words: *exousia,* "authority"; and *dunamis,* the resource or the actual exertion of the power.

Let me illustrate:

Harry Truman dropped the bombs on Hiroshima and Nagasaki that ended World War II. He no doubt saved many more lives than the bomb took. Mr. Truman had become president on the twelfth day of April 1945—the day that FDR died. He had been vice president for only a few weeks. On the twelfth of April when he became president, he did not even know the bomb existed. He was apprised of it almost immediately, and for several weeks he pondered its utilization. When he became president, he had full authority to use the power, but he did not use it until the sixth day of August.

John 1:12 says, "But as many as received him, to them gave he power [*exousia*]…." This is God's authorization for us to have the power and to use it. He hereby appropriates to us what we need.

In Acts 1:8 He says, "Ye shall receive [*dunamis*]"—the power, the resource. He is saying, 'You are already authorized to do it. Now I want you actually to unleash it. Take it and use it.'

Why does God give us this power and the authority to use it? Acts 1 says the power is given to us (1) to exalt Christ, (2) to edify Christians and (3) to evangelize the unsaved.

You see, God intends to show Himself strong. In Acts 1:8 He says, "Ye shall be witnesses unto me." That means we're to exalt Christ, hold Him up. What is our message? To exalt Christ.

The power also edifies Christians. "Ye shall receive power." He is bestowing ability upon us. He is infusing strength into us. He is making us mightier than we are.

Then, of course, He gives the power so we can effectively and successfully evangelize the unsaved. Through this power, God intends to bring sinners to salvation. It happened in the early church:

"And with great power gave the apostles witness of the resurrection of the Lord Jesus: and great grace was upon them all."—Acts 4:33.

Paul said,

"For I determined not to know any thing among you, save Jesus Christ, and him crucified.

"And I was with you in weakness, and in fear, and in much trembling.

"And my speech and my preaching was not with enticing words of man's wisdom, but in demonstration of the Spirit and of power."—I Cor. 2:2–4.

"For I am not ashamed of the gospel of Christ: for it is the power of God unto salvation to every one that believeth."—Rom. 1:16.

"For the preaching of the cross is to them that perish foolishness; but unto us which are saved it is the power of God."—I Cor. 1:18.

Real revival depends on the power and the light. When the power is turned on in our churches, the preaching gets hot.

I hope you haven't "MacArthurized" your preaching. I hope you're not locked into some simple little homilies and nice-sounding little phrases. I hope you're not content to present your message, sit down and say, "Well, it was enough."

God help us in these days to get the power turned on so the light can be given. When the power is on and the light is shining, our preaching will get hot. When preaching is hot, the church comes alive. When the church comes alive, more sinners get saved.

I have a little formula that I use: Find 'em, fetch 'em, fix 'em, feed 'em—or you may like it this way: Woo 'em, win 'em, wet 'em and work 'em.

You say, "But, man, we're having trouble in our church!" Turn the power on! Let the light shine! Go soul winning! Do it! Do it today! Do it often!

You say, "Man, we're having a business meeting, a big blowout." Turn the power on. Let the light shine brighter. Go soul winning. Preach ahead of the business meeting, give an invitation and have somebody ready to walk the aisle. Rejoicing over a sinner getting saved will do more to disrupt the disorder and the deadheads who create it than anything else you could do.

You say, "Our budget is faltering. We just can't pay our bills." Turn the power on. Send the light. Go soul winning. Remember, when Jesus needed money to pay His taxes, He caught a fish, opened its mouth and found something in its mouth with which to pay His taxes.

You say, "We just don't have any workers." Turn the power on. Keep the light on. Go soul winning. Those who have just been saved make the best workers.

One of our fellows was sitting here with me the other night. We were talking about the makeup of Church of the Open Door. One time we did a little study. About forty percent of the three thousand or so folks who called our place home had Roman Catholic backgrounds. How did that come about? We went soul winning in their territory. Up where we lived, if you couldn't get Roman Catholics saved, you probably wouldn't reach a lot of folks. Tough cases? Sure. But the power works, and the light works.

Betty and I took a little vacation in July. Among the places we went was Frankfurt, Kentucky. A beautiful, majestic Capitol building sits there in the city. Across the river, but within view of the Capitol, is a large cemetery. Several of historical note are buried there. To my surprise, in that cemetery I found the burial place of Rev. John Gano. The cemetery identified him as Washington's chaplain.

I said to Betty, "Oh, my! He was much more than the chaplain. Historical documentation says he was the Baptist preacher who baptized George Washington, and that tells me something about George Washington. I know no Baptist preacher would baptize him just to baptize him. He would have led him to Christ before he baptized him." I had my picture made by the little slab which marks the burial place of that faithful servant of God. He had the power, and he gave the light.

The power and the light are desperately needed in the darkness of this time. We need to fire and refire over and over again.

I wonder if there are not some preachers reading this book who will get determined to carry the torch in your church, to set a fire in your town.

I wonder if there are not some preachers reading this book who will start winning souls—even if nobody helps you do it.

I wonder if there are not some preachers reading this book who will decide today to resign from the "Bible-a-Month" club and preach the KJV all the time.

I wonder if there are not some preachers reading this book who will start to give invitations each time the church door is open.

You say, "But I only have a small crowd on Wednesday night." Go ahead and give an invitation.

You say, "I'd love to have a soul-winning church, but I don't know how to go about it."

If you want to go to Statesville from Walkertown, you get on Interstate 40 and go west. The right route will lead you to Statesville. If you want to have a soul-winning church, you set up a soul-winning program and start winning souls. If you don't get on the right road, you will not get where you want to go.

Let's keep giving out the light, turning on the power, making the candle burn, keeping the candlestick finely polished.

When I went to the Holy Land a few years ago, I was very surprised to learn that there would be forty-four Roman Catholics placed with me on the trip—two buses of us—forty-four Roman Catholics, including three drunken priests.

We got to Gordon's Calvary. Several begged to come with me. The Catholics will not take their people to Calvary. Instead, they take them to their shrine—the Church of the Holy Sepulchre. Several of their people wanted to come with me to Golgotha and the empty tomb. I agreed for them to come along.

We stood at Gordon's Calvary and sang "At the Cross." As we walked out of the empty tomb, we sang "He Lives." I preached a few minutes about this sacred place.

As we walked outside on that old brick street, one of those ladies from Massachusetts said to me, "That does it! That settles it! I'm getting out of that Catholic church as soon as I get back to Massachusetts!"

I said to her, "Well, that's wonderful! I'm glad to hear it—but there is something a whole lot more important." So I had the privilege of leading her to Christ, standing right there within sight of the crucifixion spot and the empty tomb. Before the tour was ended, several others had also received the Saviour.

Praise the Lord for the power and the light! It worked twenty centuries ago in Jerusalem; it still works in Jerusalem today.

I started preaching more than forty years ago. I was excited then and I'm excited today. We need the power on so we can give the light. God wants us to stay at it.

You say it can't happen in your church. It can. Don't compromise it. Don't quit. Don't be afraid. Don't stop believing God. Don't get side-tracked.

A young man came into our church and said, "I want to talk to somebody about getting in a Bible study."

"Well, come up and talk to me about it," I said.

As he sat down, I asked, "How did you happen to come here?"

"I went to___," and he mentioned a certain church across town. "The secretary there told me they couldn't help me, but they thought you could, because you are more intense about the Gospel." *Intense?* Our intensity is the power and the light!

I said, "Tell me what is going on."

"My life is all messed up. I don't know whether you can help me or not. They couldn't do anything for me at the other place."

I said, "Oh, I think we can," and, of course, I had the privilege in just a matter of a few minutes to lead him to Christ. He was so excited and so happy!

What is wrong? In some places the power is off. When the power is off, there is no light.

Let's get the candle, let's fire it, let's empower it, and let's let the light shine in order that those who come in may see the light. Don't quit, don't compromise, press on, hang tough, don't give in, stay on track, get the power and give the light.

Prospecting for Revival

"I charge thee therefore before God, and the Lord Jesus Christ, who shall judge the quick and the dead at his appearing and his kingdom;

"Preach the word; be instant in season, out of season; reprove, rebuke, exhort with all longsuffering and doctrine.

"For the time will come when they will not endure sound doctrine; but after their own lusts shall they heap to themselves teachers, having itching ears;

"And they shall turn away their ears from the truth, and shall be turned unto fables.

"But watch thou in all things, endure afflictions, do the work of an evangelist, make full proof of thy ministry."—II Tim. 4:1–5.

The need of America is a revival. As much as *America* needs revival, however, it is *our* crowd—the independent, fundamental Baptist churches in America—who most need it. Too many of our churches have dried up on the vine. Too many of our churches no longer say "Amen!" In too many of our churches it has been too long since anyone has been saved. Too many of our churches have cobwebs in the baptistry. In our independent, fundamental Baptist churches, we need real revival.

Just as there is a need for revival in our nation and in our churches, every son and daughter of the living Almighty God needs a Spirit-empowered, Holy-Ghost-anointed, sin-killing, Devil-chasing revival!

It may just be that some of us who call ourselves preachers need revival. You were once excited about preaching, but if you are not today, then you need a revival.

You preachers were once thrilled when somebody breathed the word "pastor" in reference to you; now if you shrink back, you need a revival.

There was a time when preachers were thirsty for the power of God, but now we are more concerned about our budgets, our public renown and other things. If we do not now thirst for the power of God, we need a revival.

Was there a time, dear preacher, when you were passionate about soul winning, but not today? If you have lost your zeal for souls, your compassion for those who are lost and dying and on their way to Hell, you need a revival.

There was a time when preachers pressed to build churches, but not many do so today. What we need, dear brother, is a revival!

Some of you deacons, Sunday school teachers, bus workers and soul winners—there was a time when you sat in every church service, excited about being in God's house, thrilled over what was going to happen that day inside the church, but not so today. You need a revival.

There was a time when some of you were very involved in what was going on in the church house. You were pressing to do everything, and they had to tell you that you couldn't do everything—but not so today. You need a revival.

Some of you at one time had joy bubbling like a fountain in your soul, but not so today. You need a revival.

There was a time when you had a zeal for souls, but not today. You need a revival.

There was a time when you tithed, but you do not do so today. You need a revival.

You say, "This is a day when we can't get workers. People are too busy." I know. What we need is a revival.

You say, "Sunday morning and Sunday night everybody is going somewhere, doing something, headed toward Six Flags or Nine Flags or Twelve Flags." I know. We need revival.

You preachers say, "I preach my heart out on Wednesday night, and half my deacons are at the ball game." I know. We need revival.

You say, "Folks just don't like it when we have really strong Bible preaching." I know. We need revival.

"But many who come to our place want us to use the RSV, the NIV, *The Living Bible* or some other version." I know! We need revival.

"But they don't want standards!" I know. We need revival.

"People are so sensitive. They will leave the church at the drop of a hat." Then why don't you just go ahead and drop the hat? If they get revived, then they will get over some of their sensitivities.

The Bible says that "the time will come when they will not endure sound doctrine." They will not have discernment. They can't figure out their right hand from the left. They can't figure right from wrong, spiritual from carnal. They have no discernment because they are shackled by the world. All the garbage of Disneyland and Blockbuster Video and cable TV and all kinds of other things are hanging onto them like the barnacles that stick to the ship.

Consequently, we have become dysfunctional. Deacons don't "deac." Ushers don't "ush." Singers don't sing. Since we don't do what we are supposed to do, our people have become discouraged; and out of this discouragement comes a dearth, and ultimately—probably soon—we will die if we don't have revival.

I ask you, Why don't we have revival? Is the Bible no longer true? Just suppose the pastor picked out *any* Scripture reference and preached on it; would we believe it or try to figure out some way around it?

Does God no longer answer prayer? Can we not ask Him for things and get them? Is there no power or anointing? Can souls not be saved?

These are tough times. I hear things like, "Well, this is Southern California," or, "Everybody is Gospel hardened in the South." Such talk is sheer poppycock! There are cultural differences. California is not the South; the South is not the Northeast; Canada is not Mexico; and Asia is not Europe. I understand that; but there is a God in Heaven, the Bible is true, the Gospel works, and God answers prayer!

The fact is, you and I need once again to declare, "Like it or lump it, we are standing where we ought to stand! We believe what we've always believed! We are not going with the neo-whatever crowd nor the so-called evangelical crowd! We're not going with the charismatic crowd—that Promise Keepers crowd!"

If we really want revival, how will we get it? If I want to work in my garden, I will get the right tools. If I want to pan for gold, I will get the right tools. If I need to fix my car, I will get the right tools—and if I want revival, I will get the right tools.

Verse 5 gives a little formula that will work for revival.

I. "Watch Thou in All Things"

"*All* things" means you watch the choir, the people playing the instruments, the folks sitting in the pews, the nursery workers. You pay close attention.

1. *Watch the plan of salvation very closely.* There are places all over America where they have *services* each Sunday, but they do not have

much *church*. There are places that call themselves churches, but nobody has been saved since they started.

The fact is, salvation is the business of the church. Preach salvation very simply and plainly so that even the youngest, simplest person in the crowd will clearly understand that he is a sinner who needs to be saved by simple faith and trust in the Lord Jesus Christ. The plan of salvation gets distorted, diluted, twisted and bent in a thousand different shapes. (By the way, it is not always some of the other crowd doing that. Some in our crowd are getting it tangled up.) Salvation is by grace through faith—plus nothing, minus nothing (Eph. 2:8, 9).

We need to watch very carefully what is taught on the plan of salvation. Find out if those teaching in junior church know how to teach salvation to juniors. Don't let them teach something less or more. See that they teach the plain and simple Gospel!

2. *Watch the program of the church.* We don't need to be doing everything everybody else in the country does at the church house. Leave a lot of stuff out. Just because every other church in town is doing something doesn't mean we have to follow.

Our one reason for existing is getting out the Gospel and getting as many saved as we can. We must build an oasis for helping sinners get saved. We don't have much other reason for doing what we do or gathering together or collecting money in the offering plate. Except for reaching sinners with the Gospel, we are without a cause!

You say, "But it would be nice if we had this and that." Yes, but it might take away from the main thing.

3. *Watch the pulpit.* Thank God if you have a pastor who protects the pulpit.

You may say, "My uncle from Missouri is going to be blowing in on his way to Disneyland, and he would like to preach at our church while he is here." Don't get mad at your preacher when he says "no."

Give your preacher time to get acquainted, time to check out your uncle and get comfortable with him; then maybe sometime in the future he may say "yes." Don't put pressure on him. If you fuss at the preacher and get mad at him, you are as wicked as any other wicked person in town.

Thank God that your preacher protects the pulpit, that not just anybody who calls himself a preacher or missionary or evangelist gets to preach at your church.

4. *Watch the platform where you sit.* Pastor, there is probably a ministerial alliance in your town, but if you joined it, go "unjoin" it. You don't need to be running with that cigar-smoking, beer-guzzling, foul-mouthed bunch of "clergymen"! You are not a part of that crowd. The liberals are there. Scoffers are there. In that crowd are Bible deniers. There are those who don't preach salvation sweet. Some deny a literal Heaven and Hell. That's not your crowd! Don't line up with them nor sit on the platform with them.

The problem today is, we want to sing whatever we want to sing. We don't want a preacher telling us we can't get up and sing what, when and where we want to sing! I am amazed at how many musicians say, "This is my music." Do you own it? Did you pay for it? When you come to the platform to sing, it doesn't mean that you are the president of a corporation. You don't come to the pulpit to run some sideshow just because somebody asks you to sing.

You complain: "The preacher is nothing but a tyrant!" Bless God for somebody who will guard the platform, who will keep it where God can bless.

So, watch the platform where you sit.

5. *Watch the partners you yoke up with.* The Promise Keepers in recent times came blowing into every town in America. In a lot of places they held their meetings on Wednesday nights. There is a great list of things they wouldn't talk about on their platform, as for example, eternal security. Brother, if you won't talk about that, if you are scared of that doctrine, you can't preach from my platform.

We have to watch the partners with whom we yoke up. The ecumenical crowd, the anything-goes crowd, the no-doctrine crowd, the let's-just-all-get-together crowd are not our partners. Find fellowship with the strongly fundamental, Bible-believing, Scripture-practicing crowd! Amen!

6. *Watch the perverting of the Bible.* I'm talking about the NIV, the NASB, *The Living Bible*, etc. Almost every new edition that has come out in recent years has been published for one of two reasons: it has either been produced because they had a bias they wanted to perpetrate, some false doctrine they wanted to emphasize, or those people who came out with an edition were looking for some way to make a buck!

You say, "I don't think it matters whether the verse says 'blood' or 'death.'" The fact is, the Greek New Testament has one word for *death* and another for *blood*. Where it says *haima*, it means "blood"; where it says *thanatos*, it means "death." If you switch these words around, then you are just as wicked as that other crowd I mentioned.

You say, "I still don't think it matters whether you say the 'blood of Christ' or the 'death of Christ.'" Let me help you on this so you won't ever be bothered by it again.

If someone will loan me a pocketknife, I will give you a choice: I'll cut you until you bleed, or I'll cut you until you die. Which would you prefer? Does it make any difference? It seems to me it might!

Watch the perverting of the Bible. If you have the right Bible, then don't bother with any other. It's as simple as that.

When I was pastor at Westminster, Maryland, we didn't use anything but the King James Version in our Christian school, in our Sunday school and in our pulpit. The rule was: the only mention of any other version of the Bible would be in a negative context; otherwise, keep quiet about it!

"Watch thou in all things." Watch your authority, your agenda, your associations, your attire and appearance, your attitude; watch your doctrine, your devotion, your duty, your deportment. "Watch thou in all things" covers everything!

II. "Endure Afflictions"

To "endure afflictions" means to wait. We're not talking about enduring comfort; anybody can handle that. We're not talking about enduring convenience; we can all survive that.

Some of you are working hard. Everything is going great; but when something goes sideways, you throw up your hands and say, "Listen, if that's the way it is, I'll just fold up my tent and go home!"

Someone fussed at you. This person was critical of you. Somebody else crawled all over you. You can't stand that!

Let me warn you: if you cook, there's going to be some heat in the kitchen! When you start cooking for God, there is going to be some heat in the kitchen, but when it gets a little warm, you are to "endure"! Don't run! Don't flinch! Don't shrink back! Don't go to sleep! Just say, "I'm not going anywhere! I'll stay right here and stick to it!"

What do you do? You endure the afflictions. Bless God, a few other folks have been scalded before you, and there will come some others after you.

III. "Do the Work of an Evangelist"

What does that mean? When Sunday comes, we preach with souls in mind. When we build the program of the church, we build with souls in mind. The pastor puts soul winning first on his agenda. The staff gets soul winning as number one on their agenda. The regular folks—deacons and others—get soul winning as number one on their agenda. Soul winning is *the* thing, the *main* thing.

In 1978 when I went to an area in Maryland that was predominantly Catholic and Lutheran, I had no idea what God would let us do. In the seventeen years that followed, we saw literally thousands saved.

I remember when we built that 1,500-seat auditorium. As I was driving off the parking lot about ten o'clock one night, I pulled to one side, walked to the spot where it was to be built (at that time it was nothing but a cleared dirt place), and I figured out where the pulpit would be. I looked around, and in my mind's eye, all at once, all that red carpet appeared. I could see the pews popping into place, the staircases coming down out of the balcony. I could see deacons, ushers, Sunday school teachers and others, some I didn't know, sitting in the auditorium.

It was late at night. There were cars on the highway in front of the church. There I was, standing on the dirt on the vacant lot and speaking out loud from where I thought the pulpit would be: "For by grace are ye saved through faith; and that not of yourselves: it is the gift of God: Not of works, lest any man should boast," and, "For God so loved the world, that he gave his only begotten Son, that whosoever believeth in him should not perish, but have everlasting life," and other verses like that.

Then I stopped for a minute. In my mind's eye I could see people leaving their seats in the balcony and coming down the staircases to the altar. I saw people coming down every aisle.

In a few months the building was up, and in a little while I saw the place literally fill up. People came in from everywhere; people came down the aisles getting saved and baptized at the two Sunday morning services and on Sunday night.

I was back there two weeks ago for services—Sunday morning, Sunday night, Monday and Tuesday nights. I drove around the town, and in every place I'd say, "I remember going into that house. I remember winning that family to Christ."

From every street in town people who came to Christ were in church, and I said to myself, *By God's grace, there will be nobody in my town who does not have at least one opportunity to hear the Gospel. We will do the work we're supposed to be doing!*

I told my people, "I don't care how deep the snow gets, how slick the ice is, *we will be open!*" We never closed because of weather. When it snowed, we didn't have the crowd we usually had, but, bless God, we had something for the crowd that came.

Just because your crowd is down, don't get perturbed.

"But it's Labor Day weekend, and half my crowd has gone to Arizona."

Bless God, have yourself a time with the crowd that has gathered. Don't dry up on the vine while others are absent. Stay at it! In fact, dig harder when the crowd is down and have yourself a time! Always "do the work of an evangelist"!

IV. "Make Full Proof of Thy Ministry"

We are to watch, wait, work and walk. We are to keep ourselves straight. Far too many folks are seeing how close they can get to the edge of the mountain. Find out what purity is, then get as close to it as you can. Keep strong. Get the power. Keep spiritual. Get the passion for what God wants so you can live it, breathe it, eat it and sleep it.

Keep stirred. Prioritize on what ought to be done, then keep serving and performing. Every day say, "I'm saved and I'm happy! I'm saved and I'm rejoicing! I want to be in the church house! I want to tithe! O preacher, what money do you need? I'll see if I can help you!" When the preacher wants to raise money, thank God for it. That means he is into something that is costing something!

Paul said, "I charge thee...." Some folks are always charging things; it's time *you* got charged!

Paul is saying, 'I implore you, challenge you, beseech you, adjure you. In these days, preach the word; be instant in season, out of season; reprove, rebuke, exhort.'

That doesn't sound like a lot of the silly, soapy stuff that we hear today. Paul is talking about holding the banner high—the banner of the Scriptures, of soul winning, of separation, of salvation, of stewardship. Hold it high. Cry aloud and spare not; do it with long-suffering. When the crowds are down, when the offerings are down, when people are whining and complaining, backslidden and carnal, stay at it. If every imp of Hell crawls all over you, keep doing it.

You ask, "How long are we to do this?" Until the Great Commission expires; until we hear the shout; until we hear the trumpet. Others may not, but we must. Others may fall by the wayside, but we must not. We must say, "I will watch! I will wait! I will work! I will walk!" Why? Because I want to live in a revival, even if nobody else does.

If every worker we have dries up on the vine, I want my old heart to be full of glory! Praise the Lord!

If every preacher I know gives himself away, I've got no excuse for doing likewise.

If everybody around me falls down in a lethargic state and does not care nor go nor do, I have no excuse for doing likewise. I ought to keep the fire of revival ignited and burning in my heart and soul.

God help me and God help you to have it.

You say, "But I'm off here in the desert somewhere!" Then start a fire in the desert.

You say, "I'm down here in some tough little town that is wickedness personified." Then start a fire in that town. Don't pussyfoot around; don't compromise the Book and the work. Let the people know a man of God has come to town!

If you will get on the walk with God, the two of you will make a pretty good team. Don't go the way the world is going. Don't go the way some sick outfit is going. You don't have to have a BIG church. Just go in there and do what you know God wants you to do and see what God gives you.

Preacher, quit comparing yourself to somebody else. Get up on your horse and ride when Sunday comes; then see what God will do with you.

God is so good! Let's not run out on Him. Let's not sell Him short. Let's not go cheap. Let's determine, "The world may go crazy, but I'm not going with it. I'm going to watch, wait, work and walk, prospecting for revival."

Maybe God has revealed some deficiency or reminded you of some coolness and aloofness that have gathered in your soul. Maybe He has given you a fresh, new vision of what you ought to be and can be. Maybe He has touched your heart afresh. You know you ought to find somebody on one of those streets right near your church and get him saved and get him to walk down the aisle on Sunday.

You cannot do it in your flesh alone. You need the holy anointing of God upon you. You need the power of God. Ask Him for what you need.

Redig the Old Wells

"And Isaac's servants digged in the valley, and found there a well of springing water."—Gen. 26:19.

With the early heroes of the Book of Genesis, we often find the names of Abraham, Isaac and Jacob listed together. The life of Isaac is not so well known as the others, but it is a story about which volumes could be written.

Isaac was the miracle baby of Abraham and Sarah. After they were well past their child-bearing years, God fulfilled His promise to them in an extraordinary fashion. He gave them this baby of promise and named him Isaac, which means "laughter." When God told them they were going to be parents, Sarah laughed. When Sarah told the neighbors, I'm guessing some of them laughed also.

This was the same Isaac who would go with his father to Mount Moriah, the same Isaac who would ask his father, "Behold the fire and the wood: but where is the lamb for a burnt-offering?" (Gen. 22:7).

This was the same Isaac whose father would on another day say, "We have to get this boy a wife." So Abraham sent a servant to find the bride for his son, thus beginning one of the most beautiful love stories in all the Bible. One of the sweetest romances you will ever read is the wonderful story of Isaac and Rebekah. When the bride was found, a love of great measure developed between those two. Oh, the sweetness of such a beautiful story!

There are several instances in the biography of Isaac where he did, or attempted to do, exactly what his father did; and in so doing, he made a mistake or two.

(1) In chapter 26, Isaac was among the Philistines. His wife Rebekah "was fair to look upon." She was very pretty. Likely he and Rebekah had discussed this beforehand and decided on what Isaac would say to those who asked about her. When he had to face them, he lied, saying, "She is

my sister," fearing to say, "She is my wife," for those men might kill him if they knew the truth. (He learned this particular trick of deceiving from his daddy.) So Isaac and Rebekah passed themselves off as brother and sister. Later, when Abimelech caught them together while they were romancing, he asked Isaac, "How saidst thou, She is my sister?" Then Isaac had to confess that he lied—and admit why.

I remind you of an important truth here. Think about what you do, how you do it and when you do it. There are others making steps right behind you. Every step you make, they will make. Every move you make, they will make. If you lean too far in an unwise direction, if you play it loose, very likely the generation that comes after you will play it just a little looser than you played it.

It is better to lean close to the mountain and let them—your children or your converts—loosen from the mountain a little bit than for you to run close to the edge. The likelihood is that some of the generation coming after you will not lean as close to the mountain as you do. If you lead them now on a trail near the edge, some of them will fall off the side of the mountain one day. The reason? Because thirty years before, you walked too close to the edge instead of hugging the mountain. There is security near the mountain. There is danger near the edge. The closeness of the mountain that would have been security for you would also be security for them.

(2) This chapter in Isaac's life is further complicated because the land is in the midst of a great famine. It is not the first time they had seen it. Some years before, in the heyday of his father, Abraham, famine had swept across the land. (A famine means starvation, destitution—when children die from lack of bread, when families are wiped out and funeral marches are a daily routine. The cords of life are snapped again and again.) Famine is no laughing matter. He whose name was "laughter" is not laughing now. Isaac himself must deal with the harsh realities of famine.

He carefully reviews the matter. With resilience and resolve, he says, 'I know what I will do. I'll just go down to Egypt. That is what my father did when there was a famine, and he survived.'

God then told Isaac, "Go not down into Egypt; dwell in the land which I shall tell thee of." In the Bible, Egypt is a symbol of the world. It's so easy to run to the world for help, so easy to say, "The world has it better than we have it, so we're going down there to pick fruit from their vines, eat what they eat, do what they do and act like they act. Yes sir, we like what the world has, and that is where we are going!" It's so easy! It's so tempting! It's appealing and alluring! It's often advised! The Lord told Isaac that he was better off there in the land of the famine, scratching for food out of the sand, than down in Egypt, because he was in the will of God in his land.

I. Isaac's Place

Many times folks think they have to go somewhere else in order to do something for God, but I've noticed that folks who do not do something for God *before* they go usually do not do anything for God *after* they go. Whatever they had determined to do in going, they were not able to do when they got there because they did not do it before they went.

In this case God told Isaac to sojourn where he was. There they would find a solution. "Sojourn in this land, and I will be with thee, and will bless thee." In this place, barren though it was, the promises of God would blossom like a rose.

Isaac looked around him; all he saw was the evidence of the famine. He saw no indication of fruitfulness, nothing to commend the promises of God to him. Still, God promised that if Isaac would dwell where God said dwell, He would be with him and perform for him as He had for his father, Abraham.

"And I will make thy seed to multiply as the stars of heaven, and will give unto thy seed all these countries; and in thy seed shall all the nations of the earth be blessed."—Gen. 26:4.

Listen carefully! The will of God for Isaac was to stay put. No matter what anyone else says, stay put. No matter how dark the hour, stay put. No matter how wide and appealing the exit, stay put. It was the will of God for Isaac to be right there in the place of the famine. He was not eating as well as he wanted to, things were not going the way he would have liked them to go, he was still in the place of the famine, but he was in the will of God. In the will of God, he was safe and secure, and ultimately he would be satisfied because he did not revolt against that will. There would be promise and blessing because he did not allow his discontentment to make him disobedient. There were the hope and promise of victory. God encouraged him by repeating the promises He had made to his father, Abraham, years before.

In a time when it is very hard and harsh, the Word of God will always be precious and powerful! Times may be hard, circumstances harsh, loads heavy; *but God will make His promise good.*

Isaac was encouraged by the hope of God's promise. He was not encouraged by the famine but *mightily encouraged by the promises* God gave him in the throes of the famine.

There are important things you must see about Isaac.

II. Isaac's Prosperity

"Then Isaac sowed in that land, and received in the same year an hundredfold: and the LORD blessed him.

"And the man waxed great, and went forward, and grew until he became very great:

"For he had possession of flocks, and possession of herds, and great store of servants: and the Philistines envied him."—Gen. 26:12–14.

Now we learn the story of Isaac's prosperity. We Christians have a little problem with that word. I don't believe this "prosperity gospel" that is hawked on television, but at the same time, I don't believe the "poverty gospel" either.

Some seem to think poverty is the only way that a "real Christian" can go. We have glorified the other end of the spectrum so much that when God does bless with material things, we do not know how to deal with it. I dare say there are Christians today who do not know how to deal with the blessings of God when they come in abundance. With a lot of money, they don't know how to behave. When they taste success, they lose their heads. If they have much blessing, they mismanage it.

Sometimes a church grows, and the first thing you know, it loses its perspective. The people don't know how to deal with the fact that God is actually blessing, that they are actually getting somewhere, that God is doing something.

Sometimes we don't know what to say or what to do when the blessing comes. One is not more spiritual because he is poor, and one doesn't have to be carnal just because he is doing well.

The Bible says that Isaac was very energetic and calculating. He determined he would sow in the midst of the famine. It doesn't seem a very good thing to do when there is no water, but Isaac sowed nonetheless. The result was, he received in the same year an hundredfold.

The harvest came! The Lord blessed him! Out of famine—a harvest! From nothing—everything! The miracle of Heaven's blessing came right on time!

If you invested a dollar and later that same year it returned to you in a hundred dollar bill—if it's honest and legitimate—tell me about it, and next year I'll invest two dollars. If it holds true the next year, then I'll invest three dollars. Then after a while I'll be in great shape. There is no sin in that; it's just good sense!

God blessed Isaac with an abundant harvest. God let him multiply and keep on gaining greater possessions and prosperity. He grew until he became a very powerful man in that part of the world.

I don't know very many who have gotten a harvest without sowing some seed, and not too many get ahead without working. We wish, we want, but we don't get.

Isaac went to the fields. He put seed in the ground. He sowed for the time when he anticipated a harvest.

There is a very intimate connection between the diligence of labor and the reaping of the harvest. There is a connection between what you want to accomplish and what you actually do achieve. There is a kinship between diligence and prosperity. Work ordinarily is a precedent that will come ahead of any wealth that you achieve. Very few get ahead unless they are willing to work in the doing of it. It is necessary that we sow. There is no harvest without the seedtime.

I've always thought how nice it would be to be able to play the piano. I have thought maybe I could get my daughter, Davina, to give me lessons. She is an outstanding musician and a very gifted teacher. I'm sure she might give me one or two lessons, but after that...! I have thought, *There's no reason why I can't play the piano after a few lessons;* but it was only a fleeting thought, a whim, a passing fancy.

Let me tell you why I can't play the piano. It is not because I do not have the aptitude for it. It is not because I do not appreciate music. It is because I chose to do other things, to invest elsewhere. Consequently, with the exception of a few simple little ditties, you will not find me playing much on the piano.

You cannot reap the blessing where you have not sown the seed.

Isaac was very successful. There is nothing wrong with being successful. I hope and pray that you will succeed in life, but again, there is that "failure syndrome" among Christians. We are almost comfortable with it. We can't pray and get answers. We can't win souls. We don't see the church grow. We can't pay our bills. "Well, I'm just not anything," we say in despair.

That is true—we are nothing much. You are only a man, but there is a God, and *He is everything*. Because of a great God, there is no reason why you have to fall in the pit of failure and stay there! Get up, get going and do something! Do well what you do. Serve God! It is time the world sees that it means something to belong to Christ.

So you failed! Turn to God. Receive Christ! Believe the Bible! Honor God in spite of past failure. Honor Him when you become a winner. Win, lose or draw, honor the Lord!

III. Isaac's Pressure

What happens when God blesses, as He blessed Isaac? Look at Genesis 26:14: "The Philistines envied him."

Envy is a fleshly work, and it is often the delight of evil men to be envious. Sometimes that envy is excited when we ponder what others have. We look at what someone else has achieved, and we inappropriately (lustfully, greedily) look at his prosperity. The next thing we know, something down deep inside is akin to hatred, and this inevitably leads to hostility.

The Philistine Abimelech misjudged the motives of Isaac by comparing them to his own motives. He couldn't see how anybody could be as great, as big, as powerful as Isaac and still be on the up-and-up. Because of his own lustful, greedy heart, he expected Isaac to lord his power over them with intent to hurt. Abimelech just knew Isaac was going to do something damaging with his power because that is what he would have done had he had Isaac's power.

Abimelech had seen how the Lord had blessed Isaac, how he had sowed and received an hundredfold, saw how he had become great in possessions of flocks, herds and servants and how the Philistines had envied him. Abimelech began to figure something he could do to get Isaac to move on and get out of the picture.

If you do well, there will be Philistines like Abimelech standing nearby. The Philistines will be envious of you. They will do to you what Abimelech and his crowd did to Isaac—plunder your land, pilfer your wells and shut off the water supply.

There are churches across America that had at one time wells that were open; the waters were flowing, people were refreshed there, nourished there; but the wells are now stopped up.

I received a phone call from a man in another part of the country who told me about some things that were happening in his city. He mentioned a church with which I have been familiar for many years. He said, "You remember how it used to be?"

I said, "Yes, I remember. I've been there when it was great."

He said, "I happen to know that last Sunday there were twenty-five people present."

"My, what's happened?" I asked.

I knew what had happened without asking. The Philistines had come and plugged up the wells so they wouldn't run anymore. They trashed the Bible! They trashed soul winning. They trashed a separated life. Consequently, the blessings stopped flowing.

We like for the well to run, but somebody has thrown trash in the well. They plug up the well but still want to go there when it is time to get a drink!

Isaac faced all of this. His prosperity incited the envy of the Philistines.

IV. Isaac's Patience

Isaac had stayed in the place of the famine. He had prospered greatly for his obedience; now he was the target of opposition. He would now show himself a man of great, godly patience.

"And Abimelech said unto Isaac, Go from us; for thou art much mightier than we.

"And Isaac departed thence, and pitched his tent in the valley of Gerar, and dwelt there."—Gen. 26:16,17.

Abimelech asked Isaac to leave town. Isaac packed up his flocks and his herds, his servants, his family, and moved out into the valley of Gerar. He had been to that valley years before with his father. He knew wells were there which they had dug. He knew there they could water their herds and build a life for their families. In that valley they could build little villages and survive and thrive.

When he got out into the valley of Gerar, however, he found that since the days of his father, those thwarted, carnal, worldly Philistines had stopped up the wells and destroyed the source from which the precious water flowed. They could not get even a drop of water from them.

Then Isaac started digging in those wells. He was convinced that those old wells that had once flowed still had water in them. The same wells that brought life to the flocks and to the families years before could do it again.

One day when they took out the last rock and the last piece of trash, springing water began to ooze up to the top and spill out into a little stream. They were able to build little canals so the water would flow to the flocks and herds.

After all of that was done, some of the Philistine herdsmen came around and said, "I'll declare! Those wells are running again. Isn't that something!"

Now, they hadn't lifted a hand to get them running, but they went to Isaac and said, "This is *our* place; these are *our* wells!"

"The herdmen of Gerar did strive with Isaac's herdmen, saying, The water is our's."

Not a word from Isaac—no fighting, no resistance, no mouthing, no bitterness. He simply gathered up his flocks, herds, servants and all the families and went further down into the valley where his father had another well.

Sure enough, when he arrived at the site, he found that well was also plugged. Once again they rolled up their sleeves and dug out the rocks, the sand, all the junk, all the trash. As the water began to flow and as they made little canals so the water would go out for the flocks to be watered, here came those Philistine rascals again.

They said, "Isaac, you're drinking *our* water! Remember, this is *our* territory. Why don't you move on?" (By the way, in the midst of all this, Isaac's flocks and herds multiplied, and he became even more prosperous.) As before, Isaac simply packed and moved to another area—without resistance, without being mouthy, without becoming bitter.

Isaac, remembering a third place where his father had a well, went there. He dug out the rocks, the trash, the junk. Finally they created enough water so the Philistines had all they could use.

"For that they strove not" (Gen. 26:22). Isaac said, "For now the LORD hath made room for us, and we shall be fruitful in the land" (vs. 22).

Here Isaac, with his flocks, herds, servants and families, was able to make a permanent home. The Philistines left them alone.

The first well he called *Ezek*, "the place of contention." The second well he called *Sitnah*, "the place of criticism." The third place he named *Rehoboth*, because God had made room for them.

Finally they had a place by themselves; now they were going to be fruitful.

Rehoboth is the well of conviction, of consecration, of conscience.

It had not been easy to take the unfairness of being expelled out of the town into the valley. It had not been easy leaving the wells in which he had invested, but Isaac did not become bitter. It is not easy to see things clearly in such a fog, but Isaac saw through it.

He did not quit simply because there were contentions with Abimelech. He did not quit simply because there was criticism from the herdsmen of Gerar. He did not quit simply because of the carnality of the opposition. Isaac was a very patient man.

It is not easy to take something so unfair as what I've just described to you. It is not easy to take the injustices that are leveled at you. It is not easy when you're being repeatedly robbed, mistreated, abused, maligned and cheated. It is not easy to hear the voice of God amidst the din of clamoring worldlings, but patience has its perfect work.

V. Isaac's Perseverance

Isaac was not only patient; he was persevering.

Sometimes we are patient but not persevering. Perseverance means that you stay at the task, no matter what! You don't quit; you don't give up; you stay convinced. Isaac was convinced that those wells his father had dug were still there. Energized by that conviction, he believed that their resources could be fully recovered.

Learn a lesson from Isaac. Don't quit just because of contention. Don't quit because of criticism. Don't quit because of the carnality of the Philistines.

Sometimes we ask, Where is the Lord God of Abraham? of Isaac? of Jacob? of Elijah? Where is the Lord God of Jonathan Edwards? of Charles Spurgeon? of John R. Rice?

I have a different question for you: Where are the Abrahams of the Lord God? the Isaacs of the Lord God? the Jacobs of the Lord God? the Elijahs of the Lord God?

Everybody becomes like the herdsmen; they love it when there are wells flowing. Everybody likes to walk up to the well, take a big dipper and taste that cool water coming out of the earth, but somebody has to redig the well!

Do we want power upon our pulpit? Redig the well! Do we want souls saved? Redig the well! Do we want to have a major impact on our towns? Redig the well!

Those heavy stones down in the well—who wants to lift them out?

Who wants to dig the sand out of the well, one grain at a time? We "ooh" and "aah" at the harvest, but what about the plowing and the sowing? What about the effort that goes into getting us to the harvest?

You say, "I dug one well, and I wouldn't take a million dollars for it, but I wouldn't give a dime for another one. I don't ever, ever, ever want to dig another one."

Now you have lost it, but you are not dead yet; you still have some life left. What do you intend to do? "Dr. Smith, you mean I have to get in there and dig and work and serve God again?" That's right—do it again! Do it again!

Get the trash out of the well! Clean up your act! Start doing right if every imp in Hell attacks you! Re-fire the church! Start up your soul winning again! Claim the Holy Spirit's power again!

You say, "I'm going out of the frying pan and into the fire, out of the well of controversy into the well of criticism."

Suppose Isaac had said after that second well, "Never again! Don't even say the word *well* to me. I don't want to hear it!" Had he stopped after well number two, he could never have gotten to well number three—*Rehoboth*. He would never have been in the place that God was making ready for him.

Remember, *Rehoboth* was the well of residence. It was the well of rest, the place of refreshment, the place of reward, the place of revival, the place of rejoicing! It was at *Rehoboth* that God would let them have water for the flocks, the crops, the herds, the families and the servants.

A lot of us quit at the well called *contention*—the test—and never get to the well called *Rehoboth*—the best. We never get there because after digging one well (we are so proud of ourselves; we are so thrilled at what we've done), we get hit right up the side of the head. The smack spins us silly. Dizzy from the impact, we vow, "If that's what it means to be a Christian, if that's the price I have to pay, I'll never pay it!" We thwart the victory at the well of contention. That's where we STOP!

Some of us survive the well of *contention*—the well of strife—and journey forward to well number two, the well of *criticism*. Some can't take it, so they fold up, quit and die there.

Don't you wish everybody loved you? Forget the outside world; it would just be nice if all who name the name of Christ would treat you like Christians are supposed to treat each other. I wish they would, but they won't. At the well of *criticism*, you're going to say, "I made it through the well of *contention*. It was unjust, but I made it!"

In fact, Isaac had been through a bunch of hoops even before he started digging the wells. He made it through the famine. It would have been easier for him just to do what he had seen his father do, but God gave him a set of instructions, and he honored those instructions.

Some of you will say, "Yeah, I've dug a couple of wells, but I made a mistake. I dug a couple of wells, but I fouled up!" Listen, everybody makes human mistakes. Don't falter and faint just because of some failure.

If you have failed, get out that old shovel, knock the rust off and dig another well! Do like Isaac did and put your full energy into it.

Isaac went from one spot to another each time the well was plugged. You would think he would have gotten discouraged, but he didn't.

I say to you, let no plugging of the wells discourage you! Do what has to be done and do it again and again and over again! That kind of perseverance will get you through.

VI. Isaac's Priorities

Isaac had his priorities right. He dug three wells and in a little while shifted over about twenty miles to Beersheba at the southern part of Israel. In Beersheba God again said to Isaac:

"I am the God of Abraham thy father: fear not, for I am with thee, and will bless thee, and multiply thy seed for my servant Abraham's sake."— Gen. 26:24.

There Isaac built an altar and pitched his tent. Again he had his servants dig another well! They must be getting good at it by now. I imagine their saying, "Fellows, we know what to do, so let's start building. It might be somewhere else next week! If so, we will dig a well like we've dug before."

Isaac kept his priorities right. He had God in first place. Before he dug the well of fresh water and pitched his tent, he built the altar so he could honor, serve and worship the Lord.

Before you go to work on Monday, honor God at His altar on Sunday.

I dare say that most Christians are not driven by the right priorities. Far too many of us are driven by preferences, by what feels good, by what we think, by what we feel, by what we want. We are driven by what we saw our ancestors do. We are driven by self-interest, what we will get out of it. We are driven by personal gain.

Priorities aren't always fun. Occasionally people would come into our church and see that I wasn't born wearing a tie. They would comment, "We haven't seen you without a tie before." Well, sometimes before I got to the pulpit on Sunday morning, I would take my coat and tie off because there were things to do before I preached. We must not be afraid nor too proud to roll up our sleeves and dig the wells!

Priorities aren't always cheap. They often come in the form of work. I really think a lot of men bomb out in the ministry because of all the work connected with it. They just don't want to pay the price!

Don't be content with mediocrity.

Isaac had flocks, herds, family and servants, and all were looking to him. Suppose Isaac had quit somewhere, had stopped after one or two wells. They were looking to him because they needed water.

We must remember that some folks look to us for help, for leadership. They are hoping we will succeed, hoping we will stay at it, hoping we will not stop at the well of *criticism* or stop at the well of *contention*. They are hoping we will press on to the next well, no matter what kind of lumps or licks we must endure before we get there.

I'm afraid somebody sitting here has been at the well of contention but will lose heart and not dig again. I'm afraid somebody will stop at the well of criticism.

I say to you, dig, redig; do, redo! Go for it all over again! Like Isaac, you will find a well springing up with water to meet your every need. God will bless again if we will keep digging, redigging, unplugging and unclogging those old wells where the power is, where the resources are. Don't think you have to come up with a new solution. Those old wells still have water in them.

Let us again have the wells flowing fresh with water that will bring us so many good things.

Redig those old wells!

Redig the Bible well!

Redig the Gospel well!

Redig the church well!

Redig the prayer well!

Redig the soul-winning well!

There is water in the well; dig down, and it will spring forth once again.

16

Shout It From the Housetop!

"What I tell you in darkness, that speak ye in light: and what ye hear in the ear, that preach ye upon the housetops."—Matt. 10:27.

Think with me for a little while about this: "Shout it from the housetop!"

"And Jesus went about all the cities and villages [Tiberias, Capernaum, all those cities and villages in between there along the shores of the Sea of Galilee, across to Nazareth, out over through Jezreel and ultimately down to Jerusalem and around], *teaching in their synagogues, and preaching the gospel of the kingdom, and healing every sickness and every disease among the people."*—Matt. 9:35.

Those three things were the features of His ministry: (1) teaching, (2) preaching and (3) healing.

Right about this period of time, right about the middle of Matthew, Mark, Luke and John, the ministry of healing virtually disappears. Jesus utilized that to "credential" Himself in the minds of the people; after that, He began to tell them, "Go home and don't tell anybody." He continued to teach in the synagogue. These were not great ecumenical meetings, not where Jesus preached just because He had opportunity. These were public forums. The *Torah* was read, and anyone could stand up and say what he wanted to in regard to it.

Jesus capitalized upon that, as did Paul and others who followed Him. They took advantage of any and all opportunity, but it was not under the umbrella of the scribes and Pharisees. They were not encouraging the converts to stay there at the synagogue. Jesus taught in those public forums, in those public meetings, then preached the Gospel of the kingdom.

"What is the difference between teaching and preaching?" you ask. I'm convinced that both should have a lot of biblical content. I like the preaching I do and hear to be taken from the Bible. The only difference that I can see is, when a man teaches, he dispenses information and facts and talks about the issues; but when he preaches, he cries out for a verdict. He calls men and women to a decision.

I. Look at the Harvest

Jesus went about all the cities, teaching and preaching and healing.

"When he saw the multitudes, he was moved with compassion on them, because they fainted, and were scattered abroad, as sheep having no shepherd."—Matt. 9:36.

They fainted. They failed. With all of their fright and fickleness, they couldn't stand because they didn't have a shepherd. They were scattered, like people are today. They were running different ways, trying to find peace in this and in that, putting their heads in bottles, sticking needles in their arms—all kinds of things—sheep without a shepherd. As then, so today.

"Then saith he unto his disciples, The harvest truly is plenteous, but the labourers are few;

"Pray ye therefore the Lord of the harvest, that he will send forth labourers into his harvest."—Vss. 37, 38.

I did not try in my church at Westminster, Maryland to talk people into the ministry. I prayed often that God would raise up workers out of our ranks, and we had a steady stream going to Christian colleges to prepare for the ministry.

In recent years I have heard people say, "Oh, we just don't have many going into the ministry! We just don't have many going to the mission field!" We don't need to browbeat people into the ministry.

Then how are we to get them if we don't talk them into it? We pray; God calls; He sends. When you and I build red-hot local churches where the fire is burning, then men will want to get in the ministry. Very few like to ride a dead horse.

God will get the attention of some teenagers who get into the things of God early and begin to live, breathe, eat, sleep them; and they will become preachers, missionaries and do other things in His work. Building red-hot churches will get these workers going for God. May God help us to do it so we will have more laborers for the harvest.

I am talking about Jesus' word to us: 'What you hear in the ear, shout upon the housetops.' He starts in chapter 9 by getting us to take a look at the fields white unto harvest.

Look around you today. You find on every hand people in great trouble. In one year 23,400 people were murdered in all fifty states. It was safer to have been in Iraq during the war (on our side, of course!) than to have been in any of the large cities in America. Los Angeles is like a ticking time bomb waiting to go off. Chicago, Detroit, Miami, Dallas—you name them—great trouble lurks in our land. The harvest is ripe. People are dying. People are being raped, robbed, mugged. All kinds of crazy things are going on in America.

What is the answer? Obviously, go to Washington and apply for a federal grant. That will solve almost everything. If we can just get money to pour into it; if we can just get some experts to lay out a program in a big, thick manual; if we can just legislate and tell people how all of this is to be done—and by the way, let's be sure to license it—that's going to solve it all, people think.

We must understand that what God has *us* doing is the answer. We may be hated, despised; some may want us run out of town; but we have the answer for all the troubles of America.

These boys and girls turning around—by the time they're twelve, thirteen, fourteen, they are trying all kinds of crazy and dangerous things. You and I have a great big harvest field out there.

Before saying to us, "Preach it; shout it from the housetops," Jesus first said, "Let's look at the harvest." He gets us to see all these folks out there—so many of them! He sees them like sheep without a shepherd, scattered and fainting, and He wants us to see them as He sees them.

II. Location: On the Housetop

You look at the harvest and ask, "What can I do? What can be done?"

Jesus says, "I'll give you a place to operate. I'll put you on the housetop. From this housetop shout it as loudly as you can."

In those days many houses had flat roofs. Instead of the patio being on the ground, there was a patio area on the rooftop. Those rooftops provided a place of advantage. Up there you could see better. Up there you had better perspective. Standing on that rooftop, you might get people's attention better. As people gathered, you could talk to more of them than you could if you were down on their level.

Jesus is saying, "You will hear some things in the ear as you spend time with Me in the closet." We need to go to the secret place with God and find out what He has in mind. We need to go in and listen. When we come out, then we will know what God has said.

When I stand in the pulpit, I need to have something from God. So I keep preaching from this dear old Book. Many things other than the Bible are used in churches to confuse people religiously. In Westminster, Maryland, where I was pastor for seventeen years, people would come in and say things like, "You opened the Bible. You read from it. You actually preached from it. We never saw that done in church before."

I've asked several times, "Then what have you been hearing in church?" The answer: "Well, we got digests from *Newsweek* and condensed material from *Reader's Digest*." One fellow said, "I went to this particular church and heard the best sermon on Sam Houston I ever heard."

Ladies and gentlemen, this fellow you are hearing is stuck on this Book. I'm committed to this inerrant, infallible, all-authoritative Word of God. Every time I get into the pulpit, I will have the Bible in my hands. I reminded our folks every now and then, "We may have a program, a cantata and some of these things; but you are going to hear something out of the Book."

There was a time when just some of the denominational groups had their clutches slipping, but today it seems a lot of that slipping-clutch business is taking place in our own ranks. There was a time when you went into an independent, fundamental Baptist church and you knew there was going to be a public appeal, an invitation to sinners to get saved. That's not always true today.

You preachers say, "We have only a small crowd on Wednesday night." Try preaching, then giving an invitation; your crowd might grow.

Once when I had to be away from home on a Wednesday night, I began trying to find an independent church in the town where I had gone that was having service on Wednesday night. I called about five churches before I found something. I'm talking about independent, fundamental Baptist churches. What I heard was, "We don't have anything in the auditorium on Wednesday night."

Jesus said, 'What you hear in the ear, shout from the housetop.' It's a place of visibility, a place of perspective, a place of advantage.

You and I need to get on that housetop. To that little crowd gathered on Wednesday night, give a sermon like you would give a big crowd. Do little things and you'll have little things. Do something that will look like you are going somewhere. Get on fire; then perhaps some will say, "You know what? Maybe we ought to go to that."

Jesus said, 'Shout it from the housetop.' There we can look at the harvest.

III. Line Up the Help

This whole 10th chapter of Matthew is about lining up help to do what He wants done.

We had hundreds involved in teaching Sunday school and in doing all kinds of other things—running bus routes, etc.; but I never saw the time when we had all the help we needed.

I understand the context of this passage. I know Jesus is speaking specifically to twelve men here, but there are some principles that *we* can latch onto because we've been commanded to shout it from the housetop.

This pulpit is a housetop. Every time we put an ad in the newspaper, it is like a housetop. Every time we send a soul winner down the street, we're putting someone out on the housetop and saying, "Go to it! Shout it! Tell it!"

A lot of us don't know what to do. We're scared. We're afraid to try it.

Jesus said, "Let's line up the help."

I want you to spot a few principles.

He Gives Power

"And when he had called unto him his twelve disciples, he gave them power..." (Matt. 10:1). First, He asked them to do something; then He gave them the power to do it, the energy to do it, the wherewithal to accomplish it.

What do we need? That Holy Spirit filling, that energizing of God. When the sermon is preached, it needs to be in the anointing, the unction, the power, the authority of God.

The same with the Sunday school teacher, the bus worker—all who serve in the ministry. We must teach our folks to get under the unction and anointing of God and quit worrying about all these little things that keep them from serving Him. Some are afraid to sing in the choir for fear they will hit a sour note. Listen! The world is full of mistakes; one more won't hurt. Go on. Get up and do something.

We need to ask God to fill us, to energize us, to give us His power; then when we do what we do the best way we can do it, it will work.

I have a friend in Philadelphia who has a storefront church. I preach for him every year. The reason I go? Because when I am preaching, he sits behind me and says, "That will work!" "That will work!" "That will work!" So I think up something that I would like to do, then go over there and preach it and hear him tell me, "That will work!" Then I go back home and try it.

Folks, these things God wants us to do will work because He gives us the power, the authority, the energizing and the filling of the Holy Spirit.

By the way, that same power will help you give an effective testimony and witness. You go out and tell a lost man about the Saviour, and that same power and authority will help you preach your sermons. That same power and authority will enable you to stay straight and clean, help you live right, help you behave yourself.

Sometimes we get so far from God, so distant from the throne, that we mix in all this other junk. Ten, twelve, fifteen years ago, we looked at the world. It was over there, and the church was over here. We've all slipped a notch. What the world was doing fifteen years ago, it has left for something crazier; now we have slipped into the slot where the world was.

No wonder we're suffering from anemia! No wonder we can't get up and get moving. No wonder our people are stymied. No wonder they are living like the world lives. We need the power and the unction, the authority, the anointing of God to help them.

Jesus called these men and said, 'Go shout it from the housetop. Take the message and proclaim it.' He's talking about the *Kerugma*. "Take it out and proclaim it. Give the Gospel. Tell the story."

Some little guy says, "I'm just a fisherman." God says, "I'll give you power." Somebody else says, "I have limited means." God says, "I'll give you power."

When God told Moses what He wanted him to do, Moses said he couldn't speak because he had a stammering problem. God said, "Do what I want you to do, and I'll help you." Moses couldn't understand it. God said, "You have a brother. If you can't talk, let him talk." Once Moses got into it, I don't remember his ever letting Aaron talk!

God called Jeremiah when he was just a teenager. In chapter 1 of Jeremiah, what does he say? 'God, I cannot speak, for I am a child. Not

190

me, Lord!' God said, "Yes, you." Read his weeping, compassionate, lamenting story.

Daniel, in his teenage years, down in a foreign land—I see him with limitations and many obstacles around him, but he purposed in his heart to be what God wanted him to be.

You may say tonight, "I don't know what I can do." If you will listen to the voice of our Lord and let Him show you the harvest around you and hear Him say, 'Shout it from the housetop,' He will give you the power to do what you ought to do.

You say, "What our church needs is a new pastor." This will make the pastor new.

You say, "What we need in this church is some new folks." This will give you a whole new batch of folks—and this will make some of those old folks new.

He gives power, first of all, when He starts lining up the help.

He Assigns a Place of Service

In Matthew 10:6 He assigns a place of service. He always does that. Do you want to know why I went to Westminster, Maryland? Because God put me there. In late 1978 I went on two different occasions and preached. The second time my wife went with me. In room 48 of Lee's Motel across the boulevard from the church, one afternoon we cried for two hours because in our hearts we saw what God was doing. The church hadn't voted, but we knew it was coming. We didn't know anything about Maryland nor about Westminster. We didn't even want to be in that part of the country! Still, we saw the hand of God in it. He assigned us a place of service and gave us that place with a little group of folks. I cannot describe the joy and blessing that came in those years there.

You ask, "Did you ever have any hard times?" Yes, all the time. You ask, "Did anything ever go crossways?" Yes, many times. If you wait until everything is straight and nothing is crossways, if you wait until everyone agrees with you, you'll never get anything done.

"What do you do?" Get somebody to help you do it. "Well, they didn't vote on it." Listen! Stop doing what takes voting on and go with what's already been voted on in Heaven. Our churches are voting themselves into oblivion. Cut out about nine-tenths of those business meetings and do real business for a change. If someone says, "We need to have a business meeting," I say, "Ours meets on Thursday night."

191

He assigns us a place. On this occasion He said to the disciples, "Go rather to the lost sheep of the house of Israel." He was specific. 'Don't go to the Gentiles. Don't go into the city of the Samaritans. Go to the lost sheep of the house of Israel.' He gave them a specific assignment, just like He put me in Westminster, Maryland, just like He has put you where you are.

He Commands Our Performance

In verse 16 is another principle. Are you going to shout from the housetop? God commands our performance in the doing of it. He said, "I send you forth as sheep in the midst of wolves." He said, "I send you."

In the Book of Acts they began to ask, 'What authority do you have for doing this?' Surely some of you have heard that, haven't you? Always somebody is wanting to know, "Who authorized you to do this, Brother Pastor?"

Listen again. Do what you need to be doing. "*I* send you." Jesus Himself has sent us forth. Go out into the highways and hedges, out where people are, down on the streets, out into the neighborhoods, along the byways. You and I are to go. When He said, "I send you forth," that means *go*.

Dr. John R. Rice burned this verse in our hearts through the years: "He that goeth forth and weepeth, bearing precious seed, shall doubtless come again with rejoicing, bringing his sheaves with him" (Ps. 126:6).

Jesus said, 'Go like sheep in the midst of wolves.' The great odds! People out in the world are like sheep without a shepherd; now here we are sent like sheep into the midst of wolves! What is the difference? We have the Shepherd with us, and they don't have a shepherd. They don't know where to go nor what to do. We listen to the Shepherd, so we know where to go and what to do.

Jesus said, "I send you...."

He Forbids Fear

Then in verse 26 we pick up principle number four: "Fear them not therefore." He knew we were going to be a bunch of cowards. He knew we would tremble in our boots. He knew it would cause us consternation even to think about the great assignment He was giving.

You pick up a prospect card and look at it; then fear and trepidation floods your heart. Jesus said, "Fear them not therefore."

He goes into some description about that, but He says in verse 34,

"I came not to send peace, but a sword." We are not to be afraid. Whatever we do will cause some problems. Not everybody is going to agree with you in what you set out to do. Not everybody is going to like the fact that you run bus routes. Not everybody is going to like it when you go soul winning.

You say, "Sure! Some prostitutes, bar owners, drug dealers and others like them are going to be really upset with us."

No, not them, but some who sit on the pews about three rows back. It will not be the bar owners, the tavernkeepers in town, but the folks who sit in the pew who have the road blocked. The Bible says not to fear them.

There are times when I do things and tremble inside, but I pray God will make me a person of faith, not a person of fear. "God hath not given us the spirit of fear; but of power, and of love, and of a sound mind" (II Tim. 1:7). "Fear them not." Do not be afraid of men.

"Well, I might try to do this and fail." Sometimes you will. What are you to do when you fail? Turn the corner and go on to something else. You sit around and cry about it awhile. You sit around and whine about it awhile. You sit around and analyze it awhile. You call a committee meeting. Don't do that! Do something else. Get on with it.

"But I'm afraid of criticism." Listen! You cannot keep that from happening, so go ahead and do something worth getting criticized over. Get on track; stay on track. "But they're talking about me." Don't worry about it. "Fear them not."

"Well, we won't be able to fund this. There's no way we can pay for this."

People talk about living by faith. If you have much of an operation, you're already learning about living by faith. We had fifty-two people on our church and school staff. Every one of them expected a paycheck every week.

Somebody asked me, "What kind of a stewardship program did you have in your church?" As quick as a flash (and I had never thought of it before), I answered, "We specialized in crowds."

"What do you mean?" he asked.

"We just did what we could to get the folks in. If we got them in, they would give, and we would be able to pay for what we were doing."

Some of you may do some other things, but we just specialized in crowds. We didn't get up and harp about money. If you pack them in,

God will help you pay the bills. If you get folks saved, God will help you in your funding.

You say, "But I'm scared." Jesus said, 'Shout it on the housetop, and don't be afraid.'

Then He gives us the assignment in Matthew 10:32 when He says, "Whosoever therefore shall confess me before men, him will I confess also before my Father which is in heaven."

When I became pastor at Open Door, the first husband and wife that I led to Christ, a Catholic couple, were saved after they came to my office one day and said, "We have friends who have been talking to us, and we don't understand what they're talking about. We thought you might be able to help us."

I was able to lead both to Christ. They stayed in church and were very faithful. She worked on the school staff part-time. They have a son on a short-term missionary assignment now.

What are we doing? Confessing Christ openly in our preaching, in our soul winning and in everything we do, so that people like this Catholic couple can get saved.

A little lady came to my office. She had called for an appointment several days ahead of time. I recognized her immediately when she came in and sat down. She said, "I work at the local hospital. I see you in the hall when you're visiting. For the last five years, at least once a month, you've looked directly at me and said hello. I have all kinds of trouble in my life. I didn't know where to turn. I wonder if you can help me"—and she got saved!

There was a fellow who some said was the meanest man in town. He became very ill and was in the Frederick, Maryland hospital, about thirty miles away. Betty and I were on our way out of town one night, headed somewhere over to Western Maryland to preach on a Monday or Tuesday. She was driving.

I said, "If you'll just pull in at the entrance of the hospital here, I'll visit this man. It will only take a minute because this meanest guy in our county is going to throw me out as soon as I go in."

I walked in. He was sitting up in bed. I told him who I was and why I was there. He didn't even grunt. Rather than standing there looking at each other, I said, "I hear things are not going too well." Still there was not a word. "I'm sorry that you've been sick"—not a word. "I stopped by to see you to say an encouraging word. I will have a word of prayer with you before I go, if that's all right." He didn't say a word.

"If it's all right we'll bow our heads, and I'll say a prayer for you; but before we do, let me just tell you [and I mentioned the basic facts of the Gospel to him]. Now we're going to bow our heads. If you're not saved, I think it would be a good idea, if you believe what I just told you, if you would pray it after me." He had not said a word up until then.

I bowed my head and started wording the prayer. When I said, "Dear God," for the first time he said, "Dear God." He prayed every word of it after me. I looked up and saw tears were coming down both sides of his face.

A few weeks later, when he was out of the hospital, he came to church and was baptized. We buried him a few weeks after that because his illness was terminal.

What are we doing? Confessing Christ—confessing Him in our witness and in our testimony and doing all we can do to get folks saved.

A lady had read about our church from the SWORD. She wrote from Alabama and said, "My mother-in-law is in the hospital at Johns Hopkins in Baltimore. Maybe you would go see her. She's not saved."

Just three or four days after that I went to see this lady. Way up high in the hospital I went in a little room. A very sophisticated looking lady, very nicely dressed, was sitting there. I was told she had a terminal illness. Doctors were coming and going. Every time I would say "Hi," a doctor would push me out of the way. Every time I would say, "Uh, Mrs. ___," and try to start a conversation again, a nurse would come in and take her temperature or do something else.

All the while another nurse was standing over to one side. She seemed to be a permanent fixture in the room, standing there like a Sherman tank. I knew she was just about to unload on me and throw me out.

One of my associate pastors was with me. All the time I was thinking, *I'm not making such a good showing here. He's going to see how this isn't to be done, and he'll never get it done again. Jim will follow this example, and we'll both be ruined.*

Finally, I reached over, got that lady by the hand and said to her, "Do you believe Jesus died for you?"

"Yes, I do," she answered.

After I had said a few other things to her, I suggested we bow our heads. I said, "I want us to pray." We prayed. When we finished, she too had tears. She grasped my hand, shook it and said, "Thank you! Thank you! Thank you!" Three weeks later she went to Heaven.

After walking out of that room, I said to my associate, "Jim, don't ever do it like that."

Just every little bit I get a letter from that lady's relatives who live down South. There will be a $25 or $50 check in it because that patient, almost from the time I walked out of the room, began calling people all over the country and telling them, "I just got saved!"

I went to St. Joseph's Hospital, a Catholic hospital in Baltimore, to see a man who I knew was lost. I had talked to him before and couldn't get him saved. His was a similar situation to the lady at Johns Hopkins. I just said, "Sir, before I leave, I want you to bow your head and pray after me. I really want to see you get saved."

I began to pray out loud and word the prayer. He prayed after me. He too got saved that day. We buried him two weeks after he got saved.

What are we doing? All over this land, wherever we go, we are telling the same old story—of Jesus and His love. In one year we had more than two hundred people saved at funerals. You ask, "How in the world do you get folks saved at funerals?" You ask them!

There are people all over this land who need to and who will get saved if you and I will keep shouting it from the housetop. God has located all of us up on a housetop somewhere, and He says, "Open your mouth. Speak out. Shout it." What am I saying? All the time we need to confess Christ openly before men.

A fellow just asked me, "How did you get your work going?"

When I arrived in Westminster, I got a handful of prospect cards my first day at work and went out to get somebody down the aisle the first Sunday I was there. I got one. The next week I went out and got another. The third week I went out and got three.

That's a good plan, and it will work. I did it those years while there. Then I had a whole army of people helping me win souls and bringing them in.

"Well, do you do thus and so?" No, I don't. "Do you do thus and so?" No, I don't. A lot of you do this and that and something else. I'm not against that, but I zeroed in on some things.

I was preaching in the upper Midwest. A fellow came to me after the service and said, "You seem awfully excited about things. Can you tell me why?"

I said, "I think I can. Number one: I can be excited and I can shout because I'm saved.

"Number two: I've been married to the same woman for thirty-eight years. She still likes me, and I still like her, and that excites me.

"Number three: We have two grown kids. Both are married now. Both think Mama and Daddy are about the greatest things that ever came down the pike, and that excites me.

"Number four: I pastored a whole passel of people. Hundreds and hundreds and hundreds of them called our place 'home.' I loved all of them, and most of them loved me, and that excited me."

God let me have some of His power and energy, and He said, "Shout it."

There is a God in Heaven, and I ought to shout it. He sent His Son to die upon the cross, to be buried, to rise from the grave for sinners like me; and I ought to shout it.

One of these days, and maybe soon, He'll break through the blue of the azure sky. He's coming, and He's coming for all of His own; and because He's coming, I ought to shout it.

I ought to get on my housetop and tell people there is a God in Heaven. His Son came down to earth, lived, died, was buried and rose from the grave for my salvation and justification—and He is coming again one day. In the meantime, we are to live for God, love Him, serve Him and shout it from the housetop.

Oh, shout it, shout it from the housetop!

17

Stay on Track!

"Thy word is a lamp unto my feet, and a light unto my path.

"I have sworn, and I will perform it, that I will keep thy righteous judgments.

"I am afflicted very much: quicken me, O LORD, according unto thy word.

"Accept, I beseech thee, the freewill-offerings of my mouth, O LORD, and teach me thy judgments.

"My soul is continually in my hand: yet do I not forget thy law.

"The wicked have laid a snare for me: yet I erred not from thy precepts.

"Thy testimonies have I taken as an heritage for ever: for they are the rejoicing of my heart.

"I have inclined mine heart to perform thy statutes alway, even unto the end."— Ps. 119:105–112.

Every year at a certain time in Indianapolis, a world-famous auto race is run, the Indy 500. It is run at a very grueling pace. Those cars run on a well-designed, well-laid-out, well-defined track. Even though there's a great pace involved, it seems fairly easy for them to know how to get to the finish line because the track is well laid out.

In that same season of the year, in my home state of Kentucky, they run a horse race, the Derby. Two weeks later the Preakness is run in Baltimore, and two weeks after that the Belmont is run in New York— the famous Triple Crown of horse racing.

It's very easy for the riders and horses to get on track, to run the race, to make the finish line, because the courses are very specific, and the participants know exactly where they're going.

In Boston, New York City, and several other cities around the country, marathons are run every year. At the one in Boston, thirty thousand sets of human feet are plodding together, running twenty-six miles—a hard race, one of great endurance. The track is well defined and well marked along the way. The runners know exactly where the course is set. There are ribbons and markers to keep them on the track. It is important that they stay exactly where they need to stay for all the twenty-six miles. They must run it until the finish. They must pass the ribbon to finish.

For Christians, the race is on a well-defined track. Sometimes it's a tricky course and over rough terrain. There is a narrow path, with very few on the trail. We run it through darkness, with all kinds of conspirators who have evil designs waiting along the way to get us off the course and off track.

Unfortunately, many today are getting off the track. Some stay on, but many get off. There are those who get off the track spiritually. Others get off track morally. Some get off ministrywise. The options for off-the-track detours are myriad.

There are seven things I mention that will assure that we get on track and stay on track:

1. I've said to my members at Open Door Church in Westminster, Maryland, "The Bible is the Word of God. That's what we preach here. It is the same Bible every week—God's preserved, infallible Word; no new twists, no new wrinkles. It is the same God; His same Word; the same Bible in the pulpit, in the Sunday school classes, in the Christian school—none of the fouled-up, dissected, diluted, polluted versions.

"We use the King James Version by conviction and without apology. If you are not interested in hearing the Bible, you're probably in the wrong church. We believe all of the Scripture is given by inspiration of God—and is *profitable*. It's profitable for the preacher, for the deacons, for the singers—for everybody."

I believe that if you get on track about the Bible and don't get off track, so many other things will be right too.

2. I've tried to get our people to see that the church ought to be the epicenter of their lives. Build everything you do—your family, your home, your recreational life—around the church. The church is the most important place in town—not the mayor's office nor City Hall nor the public school building nor the civic center. The church ought to be the epicenter of my life and yours.

3. I have said to our folks, "There are three *L*s that belong to Jesus—your love, loyalty and labor." If you love like you ought to love, you will love Jesus. If you are loyal like you ought to be loyal, you will be loyal to

Jesus. If you labor like you ought to labor, you will be laboring for Jesus.

We sing that sweet song:

> Turn your eyes upon Jesus,
> Look full in His wonderful face,
> And the things of earth will grow strangely dim
> In the light of His glory and grace.

As surely as we sing it and mean it, we tie our love, our labor and our loyalty to the light of our wonderful Lord; and we shall sing all the more:

> Jesus, Jesus, Jesus—
> Sweetest name I know;
> Fills my ev'ry longing,
> Keeps me singing as I go.

We've tried to stay on that track—to get the people to stay focused on Jesus with their love, their loyalty and their labor.

4. I've said to our people, "You stay clean, morally clean, upright, decent, separated. Keep your hand out of the cookie jar. Do not do the things you ought not do."

Our folks were like your folks. They didn't always like to hear what needed to be said. Some thought we shouldn't talk about this and talk about that (especially if "this" or "that" was close to their heart); but the pulpit is a very private spot in a public arena, and when the preacher gets in it, he should talk about everything that's going on in his town.

We need to live right, stay clean, do right and do what we're supposed to do.

5. I've said to my people, "You ought to pray and walk with God. Get the power of God on your life."

These are mere hands of clay. They cannot do everything; in fact, they can do so little, especially of any lasting or eternal value. Whatever they can do, they will not do for long. Life is short and fleeting. We must have not just what human energy can achieve and not just what a human being can do in the energy of his own flesh. We need the power, the anointing, the filling of the Spirit of God upon us. In order to get that, we have to pray and walk with God.

There is no greater need than His power upon our lives. To stay on track, we must have it.

6. I've said to our people, "We need to stay on track as soul winners"—not just the preacher (although the preacher ought to be a soul winner), but all of us on the trail, on track, for souls.

I have an article on my desk right now out of a Texas newspaper which says in the Convention last year [1994] 10,000 churches did not baptize a single soul. That means one out of four Southern Baptist churches went an entire year without baptizing a single soul. All total, they baptized 378,000. Divide that by the almost 40,000 total churches, and that's fewer than 10 baptisms per church throughout the Convention, which, in other words, is fewer than one per month per church.

I said to myself, *If nobody else is doing anything, what on earth are the preachers doing?*

Dr. John R. Rice used to say, "If a preacher doesn't go out and win souls, he ought to get out of the ministry and make an honest living doing something else." It would seem to me that if nobody but the preacher did it, there ought to be more than one person per month walking the aisle and getting baptized. In every church, everywhere, all the time, the preacher should lead the way in getting somebody saved every week.

The preacher ought to be a soul winner. The deacons, the Sunday school teachers, the bus workers, the choir members, the ushers—all ought to be soul winners. In fact, every single blood-bought, born-again son and daughter of the living God ought to be a soul winner. We have a mandate from God to go after the lost and bring them to the Saviour.

I parked on it. I invested in it. I majored in it. I preached it to our people over and over again: "Every Christian ought to be a soul win- ner." Stay on track.

7. I've said, "You ought to tithe and give. Don't just tithe when you're at home. What about when you're on vacation? when you are going to Six Flags Over Montana? Tithe all the time."

Some of you tithe when you are in town; then there are another ten, twelve, fifteen weeks a year when you are not in town and don't tithe, which says you really don't tithe any of the time. Compute what you gave over the full twelve months.

I'm simply saying, get on track and stay on track.

In this passage in Psalm 119, he said, 'I will swear to you'—meaning by that, "I aver," "I declare unto you," "I promise to you"—"I will per- form what I am supposed to perform." It is a weakness (if not worldli- ness) when we shy away from commitments and vows to God.

"I don't want to promise." Why on earth not? I know why! You're not serious! Your faith is flimsy! You can't be counted on.

Psalm 119:112:

"I have inclined [given] *mine heart to perform thy statutes alway, even unto the end."*

In other words, "I'm going to do it and continue doing it until I die. I will do exactly what I am supposed to do as long as I live. I'll stay at it as long as God gives me breath. I'll stay on track."

What a saint of God! It is nothing extraordinary, though; all of us, young and old, can make those same kinds of vows anytime we decide to give the Lord our all.

There's an outline in this chapter you might like to see.

I. God Charts the Course to Keep Us "on Track"

I didn't decide to be a preacher just because it was something to do. When I was a teenager, I believed in my heart that God had called me to be a preacher. I didn't know anything about it, but I believed God had called me to do it. Just as I believed the call of God, I also believe He charts the course for His calling.

Whether you're supposed to be a preacher or whatever you're supposed to do, God charts a path for you. He lays it out and says, "There ought to be prayer, power and preaching. There ought to be a surrendered heart, a separated life and soul winning." God has charted the course for us.

I didn't decide to become a soul winner just because I thought it was a grand thing to do. I was convinced it was a command of God, and I knew I ought to follow His command.

God lays out the path. He charts it, maps it out so we can know exactly where we ought to go. When God holds the lamp, don't ever be afraid to put your feet down. When God puts light on the path, go ahead and walk in it. You will step in potholes or fall and skin your shins or wind up with mud on your face when you're not walking on the path where God has the light.

II. The Commitment We Must Make to "Stay on Track"

In verse 106, the commitment to the course which God has set is clearly defined:

"I have sworn, and I will perform it, that I will keep thy righteous judgments."

In other words, "I'm telling you, I swear to it, I've dedicated myself, I've put my heart in it; and with full dedication, with all seriousness and with the utmost commitment, I will perform it." God has charted a course for us.

I read in the paper the other day about a famous baseball player who has a .315 or .320 lifetime batting average. He told how he had become such a great hitter: "I get up on the day of the game and remind myself, 'I am a hitter.' I have that conviction in my heart. I know I can hit. It matters not who the opposing pitcher is, I can hit off him. I am not afraid of whatever he may throw. I go to the batter's box not hearing the applause of the crowd but saying to myself, *I'm a hitter! I know I can hit.*"

Some of us need to learn from that baseball player.

He continued, "Not only do I have the conviction of it, but I am committed to it. Bench me, and I'm going to be unhappy. I want to play in every game. When somebody else is batting, I want to bat. When others are out in the field at play, I want to play."

To have the conviction that you are who you are and what you are and God has you where you are is exciting; and when you get committed to it, you say, "It's my time to bat. Sit down; I want to preach. Sit down; I want to sing. Sit down; I want to be the one leading in prayer. Let me go soul winning. Let me have that prospect. Let me be the player."

That same ball player went on to say: "When I get up to bat, I concentrate on what it is I'm there for. I look at the bat. I look at that pitcher's hand. I watch that little ball as it hurls toward me. I watch as it comes all the way to where it meets the bat and the contact is made."

That kind of concentration will shut out everything else.

There are storms brewing in your life. Things are happening in your church, and you don't know what to do about it. You wonder if this can be done in your town.

Shut it out! Get your mind on your preaching. Say, "I'm going to preach when preaching time comes." Get your mind on soul winning. "I'm going soul winning when soul-winning time comes. I'll get somebody to walk the aisle this Sunday."

You say, "But I have some deacons and some choir members who are unhappy." Concentrate! Remember, you're a hitter. You're the player.

You're in place. Shut out the noise and concentrate on preaching, on soul winning.

Somebody may have chewed you out and cut you up. Forget it and concentrate on who you are and what you are and what you're about.

The same ball player said, "No matter what kind of a bad call is made by the umpire, I never turn around to him and fuss over the call, because I must stay concentrated on the next pitch."

He went on: "I have this one goal, and it's always the same one—contact the ball with the bat."

I too am a ball player. I love playing softball. We had a fast-pitch softball league that I played in for sixteen summers. When some of the guys went up to bat, I would shake my head and say, "That guy stands so funny. There's no way he can bat like that!"

The one who is convinced he is a hitter and is committed to being a hitter is concentrating on being a hitter. He stays in control of himself and stays determined to make the contact. It doesn't matter how he looks when he stands to bat. Stand on one foot if you like. Stand with feet wide apart if you want. Stand on your head if you think it will help. Just stand in there, be a hitter, don't be intimidated, and don't forget the goal.

You say, "I can't do it like Dr. Roberson or Dr. Malone, but I can do it—and by God's grace I will do it. I will. I'm a hitter."

God will let you do it. Remember what the object is.

You say, "Why is that guy standing in that little white box with the bat in his hand?"

He's a hitter! He's going to hit the ball.

You say, "That funny-looking guy? That odd crouch! The bat's too big, the pitcher's too fast, and he's too small! No way can he hit the ball"—but he does.

Aren't you amazed at some of the folks God can use in His business? Some folks have come forward and said, "God has called me"—I've argued with some. Of some I've said, "No way is God going to use that person! I just can't believe He has called this one to the ministry!"

However, God sometimes picks people we would never pick.

Look at the twelve apostles. Such a motley crowd they were! If you could have a staff of twelve men, you wouldn't pick the twelve Christ chose.

No matter how you crouch at the plate, the object is to hit the ball.

"But," you say, "the last time I was up to bat, I hit a ground ball." Okay, so you wanted to hit it up against the wall; but when you hit a ground ball, run, run, run! You might beat it out.

You say, "Well, everything's against me. They're going to throw me out. They're faster than I am." Run! Beat it out!

You say, "But the last time I was up to bat, I struck out. I made an absolute fool of myself." Get up there! Hit it again. Just because you struck out the last time and the time before that and the time before that doesn't mean you're going to strike out every time.

The team I played with—the gray team—played together three years before we won anything. Then we had one season where we were 23 and 1. The next year we were 24 and 2. We played together, pulled together, fought together as a team.

When some of those guys got up to bat, I would say, "Man, does that guy have to bat? Do we have to play with him tonight?"

When he gets up there, though, everybody cheers for him. They say, "Get up there and get at it! Get at it! Hit it! Hit it!"

I'm saying to you, this kind of commitment is what we have to have. We have to decide who we are, then say, "This is my team. I'm here to play, and we're going to play."

III. The Circumstances Offer No Excuse for Getting "off Track"

Verse 107 makes it abundantly clear there's no excuse for getting off the track:

"I am afflicted very much: quicken me, O LORD, according unto thy word."

You say, "I'm afflicted." That's no excuse. "I've been hurt." That's no excuse. "I don't have any friends." That's no excuse. "Nobody loves me"—no excuse. "I'm located on the wrong side of town"—no excuse.

Let no circumstance foul you up or strike you out.

IV. The Certainties of God Must Always Overshadow the Uncertainties

"My soul is continually in my hand: yet do I not forget thy law."—Ps. 119:109.

There are always uncertainties. What is always certain is that the Word of God will see you through. The psalmist said, "My soul is continually in my hand [a lot of things I can't control]: yet do I not forget thy law."

Whatever uncertainties there are in your town, church, life or ministry, the Word of God is always certain.

The uncertainties, though they be strong, are not as strong as the certainties. No matter what is happening around you, no matter if rain is falling on your parade, the certainty of God is stronger than any uncertainty you may have.

The certainty of salvation is stronger than the uncertainty of your situation. The certainties of the Bible are stronger than the uncertainties of your present battle. The certainty of God's commands is stronger than the uncertainties of your circumstances.

V. Conspirators Will Create Detours to Get You "off Track"

You say, "There are certain conspirators who lay traps for me."

"The wicked have laid a snare for me."—Psalm 119:110.

That will be true sometimes. Though they lay a snare, don't step into it. The hook may be out there, but you don't have to bite it.

You say, "Well, everybody is saying we ought to have a contemporary church." Don't bite the hook.

"Everybody is saying we ought to have this dressed-down, honky-tonk music in our church." Don't bite the hook.

"Everybody is saying now that we ought to go with the lifestylers on evangelism." Don't bite the hook.

"Everybody is saying the 'Bible-a-Month Club' has a new translation this month." Don't bite the hook. Stay with the same Book, the same Bible. Stay with the same program you found in the Book of Acts. Stay on course. Don't get off the well-defined scriptural track.

It's true that there are those who are trying to waylay you, trying to lay a snare for you, trying to get you off course, trying to trap you. They're very devious sometimes, very deceptive and deceitful—but don't fall for it. Don't get off track. Stay the course.

VI. The Consequences of "Staying on Track"

The consequences of staying on track are pretty good. The psalmist says,

"Thy testimonies have I taken as an heritage for ever: for they are the rejoicing of my heart."—Ps. 119:111.

God's heritage is pretty good. God treats His workers pretty well. The rejoicing of your heart is pretty good. I like being happy. I like the sweet joys that come from working in the Lord's vineyard and walking side by side with the Saviour.

VII. Complete the Course

So what is ahead? What's our future? What are we going to do? Complete the course.

"I have inclined mine heart to perform thy statutes alway, even unto the end."—Ps. 119:112.

The course is laid out. It has been charted and well defined. What are you going to do? As for me, I'm going to complete the course.

You say, "I'm hurting. Nobody loves me. Everything is going awry." Complete the course.

They enter that horse in the Derby, and he wins. They enter him in the Preakness, and he wins. Then they enter him in the Belmont, the longest of the three, and he decides, "I don't want to run this race!" So he jumps off track into the infield, runs up in the grandstand and out on the street.

Somebody asks him, "Where in the world are you going?" He answers, "I'm running the race my own way. I have run those other races. I did it the way it had always been done. I won a few of them. I've come to a new time. This is the last of the 1990s. I'm entitled to run it the way I want to."

Sir, it doesn't matter how many races you've won. If you don't run it like it's supposed to be run, you're not going to win this one.

I'm urging you, stay on track.

The day of the Boston Marathon comes, and some runner with resolve starts with the crowd at the starting gate. Then he runs from Boston down to Connecticut, across to New York City, down to

Baltimore, through Richmond and even to Winston-Salem. He circles the building here, heads back to Richmond, up to Philadelphia, through New York, past Connecticut and back to Boston—about six weeks later.

When asked, "What are you doing, man?" he replies, "I'm running the Boston Marathon."

They say, "But you got off the track. You're not on the track."

He says, "But I'm doing it a new way—my way!"

They say, "No, you're not on the track!"

I'm saying, you can't win the marathon if you run it that way. Stay on the track!

Those guys in Indiana can't win the Indy 500 by driving to L.A. and back or to Florida and back. They have to stay on the track until the course is completed.

What I am saying to you now is: Find the course, focus on it, be faithful to it and finish it.

Be a Joseph. Stay on track when you've been betrayed. Stay on track when you've been sold out. Stay on track when you've been abused.

Be an Elisha. Stay on track when you're young and inexperienced and lonely.

Be an Elijah. Stay on track when you're outnumbered 850 to 1.

Be an Ezekiel. When your mate dies ("At even my wife died," Ezekiel says, "and I did in the morning as I was commanded"), stay on track.

Be a John the Baptist. When your very life is at stake and they're about to take your head off, stay on track.

Be a Paul. When you're criticized, chased, beaten and left for dead, stay on track.

Be a Lee Roberson. When a little baby dies in the midst of your ministry and your heart is broken, stay on track.

Be a Charles Spurgeon. When you're sick and depressed and you can't stand up to preach and all kinds of things are coming down around you and you're much too young to die, stay on track.

Be a Moody. When a great fire comes and destroys everything for which you've worked, stay on track!

Be a Ray Hart whose mighty voice blessed us in these conferences so many times. With the health problems he had, he knew that he should not travel alone; but he did, to be a blessing to audiences like this. Stay on track like Ray did.

Be a Dr. John Rice. When the stands he took were not popular, when people threw verbal assaults at him from every direction, he stayed on track.

Be a Curtis Hutson. Even though his body was racked with unbelievable suffering for so many months, he stayed on track. People would come into his room, and he would ask them one after another if they knew the Saviour. The last week he lived, a new nurse came on duty. The first thing he wanted to know was whether she were going to Heaven when she died. Unable to sit up in the bed or even hold a Bible, he had someone else sit down by her and hold the Bible while he quoted verses and led her to Christ.

Even though he was sedated there three or four days before his graduation to Glory, he came out from under the sedation for a while and repeatedly said for almost twenty-four hours without stopping, "I was born a preacher. I've lived a preacher. I'll die a preacher. I'll fight the Devil as long as I live."

I'm saying, be like Curtis Hutson and stay on track until your last breath comes. Keep preaching the Book. Keep telling people how to be saved. Keep holding up the standard.

Hold the banner high for separation and godly, clean living. Hold the banner high for the church. Hold the banner high for soul winning. Hold the banner high for prayer and Bible reading and sanctified, godly, Spirit-filled living. Hold the banner high. Keep your heart warm and sweet and right.

Stay on track. Don't let anyone sidetrack you. Don't let bitterness, depression or criticism get you off. Don't let somebody's new game plan get you off. Revival, soul winning, separation, salvation—stay on it.

They say, "You're playing the same song you played last week." Play it again. They say, "It's the same song you played last year and the year before and the year before." Play it again.

Stay on track. Be as David and say, 'I aver, I declare unto you, I state to you, I'm staying on the track—and I will perform it until the end.'

What Will It Take for America to Have Revival?

"And he said unto him, If they hear not Moses and the prophets, neither will they be persuaded, though one rose from the dead."—Luke 16:31.

On Sunday, September 16, 2001, church facilities across America and around the world were considerably fuller than they had been the week before. In the throes of fear and with a war having been launched upon us in a sneaking, cowardly and murderous fashion, suddenly there was a renewed interest in God, in prayer and in other things spiritual and eternal. It was a natural response in the midst of the burden, the crisis, that had been thrust upon us.

One could not help but ponder the situation and speculate as to its long-term impact upon the nation. Was it a genuine turning to God; or was it merely a spiritual knee jerk, a reaction to the shock, a desperation driven by fear?

In the November 3, 2001, *Nashville Tennessean*, a Knight Ridder News Service article addressed the matter:

Hope for a Mass Spiritual Awakening After Attacks May Have Aimed Too High

From so many pulpits in the wake of September 11, the message was the same: Terror can be transformed into a spiritual wake-up call.

In the first few weeks, there was evidence that Americans were turning to traditional and newer sources of spiritual guidance: Churches were filled. Books about faith and spirituality flew off the shelves. Neighbor reached out to neighbor.

But hopeful predictions of a great faith-based awakening seem to have overstated the case. Yes, some people are praying more....Some people report that their faith is stronger, others that their beliefs are more confused. Worship attendance in many places has dropped back to levels similar to those before the attacks.

Almost eight weeks after the horror of that first day, spiritual changes may be more subtle than startling.

A further article appeared November 28 in *USA Today* which affirms that "...spiritual routine..." has resumed:

Many Americans who crowded pews and bought new Bibles in the aftermath of September 11 have settled back to their routine religious beliefs and practices—with one significant shift.

We're less likely to believe in absolute good and evil, according to a new survey by Barna Research Group....

"People are asking more questions, moral questions. 'What is right? How should we react?' Everyone seems involved in raising questions about faith. They're taking it more seriously now," [says a New Hampshire minister].

Most measures of religious belief and behavior, however, showed no change from a similar Barna telephone survey in August.

"It proved the old saying: People came back to church and rediscovered why they didn't come in the first place," says Pastor Rod Loy....

"People like to acknowledge the existence of God, someone or something in control, at Christmas or Easter or in a crisis; but to keep coming, they have to be convinced that the church is relevant to their everyday lives," Loy says. "That's where absolutes matter."

You would think perhaps in fundamental churches the pews would be packed and the altars filled at every invitation. You might expect that the Sunday-morning-only crowd would have a hunger for God that would get them to come back Sunday night and Wednesday night. Surely there would be a stirring among God's people that would be reflected in the offerings, in the folks going soul winning, in the attendance at special meetings, etc. Alas, it is not yet evident! Why not?

Note carefully the text and its message:

"And he said unto him, If they hear not Moses and the prophets, neither will they be persuaded, though one rose from the dead."—Luke 16:31.

So if something so dramatic, so startling, so incredible as one's rising from the dead will not capture the interest of the wayward, the indifferent and the self-centered, what will it take?

Well, this verse has a very profound and practical message for us— namely, if they will not hear the message of the Word of God, don't expect crisis or conditions or circumstances to persuade them!

Revival will not come because of the atrocities of September 11!

Revival will not come because of this war on terror!

Revival will not come because of our fear!

Revival will not come because we have a great need!

Revival will not come because of anxiety or worry! It will not come from our desperation or our helplessness!

Oh, here and there, once and again some individual may be thus motivated and come to Christ and salvation. There may be a preacher, maybe one in a thousand-mile radius, who will awaken with new zeal, catch fire and start to do the work of God in a powerful way.

But these are rare, isolated examples! It is not the norm; it is not a trend; it is not catching hold across the country. In other words, it is not a national revival!

Believe me, I'm excited when I hear of any hint of revival! If a church begins to grow dramatically (and I know of several that are), I am indeed thrilled. If a dear man of God somewhere gets the fresh winds of God caught in the sails of his ministry, we rejoice! Amen! If there's a place where soul winners work successfully every week and people are often being saved and baptized, we praise God! Amen!

However, we're looking for a revival the size of which will have a mighty impact on millions of our citizens, where people stand in line for the church doors to open on Wednesday night, where towns are so caught up in the things of God that beer joints close for lack of business, where drug dealers get converted and flush their vile business down the sewer, where the police force has layoffs because the town is so quiet, and where the plans for the new jail are canceled because there are so few people in the old one! I'm talking about a Heaven-sent, anointed, powerful movement that sweeps across a town, a county, a region, and sweeps it clean!

Could such a mighty revival happen? Indeed it could—but *will* it? If it does, it will come on God's terms, not ours; so, perhaps we should review His ideas on this.

Revival Is Not As Many Expect

1. A genuine, Heaven-sent, Holy Ghost revival will not come as a result of legislation.

You say, "You cannot legislate morality"; but in actuality, all legislation is an attempt to effect some degree of morality. The Congress passes and the president signs thousands of laws, yet the people—

rebellious in heart, in defiance of God, wandering aimlessly—find a thousand new ways to do wrong.

The real truth is, you cannot pass enough laws to produce the utopia, a Garden of Eden, where everything is wonderful all the time! Legislature, laws, edicts, fiats, rules, regulations and such are not the vehicle on which revival will be borne in our midst. Never before has it been by legislation, and it will not be so now!

2. A genuine, Heaven-sent, Holy Ghost revival will not come as a result of reform.

Reform has its place. An industry or an institution which operates by certain guidelines over a period of years may grow careless, or the guidelines may no longer be as suitable or helpful as they once were. So we take notice and we reform it!

It's an old, old story. Everything men do can be improved, upgraded and changed! Since we don't have infallible wisdom, we make lots of mistakes, and we keep trying to reform things and get them right. All the while what we need is revival, and revival cannot come of reform. Reform itself will need to be reformed soon!

3. A genuine, Heaven-sent, Holy Ghost revival will not come as a result of patriotism.

My level of agitation is increased considerably by the unpatriotic yokels in our land. I'm talking about newscasters who refuse to wear the American flag lapel pins, the educators who have eliminated the Pledge of Allegiance to the flag because of "one nation under God," the flag-burning crowd, etc. Very candidly let me say, I have no time for and nothing good to say about any of the unpatriotic crowd.

There was a big article in one of our Midsouth dailies about the conflict some churches created when they took the American flag into their church houses after September 11. The reporter made it seem like some new and novel thing that these liberal churches had just invented! What a bunch of wimps and Johnny-come-latelies!

The crowd I run with has always made a to-do on Memorial Day weekend, the Fourth of July and Veteran's Day. Fifty years ago as a small boy I attended Vacation Bible School, and it was there that we learned the Pledge of Allegiance and saluted the American flag every day. When I was a pastor for more than thirty years, there was never a Sunday when the American flag was not displayed in our church.

To the Bible-believing Christian crowd, patriotism is not new. We didn't just start waving the flag on September 11—we never stopped waving it. It's always been a part of the fabric of our being!

Listen now. Patriotism will not produce the revival we need. It will have some good effect, but it will not do long-term what is needed. Only revival can take us where we need to be and generate for us what we need to have.

I've seen some pretty wicked people patriotically waving the flag in recent weeks, and I'm glad they have. Just don't imagine that they've changed! They'll soon set the flag aside! The ugly head of their godless ways will soon reappear, and they'll be back in business as usual. Oh my, we need a revival—the kind like God can give!

4. A genuine, Heaven-sent, Holy Ghost revival will not come as a result of prosperity.

America is the most prosperous nation in the history of the world. We waste more on trinkets and toys in an average week than some people would make in a year in a lot of countries.

It is true that "every good gift and every perfect gift is from above, and cometh down from the Father of lights, with whom is no variableness, neither shadow of turning" (Jas. 1:17); and we rejoice in the provisions of God's goodness and His gifts. Yet they are not the impetus to bring revival! We bask in the sunlight of His blessings! Abundance has often been bestowed, yet revival lingers!

5. A genuine, Heaven-sent, Holy Ghost revival will not come as a result of technology.

Cars, airplanes, radio, television, the Internet and thousands of other things have become commonplace in the past hundred years as technology has exploded on the scene to provide us so much! Are we grateful? Do we realize God's good things are for His purpose? Do we use them well? Often we do not!

Even if the whole world acknowledged the creation of God in all this technology, it is not the key to revival.

6. A genuine, Heaven-sent, Holy Ghost revival will not come as a result of "religion."

Religion is everywhere! The most sinful of nations will sport its share of religion, and the most insane of things religious will engender the follow-ship of committed devotees.

Religion works feverishly to appease and please God, but to no avail!

Works are empty and vain, like filthy rags (Isa. 64:6), until the heart is turned toward God.

Religion sacrifices valued things, even life, but fails to gain Heaven's attention! Is God impressed by a religion that takes lives so carelessly, so coldly, so ruthlessly! Not at all!

Religion sets aside God's revealed plan and postures its own self-centered way and, in doing so, plays the fool!

Religion is "do and doing"; God says, "Done!" The whole scheme of the various religions spawned out of human experience cannot secure for a moment what God alone can provide.

Religion has never been and is not now the answer. Real revival is the antithesis of man's religions. Real revival by its presence and power will decimate these flimsy, fumbling efforts of men.

Wherein, then, is revival? When does it come? What is the way? What will it take for America, or any other nation, to have revival?

I. It Will Take Repentance!

"Testifying both to the Jews, and also to the Greeks, repentance toward God, and faith toward our Lord Jesus Christ."—Acts 20:21.

"Because he hath appointed a day, in the which he will judge the world in righteousness by that man whom he hath ordained; whereof he hath given assurance unto all men, in that he hath raised him from the dead."—Acts 17:31.

Repentance by definition is "a change of mind"; and specifically, for the unsaved, it is a change of mind about God (vs. 21). Until a man gets a proper view of God, he'll never understand his own sinful nature. When he compares himself to himself or to other people, he only makes himself a competitor in a race of pride and performance. When he sees God as God is, his own personal best shows itself transparent, and the dirty, rotten core of his sinful heart is exposed.

"And one cried unto another, and said, Holy, holy, holy, is the LORD of hosts: the whole earth is full of his glory.

"And the posts of the door moved at the voice of him that cried, and the house was filled with smoke.

"Then said I, Woe is me! for I am undone; because I am a man of unclean lips, and I dwell in the midst of a people of unclean lips: for mine eyes have seen the King, the LORD of hosts."—Isa. 6:3–5.

216

Isaiah got the picture of his own need and plight when he saw the Shekinah glory of God. His darkness was clearly manifest when he saw the brilliance of God.

Consider the first item in the great formula of II Chronicles 7:14: "If my people...shall humble themselves...." Humbling ourselves before God is what happens when we come to grips with who He is.

As long as we strut around like a pompous peacock, saying, "I am rich...and have need of nothing" (Rev. 3:17), we are playing the fool. We may strut our pride and boast our exploits, but it is empty rhetoric—vanity at best! Cloak it in religion if you will, but you are all the more foolish. We are but "a vapour, that appeareth for a little time, and then vanisheth away" (Jas. 4:14).

Who are we? Absolutely nobody except by the grace of God! So down with our crowing and honking, and give God the place, the credit, the glory that are due!

Let's get a right mind about God! It's called *repentance!* It is the first step to revival! When you think right about God, it will affect your thinking about yourself and your sin. Think right about God, and you'll settle the issues of humanism, of alcohol, of pornography, of dishonesty, of the plunderings of your self-will and of other godless matters.

II. It Will Take Salvation!

"For all have sinned, and come short of the glory of God;

"Being justified freely by his grace through the redemption that is in Christ Jesus:

"Whom God hath set forth to be a propitiation through faith in his blood, to declare his righteousness for the remission of sins that are past, through the forbearance of God."—Rom. 3:23–25.

Man is by nature a sinner—a vile, wicked sinner. Apart from salvation in the Lord Jesus Christ, the very best of human efforts soon sputter in lifeless failure. You cannot make a sinner a saint with a bath and a new suit of clothes. No amount of polish and paint can "spiffy up" the old, unregenerate nature.

Love and peace, though universally desired, are elusive, just out of reach from the grasping fingers of philosophy, philanthropy, psychiatry, prosperity and productivity. Look not to Buddha! Forget Mecca! Be not enamored with Joseph Smith, Mary Baker Patterson Glover Eddy,

Ellen G. White, the various popes and others who may clamor for a place in your life which they do not deserve. Every one of us needs the wonderful salvation that is available only in the Lord Jesus Christ.

"For by grace are ye saved through faith; and that not of yourselves: it is the gift of God:

"Not of works, lest any man should boast."—Eph. 2:8, 9.

"For there is one God, and one mediator between God and men, the man Christ Jesus;

"Who gave himself a ransom for all."—I Tim. 2:5, 6.

If there is to be forgiveness, you must come to Christ for His salvation. If there is to be Heaven, you must come to Christ to be saved. All that you want and all that you need can be found in just one source: the Lord Jesus Christ.

We cannot have a real Heaven-sent revival anywhere unless we get in the blood-bought, born-again, salvation business! The do-gooders fail! Works cannot avail! It takes salvation to prevail! Salvation gives you a *new* nature which fights against your *old* nature! There's a fierce battle for control of your life! Without salvation you'll never succeed in conquering sin, self and Satan! It takes the new birth, regeneration, salvation!

"For I am not ashamed of the gospel of Christ: for it is the power of God unto salvation to every one that believeth; to the Jew first, and also to the Greek."—Rom. 1:16.

We will not have Heaven-sent revival apart from a big to-do about the salvation of sinners! That's why churches, *all* churches, should get their houses in order. Make the Great Commission of Jesus (Matt. 28:19,20) the main event in your ministry and start winning souls in your area.

That's why you and I, every single one of us who are saved, should be giving ourselves to the task of winning others to Christ!

III. It Will Take Surrender!

When the people of God ignore the Word of God and are inattentive to the will of God, there can be no revival! Who among us does not want the blessings, but how many of us are willing to shoulder the burden of it?

It requires a surrender of our will to His will—a surrender of heart, of spirit and attitude. "Yes, Lord," must be our innermost and immediate reaction to every divine prompting. "Not my will, but Thine" must be emblazoned over the doorposts of our lives. Confronted by the mandates of His Word, there can be no place, no safe harbor, for self, for carnality, for ambition, for disobedience! We must surrender!

D. L. Moody said, "It remains to be seen what one man wholly dedicated to God can do, but with God's help, I will be that man." That's a yielded heart, a surrendered life!

If revival is to come in our lifetime, a host of us need to lay down our own agendas, lay aside every personal determination and totally give ourselves up to Him—I mean a full surrender to every known truth of God and to every established task of His choosing. Get up, put yourself on the altar, give yourself as a sacrifice to Him, and then, by your yielded heart and surrender, get out of the way to allow His will to be fully effected in your life.

Don't hedge! Don't hold back! Hear the Word of God without hesitation or delay! Yield! Believe what He has said, trust Him and do what He instructs!

It is the stuff out of which revival comes!

IV. It Will Take Obedience!

"And Samuel said, Hath the LORD as great delight in burnt-offerings and sacrifices, as in obeying the voice of the LORD? Behold, to obey is better than sacrifice, and to hearken than the fat of rams."—I Sam. 15:22.

Despite the urgings of Scripture, disobedience to God and to His duly appointed deputies is a reserved right and a protected privilege among many carnal Christians. On one hand, there are Christian talk and spiritual activity; but on the other hand, many Christians are openly rebellious to their parents and seemingly oblivious to the responsibility to follow their pastor.

"Children, obey your parents in the Lord: for this is right."—Eph. 6:1.

"Obey them that have the rule over you, and submit yourselves: for they watch for your souls, as they that must give account, that they may do it with joy, and not with grief: for that is unprofitable for you."—Heb. 13:17.

But immediately these folks object with hypothetical cases of "what if?" They see all kinds of supposed danger in following someone else.

Their presumption is that God did not have the wisdom when He wrote the Bible to see what practical problems you and I would have with His instructions. Such presumption is only further carnality and the apex of foolishness!

"Then Peter and the other apostles answered and said, We ought to obey God rather than men."—Acts 5:29.

The Bible never instructs us to follow blindly any leader who has betrayed his position to ask us to do something which violates the Word of God. So we follow those who follow Christ (I Cor. 11:1) as long as they follow Christ and are themselves honoring God. If they ask us to do something outside the revealed will of God, we are within the Lord's guidelines to resist that leadership at that point and continue on with the Lord.

So you see the Lord was not napping nor intellectually deficient when He outlined and detailed His instructions on obedience. Revival is stymied by our disobedience. We must not expect that the strong winds of spiritual refreshment will blow upon us as long as we reject God's Word and resist His will. Disobedience is a hindrance that we must not permit. Self-will must be laid aside for full obedience to His will. It is a vital ingredient in the formula for revival.

V. It Will Take Prayer!

Jesus taught us that God's children have the privilege to "ask...seek, and...knock" (Matt. 7:7). For us it is the lifeline of our communication with Heaven.

Prayer is not God's talking to us. Prayer is the expression of our voice lifted up to God. It is our opportunity to talk to God, a special privilege afforded because we are saved. If we fail to talk to God, the dynamics of our relationship wax dull. When the relationship weakens, the excitement wanes. When the thrill of being saved is not fresh, there's little or no energy to do the great bidding of God.

Prayer admits need! By its very nature, the act of prayer shows us to be needy, admittedly helpless, but looking for answers to our lack.

Prayer acknowledges God! It is not a prayer to one another that we utter, but to God! Our posture in prayer—eyes cast upward and knees bent downward—defines the yearning of our heart. By calling on Heaven, we attest to our consciousness of the presence and the power of God.

Prayer accesses the heavenly storehouse! What resources, what amazing supply are contained in the inestimable, inexhaustible inventory of God's resources! Whatever our dilemma, the divine supply is ample—yea, abundant—to provide. When we in prayer call out to God, we are given access to the Lord's bounty of provisions.

If we expect to have a revival personally or nationally, it will not come from our pompous perch where we proudly proclaim our prominence and preference. Instead of strutting as though all is well, we rather need to surrender ourselves to the will and wisdom of God. On our faces, we must invoke a prayer of yieldedness to declare ourselves humbled and dependent upon God.

VI. It Will Take the Anointing, the Power, of the Holy Spirit!

"But ye shall receive power, after that the Holy Ghost is come upon you: and ye shall be witnesses unto me...."—Acts 1:8.

We live in a society where paganism, humanism, hedonism, secularism, atheism and a host of other crackpot ideas are holding sway. Self-will articulates itself loudly with a brash defiance of God's will. The environment of our culture is not entirely friendly—in fact, sometimes it is hostile—to God, the Bible, the old-time way and all that is precious to us.

When we wade into the arena where we live and work with a full dedication to the Great Commission of our Saviour, these isms often meet us with angry resistance. They do not like the efforts we make for Jesus' sake.

If our effort is merely intellectual or emotional, if it be no more than humanitarian or patriotic, it will falter quickly and flop around helplessly in defeat. What is needed is an infusion of supernatural power, the dynamic empowerment of God's Holy Spirit!

"And be not drunk with wine, wherein is excess; but be filled with the Spirit."—Eph. 5:18.

That filling is for the purpose of power! It is a necessary filling for the Christian who expects to do God's work.

It is not easy to confront the philosophies of men. They're bold and they're aggressive. They're heady and high-minded. They dislike the very idea of God, and they will fight you when you raise the issue.

Your puny hands are not much! What you need is something mighty. Only the Almighty can provide it! Revival like we need will confront the crowd marching the broad road in their militancy against God! No such revival can be energized by our feeble ability. It's God's power we need!

VII. It Will Take Preaching!

"It pleased God by the foolishness of preaching to save them that believe.

"For the Jews require a sign, and the Greeks seek after wisdom:

"But we preach Christ crucified, unto the Jews a stumblingblock, and unto the Greeks foolishness;

"But unto them which are called, both Jews and Greeks, Christ the power of God, and the wisdom of God."—I Cor. 1:21–24.

Not just teaching—preaching!

Not dialogue—preaching!

Not forums—preaching!

Not "sharing" times—preaching! Preaching, dear ones, preaching!

Would to God that every preacher would with faultless memory recall:

"Preach the word; be instant in season, out of season; reprove, rebuke, exhort with all longsuffering and doctrine."—II Tim. 4:2.

If God has called you, then stand up and speak up! Be the preacher! Let the sense of urgency envelop you every time you approach the pulpit. It is no small task to do as instructed, to follow the clearly revealed plan of God! It is not "trivial pursuit" to which we are pledged! This old world, sin-laden and Hell-bent, needs to hear the eternal truths, the old-time religion, the blessed Gospel! "How shall they hear without a preacher?" (Rom. 10:14).

"But watch thou in all things, endure afflictions, do the work of an evangelist, make full proof of thy ministry."—II Tim. 4:5.

Why is it that everything else in the world gets shoved to center stage (music, announcements, promotion, fund raising, programs, etc.) and preaching time is treated like table scraps? Why doesn't somebody fight off the usurpers and shake off the intimidation and give full measure to preaching? Is there a preacher? Then why don't we have preaching?

Why don't we prepare and then preach?

Why don't we pray for power and then preach?

Why don't we get a vision for our city and then preach?

Why don't we get excited and then preach?

Why don't we do as we have biblical instruction to do—preach? Preach! Preach!

You'll bless hearts if you'll preach!

You'll stir the church if you'll preach!

You'll convict and convince sinners if you'll preach!

You'll solve trouble in the church if you'll preach!

You'll get the attention of your town if you'll preach!

You'll be the catalyst of revival if you'll preach!

God bless our politicians, our public servants, our carpenters and plumbers, our bakers and tailors, our farmers and our builders. God bless them all! We need all of them, and we are thankful for them!

However, revival necessitates some preachers—preachers who will preach! Amen! Sunday morning, Sunday night and Wednesday night, mount that pulpit, breathe a prayer, open the Bible, take a text, open your mouth and PREACH!

Conclusion...

The revival we need cannot be invented in a church growth seminar. It is not the product of diplomacy nor the result of dialogue!

Revival is neither manipulated by the media nor manufactured by religious machinery at work.

Superficial, half-baked, whimsical, fledgling, immature, unseasoned, carnal, fleshly, worldly reasonings are empty human attempts which shall ever falter and fail.

Churches whose unprincipled character checks the polls, the trends, breathless to accommodate the latest lustings of the culture, will not know the fresh breath of God.

When contemporary is given the place of convictions, there'll be no revival.

Without revival the people delight in psychology instead of preaching, and they demand counselors instead of preachers.

In the absence of revival, the people wear their feelings on their sleeves; someone is always up the miff tree. Churches squabble and split. Everybody wants to have his or her say and press for his or her rights. Power struggles abound in the churches, and the pastors are relegated to being errand boys.

Local churches are turned in on themselves, oblivious to the divine mandates, the biblically defined agenda. They have lots of activity, spinning 'round and 'round like the merry-go-round at the city playground. Revival would change all such!

Everybody turns out for pizza, softball and the gospel sing, but only a few of the very faithful are at the Wednesday night service, and even fewer attend the soul-winning times. It's symptomatic of the need, the dire straits of our times. We need revival to change it around and get priorities in place.

What will it take for us to have revival? It will take repentance, salvation, surrender, obedience, prayer, the power of the Holy Spirit and preaching. Are you listening? Is there somebody right now who will say, "I will give myself and do what it takes to have a revival burning in me"? Amen!